The Evolution of the Southern Backcountry

A Case Study of Lunenburg County, Virginia 1746–1832

Richard R. Beeman

University of Pennsylvania Press
Philadelphia

Designed by Adrianne Onderdonk Dudden

Library of Congress Cataloging in Publication Data

Beeman, Richard R.
  The evolution of the southern backcountry.

  Includes index.
  1. Lunenburg County (Va.)—Civilization. 2. Virginia
—History—Colonial period, ca. 1600–1775—Case studies.
I. Title.
F232.L9B34   1984   975.5'643   83-27397
ISBN 0-8122-7926-3

Printed in the United States of America

*For Kristin
and Joshua*

Contents

List of Figures

List of Maps

List of Tables

Acknowledgments

I have drawn heavily on the advice, expertise, and goodwill of many friends, students, and professional colleagues over the course of this project. Three undergraduate research assistants— Pamela James, Scott Oleson, and especially Fred Rollman—provided invaluable help in gathering data from the county court order books, tax lists, and land records. Two longtime residents of Lunenburg, Grace Marshall and Virginia Redd, were particularly hospitable during my trips to the county. The members of the staffs of the Virginia Historical Society, the Virginia State Library, the Virginia Baptist Historical Society, and the library of the University of Pennsylvania have been consistently helpful to me. I only regret that Will Rachal, longtime editor of the *Virginia Magazine of History and Biography* and an important presence in the manuscript room at the Virginia Historical Society, passed away before this project was completed. Mr. Rachal was always generous in sharing his unparalleled knowledge of Virginia's manuscript sources and kind in his advice and criticism, and I lament his passing.

Some of the evidence and arguments in this book have appeared in a different form in various scholarly journals. My initial formulation of many of the problems discussed in Chapters 1 through 4 was published as "Social Change and Cultural Conflict in Virginia: Lunenburg County, 1746–1774" in *William and Mary Quarterly,* 3d ser., 35 (1978): 455–76; the discussion of Lunenburg's political style in Chapter 3 appeared in a more extensive form in the *Journal of American Studies* 12 (1978): 169–83; and portions of Chapter 6 appeared in "Cultural Conflict and Social Change in the Revolutionary South: Lunenburg County, Virginia," *Journal of Southern History* 46 (1980): 525–50 (co-authored with Rhys Isaac).

The list of individuals who have helped me sharpen my conception and execution of this project is a long one. Lois Carr, Paul Clemens, Drew Faust, Mike McGiffert, John Modell, Michael L. Nicholls, Thad Tate, Lorena Walsh, and Michael Zuckerman have all been generous with their advice; Allan Kulikoff has been not only a source of useful advice and constructive criticism but also unfailingly open about sharing his own research with me. My manuscript benefited from careful readings by other scholars at several different stages. Jack P. Greene, in addition to reading and commenting on the final draft, has in his own work proven to be a constant source of stimulation. My colleague at the University of Pennsylvania, Richard S. Dunn, read two different versions of the manuscript and on each occasion offered both useful criticism and, at a crucial stage, much-needed encouragement. And I am especially grateful to Gary B. Nash, who managed to be both appreciative and relentlessly critical in his reading of the manuscript. My final revisions may not satisfy Professor Nash on all points, but I will always admire the combination of seriousness and collegiality with which he approached my work. At the University of Pennsylvania Press, my copy editor, Peggy Hoover, worked both speedily and constructively in improving the clarity of the manuscript. And finally, I want to acknowledge my deep debt—both professional and personal—to Rhys Isaac. We met and fast became soul mates in the enterprise of eighteenth-century Virginia history at the very beginning of this project; he has throughout the course of it all been the best of friends and the most inspirational of colleagues.

In the space of time that it has taken me to finish this book, my wife Pamela has completed two advanced degrees and embarked on a promising career of her own, while at the same time continuing to be the glue that holds our family together. My children, Kristin and Joshua, were barely walking when all this began, and now, as obstreperous teenagers, they are actually in a position to read this book and figure out some of what their father does for a living. For that reason, and for many others, I dedicate this book to them.

*The
Evolution
of the
Southern
Backcountry*

Prologue

If we were to travel today to the towns of Andover, Dedham, or Concord, Massachusetts, in search of the remnants of seventeenth- and eighteenth-century community life, we probably could—through the clutter of gas stations, shopping malls, and fast food emporiums—still catch a glimpse of those institutional and physical structures that tied the people of the much simpler world of colonial New England together in a network of shared values and aspirations. Be the year 1783 or 1983, our search for those institutions and activities that define community life in the Virginia Southside is a far more perplexing endeavor.

Embarking on our quest to discover the character of community life in Lunenburg County, Virginia, today, we would probably take the South Hill turnoff from Interstate 85, sixty-five miles southwest of Petersburg and about twenty miles from the North Carolina border. Traveling toward Lunenburg on Route 40, we would find ourselves immediately removed from the mass-market world of McDonald's, Colonel Sanders, and Holiday Inn along those concrete ribbons that traverse our land. There is a new Tastee Freeze in Victoria and something called the Golden Skillet in Kenbridge, but for the most part the people of Lunenburg County have been spared those corporate symbols and points of congregation of the fast food kingdom which have so homogenized the American landscape.

The county seat of Lunenburg, bearing the same name as the county, is situated in the geographic center of the county and is not so much a town as an historical artifact.[1] It consists of the county courthouse (which was rebuilt in 1827 after the 1787 edifice burned to the ground), the sheriff's office, the health and welfare department, and directly across the street, a general store and filling station. If we have an hour to spare and enjoy sitting in the hot summer sun leaning against the Confederate soldiers' monument outside the courthouse, we might see a dozen people go in or out of those town buildings. Inside the courthouse, Mr. Roy Moore, clerk of the court, and his deputy, Grace Marshall, are pleased to spend some time with an inquiring stranger. The county sheriff and his deputies have little difficulty maintaining order in a county where the incidence of serious crime is relatively slight. The welfare department building, which used to serve as the library until insufficient use caused the county's residents to abandon the library in favor of a bookmobile service from a neighboring county, is quiet by big-city standards. And across the street there is seldom need for Mark Osborne to put on extra help to pump gas while he is selling groceries.

Driving northeast toward Victoria, we do come across something more akin to the community for which we are searching. It is not a strikingly pretty place; in fact, it looks as if there has been little new construction in the town since the Depression, but at least there are some shops, a bank, and a few restaurants. There are even a few factories in Victoria (a small shoe company, a division of the Scovill Manufacturing Company which makes zipper tapes, and a knitwear factory) which provide jobs for some of Lunenburg's residents.

Just a few miles farther up the road, in Kenbridge, there are several large warehouses run by the Commonwealth Tobacco Company, but many of the local residents fear that the town's days as a center of Virginia's tobacco trade are numbered. Most of the warehouses are now located to the west in Danville, and the Kenbridge warehouses seem to be losing ground. Kenbridge folk do, however, consider themselves just a bit more sophisticated than their Victoria neighbors. It's often said that Kenbridge residents will go out to one of the town's three restaurants to eat dinner late in the evening, while Victoria residents nearly always eat an early supper at home. And while most businesspeople visiting the county would probably choose the Holiday Inn over in South Hill in Brunswick County, Kenbridge does have one small motel while Victoria has none. Many years ago, the Patrick Henry Hotel served as a stopping place for visitors to Victoria, but that building, which stood empty for many years, has finally encountered the wrecking crane and bulldozer, and there is only a vacant lot where it once stood.

In both Kenbridge and Victoria, closed stores and factories— the classic signs of a town in decline—are not so much in evidence as vacant lots, a sign that neither center ever achieved a full concentration of commercial and social activity. While these "urban centers" in Lunenburg provide jobs, a few places to eat, and a locally owned department store and supermarket (there are, however, no A&Ps or Winn-Dixies in Lunenburg) in which the county's residents can purchase most of their daily necessities, they cannot be considered the most meaningful focus of community activity. Indeed, the saying "Heaven is just seventy-five miles away" (oft-repeated by Lunenburg's residents) tells us much about how Lunenburgers perceive their community. "Heaven" is Richmond, and in the age of the automobile the people of Lunenburg are just as likely to drive the seventy-five miles to that capital city to make a major purchase or see a movie (there are no movie theaters in Lunenburg) as they are to drive the fifteen miles to Farmville, the next biggest town in neighboring Prince Edward County.

Ambling along one of the dozens of state and county roads serving Lunenburg, we are struck not only by the absence of the obvious signs of progress represented by the Big Mac, Colonel Sanders, and The Whopper but also by the relative plainness and small scale of virtually all the surrounding architecture. In twentieth-century Williamsburg, the visitor can view in handsomely restored and carefully sanitized form many of the architectural artifacts of eighteenth-century Virginia's political culture, and in that stretch of the Northern Neck lying between the Potomac and the Rappahannock rivers it is easy even today to gain an impression of eighteenth-century Virginia's plantation culture by touring the magnificent homes of the Lees, Carters, or Tayloes. In Lunenburg, however, neither the eighteenth century nor the twentieth century produced a level of affluence that permitted the county's residents to build such imposing monuments to their political achievements or personal economic success. Local history buffs may point with pride to Magnolia Grove, John Ravenscroft's old homestead, or to Pleasant Hill, the Garland family home, but they are really quite simple frame structures, standing unimposingly amid the rolling hills and lush forest that characterize the terrain of the county.[2] While those simple residences may have served as lively centers of family life, they seem unlikely gathering places for the activities of an entire community, either in the eighteenth century or the twentieth.

There is, however, one striking aspect of the architectural landscape of the county that brings us closer to our search for "community." Lunenburg's sixty-four churches, though unimposing in their individual structures, seem to crop up along every intersection of every road. The roster of churches—thirty-five Baptist, seven Methodist, six Church of Christ, three Nazarene, two Presbyterian, two Episcopal, and so on down the line—is weighted heavily toward fundamentalist denominations, and one suspects that there are still other, smaller sects with even less-imposing houses of worship that might escape the attention of a casual visitor to the county. Judging from the hand-lettered banners visible on many of the church buildings (announcements for buffet suppers, cookouts, and yard sales), the church meetinghouse serves more than a once-a-week function for its congregants.

Those sixty-four churches, serving a population of only a little more than twelve thousand souls, suggest both a diversity and an intensity of religious experience that is not common in most regions of the United States today. And if one looks at the membership of those churches, it becomes apparent that the religious experience of twentieth-century Lunenburgers, like that of their counterparts in earlier years, occurs in two still largely separate spheres—black and white. Not long ago there were many more Afro-American churches in the county, but the number of Lunenburg's black citizens (who as recently as 1960 constituted almost 45 percent of the population) has been steadily declining since that time, a sign in part of the relatively poor prospects faced by young blacks in the county. Still, those blacks who have stayed in the county continue to worship largely among themselves, and their churches—like their white counterparts heavily weighted toward fundamentalist sects—are important centers of black community life and cultural identity.

In the prerevolutionary era, Lunenburg's white population was at least technically committed to the precepts and established ritual forms of the state-supported Church of England, but today it is overwhelmingly committed to the more enthusiastic and emotional forms of fundamentalist religion. Although there are Episcopal churches in Kenbridge and Victoria, they are dwarfed in numbers and total members by the meetinghouses of Baptists, Disciples of Christ, and Methodists. The very number and diversity of the individual congregations within the county suggest a considerable diffusion of community spirit, but those congregations also embody a cluster of shared values and experience that equals more than the sum of the individual activities of each of those families spread across Lunenburg's lush but sparsely settled landscape.

Yet something is still missing from this view of the contemporary character of community life in Lunenburg. We cannot really see it, we cannot locate it precisely in any one visible institution or social center, but there is a general acceptance among at least most white Lunenburgers—be they Baptists, Methodists, or Episcopalians—that they are fellow county-folk. When asked where they live, they do not answer "Kenbridge" or "Victoria" or "Meherrin," but rather, "Lunenburg." And they have a good sense of the historic roots of their county, chortling with some measure of defiant pride as they recount the story of Lunenburg's threat to secede from the state of Virginia in the early months of 1861, when it appeared that Virginia might be having second thoughts about seceding from the Union herself. That tradition of stout localism, embodied in the county's identification of itself as "The Old Free State," plainly gives to Lunenburg's citizens a continuing sense of place and perspective.

That sense of identification contains powerful doses of fundamentalism, localism, and conservative Southern populism (it was no accident that Lunenburg gave heavy majorities to George Wallace in 1968, to Jimmy Carter in 1976, and to Ronald Reagan in 1980), and those elements no doubt provide much of the cement that binds together different religious groupings within the county. In sum, that identification is not very different from counties in western Tennessee, Mississippi, or Arkansas.

The social world of late-twentieth-century Lunenburg, a world in which Billy Graham, Jerry Falwell, the camp meeting, and George Wallace's populism of fear have become the dominant cultural norms, bears little resemblance to the genteel, cavalier world of Anglican gentry such as William Byrd or Richard Randolph, who were among the most prominent of the early pioneers of the region, yet it is that much earlier world—stretching back into the past nearly 250 years—which this study seeks to comprehend. When I first embarked on this project, I drew much of my inspiration from the methods and perspectives of the "new social history." My previous work on eighteenth-century Virginia politics had revealed to me the full level of unconcern that most Virginians felt toward the great political issues of the period, and thus the prospect of studying the daily lives of ordinary Virginians, learning about those things that truly did concern them, seemed not merely voguish but the very essence of the historian's craft.

The immediate models for this study were close at hand, for like so many others I was impressed by the way the New England town studies of Kenneth Lockridge and Philip Greven had been successful in retrieving "the world we had lost," and it seemed plain that I too should study the lives of my Virginians, at close range, within the bounds of their individual communities, as part of that same quest.[3] It was equally plain, however, that the social organization of the closed, corporate seventeenth-century New England town was drastically different from anything existing in the more expansive and mobile society of eighteenth-century Virginia, and that the closest comparable unit of political organization in Virginia—the county—might well require strategies of investigation different from those used by historians of early New England. Indeed, it seemed to me then and even more now that the New England historians themselves had erred in assuming an identity between the geopolitical unit of the town and the "community" for which they were searching. As anthropologist Robert Redfield noted, the principal force holding members of a particular community together is not simply physical space but communication, and the pattern of association and interaction even in the relatively compact seventeenth-century New England town transcended the bounds of any single locality. Redfield's notion of community as a variegated communications network has an even more obvious application to the world of eighteenth-century Virginia, where patterns of association often extended far beyond the boundaries of a single county, as in the case of the planters' commercial dealings with London or Scottish merchants, while at the same time encompassing interactions—such as those at the local tavern or general store—that were even more narrowly bounded than the geographic lines of the county itself.[4]

But Redfield did not abandon the notion that the primary focus of investigation of community norms and activity should be a particular locality. In the end, a community is more than the sum of a series of interconnections along a far-flung communications network, and in order to create for itself some distinctive sense of identity as a community, it must generate within a particular geographic space sets of institutions and associations around which the people of a locality might cluster. In colonial New England that geographic space was the political and social unit of the township; in colonial Virginia—though lacking a political subdivision as compact as the town—the county, which provided such important institutions for group cohesion as the parish church and the court, was the one locally based political unit around which the people of the colony gathered most frequently and intensely. Though hardly the stopping point in the search for community, a locally based political unit was the obvious starting point.

All of which brought me to Lunenburg County. King George II, who listed among his many titles that of the "Baron of Brunswick-Lunëbürg," was probably not even aware that the 1745 session of the Virginia House of Burgesses had named a new county in the wilderness of the Southside in his honor. I was equally ignorant of Lunenburg's history or present circumstance until I began the task of determining which of Virginia's ninety-six counties had the best combination of local records from which a portrait of everyday life could be reconstructed. With its full set of court records, deed books, wills and inventories, tithable and tax lists, Anglican parish vestrybook, and assorted other denominational records, Lunenburg County seemed the best place to start.

No sooner had I begun my study of Lunenburg, however, than I realized that my conception of the project had to change. Settled in the mid-eighteenth century and situated far to the south and west of the traditional centers of political and economic life in Virginia, Lunenburg County was distinctly different from the long-settled parts of the colonial Chesapeake. A "community study" of Lunenburg could therefore not stand as representative of all Chesapeake society. It became clear that in addition to being the starting point for my search for the character of "community" in eighteenth-century Virginia, Lunenburg must also serve as a site in which to observe a more general and far more dynamic historical process—the transmission of culture from older and more settled regions to the frontier.

That process of cultural transmission had begun in the early seventeenth century with the first settlements on Virginia's eastern coastal plain, and when extended farther westward, it was plainly more complex, and its results more ambiguous, than generally recognized. The great weakness of most existing studies of the western regions of Virginia, a weakness that also afflicts treatments of the backcountries of North and South Carolina, is the tendency to regard the histories of those regions merely as fragments of the histories of the colonies to which they were legally attached. But the sources from which Lunenburg County, in common with those counties in much of the Southern backcountry, received its institutions and cultural values were more diverse.

One can perhaps best discern those sources by conceiving of a series of overlapping maps depicting a series of simultaneous but not always compatible streams of influence. Those streams of influence, together encompassing the transplantation of Virginia's political institutions, the expansion of the Chesapeake tobacco economy, and perhaps most decisive, the migration of settlers carrying with them a multitude of cultural traditions, would combine to shape the history of the Virginia Southside in a manner altogether different from that of the eastern Chesapeake a century earlier.

The first of those streams of influence—the transplantation of the political institutions and laws of first the colony and later the independent commonwealth of Virginia—encompasses that aspect of cultural transmission in which Lunenburg's destiny was most closely tied to the history of Virginia itself and in which the direction of influence moved from east to west, from the provincial capital in Williamsburg to the hinterland. The men who were instrumental in Lunenburg's official creation—Anglican gentry such as William Byrd and Richard Randolph—clearly intended that that region be incorporated into the normative framework of the culture in which they played such a visible and dominant role. Those men had invested their resources in the area not only in hopes of pecuniary profit but also at least secondarily in the expectation that their own values would be emulated by others in the as yet unsettled region.[5]

Even in the operation of its political institutions, however, Lunenburg would fail to conform precisely to the expectations of those genteel Virginians in the House of Burgesses, and the reasons for that failure can be understood only with reference to those other streams of influence affecting the county's history. The second of these streams—the extension of a slave-based, agricultural economy to the Virginia backcountry—was not felt by most citizens until long after the political institutions of the parent culture had taken hold, and even when Lunenburg did wed itself to the tobacco culture, the pattern of investment in that crop would be markedly different from that prevailing in those Chesapeake counties which had made the commitment in 1650 or 1700 or even 1750. Lunenburg's increasing commitment to tobacco would gradually bind that county's citizens more closely to the rest of the colony of Virginia, for many of the regulations governing the operation of the tobacco economy were organized around the political unit of the colony. Even here, however, fundamental facts of geography often took precedence over political influence. No amount of regulatory legislation emanating from Williamsburg could transform the shallow, rocky Appomattox River into a main artery of transport connecting west to east, nor could that regulation change the fact that the other major river systems of the county flowed not eastward into Virginia but into Albemarle Sound, in North Carolina.

Those obstacles would merely retard, but not irrevocably block, Lunenburg's entry into the world tobacco market, but by the time Lunenburg had marshaled the resources sufficient to play an important role in that market, the cultural values and styles of those citizens who resided in the county had come to differ irrevocably from those that had prevailed in the prerevolutionary world of the Tidewater and Northern Neck. Part of the explanation for this divergence rests in the unceasing flow of history. While places like Lunenburg were in some ways becoming more like their Chesapeake neighbors to the east, those eastern areas themselves were undergoing changes, which made it impossible for the western counties ever to duplicate the eastern experience at precisely the same point in time. In the area of economic development in particular, Robert "King" Carter's Lancaster County in Virginia's Northern Neck and a Southside county like Lunenburg may have been traveling on roughly the same path, but their schedules were so vastly different that they would never travel over the same landscape at the same time.

The fundamental differences between the world of Robert Carter's Lancaster or William Byrd's Charles City County and Lunenburg were not simply the consequence of disparate timing, for a third stream of influence was also at work, shaping the character of the Virginia Southside in ways that connected the history and culture of that region not to that of colonial Virginia but to the vast expanse of territory running from Frederick County, Maryland, down through the Great Valley, Central Piedmont, and Southside of Virginia, and into North and South Carolina between the Fall Line and the Great Smokies. The history of that region—the colonial Southern backcountry—has too often been written as several histories, as fragments of the history of each of the original Southern colonies, but in fact the people of mid-eighteenth-century Lunenburg were part of the same great wave of settlement which often bound them more closely to the residents of Anson County in North Carolina or the Ninety Six District in South Carolina than to the Anglican-gentry world of William Byrd or Richard Randolph. As we will see, that pattern of settlement was marked by unprecedented rapid population movement in and out of the county, a strikingly diverse (at least by Virginia standards) ethnic and religious mix among the incoming settlers, and—in part a consequence of the previously named conditions—a social and political order that was markedly more egalitarian than that existing anywhere else in the Old Dominion. All these features of settlement are strikingly reminiscent of Frederick Jackson Turner's *American* frontier, but occurring as they did within a structure that was *Virginian*, and with a social and economic system of labor organization that was dependent on racial slavery, the course of the history of Lunenburg would, by the mid-nineteenth century at least, turn in a direction that was distinctly *Southern*.

We can now return to the problem with which I started this project—that of "community." In the midst of this pattern of dynamic historical development which simultaneously bound Lunenburgers to and differentiated them from the traditions of the Old Dominion, the people of that county, like residents of any locality, endeavored to create locally based institutions and networks of association that would serve to bring them together in a system of shared values and aspirations. As we shall see, the initial process of community formation at the local level in Lunenburg was consistently thwarted by the conditions of the frontier. And although the social networks that gave definition to the community grew more dense and varied over the period from the official establishment of the county through the common cause of the Revolution, it would not be until the mid-nineteenth century, when Lunenburg's white residents wedded themselves to a system of values which was explicitly and even virulently racist, that those citizens would embrace a conception of community on which they all could agree. The story that follows is about the creation of bonds of community within a discrete local entity, but ultimately, and more important, it seeks to describe how that local entity, affected by those staples of American historical development—opportunity, mobility, democracy, and ethnic pluralism—came to link its destiny first and foremost to that of the South.

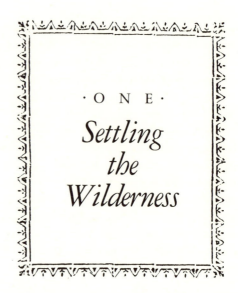

· O N E ·
Settling
the
Wilderness

At the beginning of the eighteenth century the Virginia Southside, extending nearly nine thousand square miles from the Fall Line of the James River to the base of the Blue Ridge Mountains, remained nearly untouched by the political institutions of eastern Virginia, the economic arrangements of the Chesapeake tobacco economy, or the influences of European immigration. It was, at least in the eyes of those white Englishmen who sought to bring it under their domain, a rude wilderness that needed to be tamed and mastered.

• THE SOUTHSIDE FRONTIER, 1700–1746

In 1733, William Byrd II, while surveying his lands in the Southside region that would later become Lunenburg County, recorded some impressions of the character of the area. Byrd had invested in over 100,000 acres of land in the Virginia Southside in hopes that he could lure Swiss and German immigrants to buy tracts and settle there, so it is not surprising that his account of his first thorough survey of the region should stress the potential bounty offered by the new lands. Byrd praised the rich soil, the quality of the timber, and the beauty of the countryside, and he even held out hope that the several copper mines in the area might someday yield substantial returns. But he was unable to subdue his impression of the rudeness and remoteness of the place, believing it "quite out of Christendom." Describing one of the principal plantations of the Southside, he noted that it "was a poor dirty hovel, with hardly anything in it but children that wallowed about like so many pigs." His own house in Lunenburg, where his manager Henry Morris lived, was a modest structure; during the 1733 expedition Byrd's entire party of nine was forced to sleep in one room. Nevertheless, that modest dwelling seems to have been one of the grandest in the Southside. When a neighboring family came to visit they "admired it as much as if it had been the grand Vizier's tent in the Turkish army."[1]

Byrd was hardly more flattering in his comments about some of the "leading citizens" of the region. Cornelius Cargill, founder of what would become one of Lunenburg's principal families, was described by Byrd as a less-than-honest horse trader living in "comfortable fornication with . . . a young woman" of the area. Captain Henry Embry, who would later become one of Lunenburg's first elected burgesses, lived in a "castle containing of one dirty room with a dragging door to it that will neither open or shut. . . . We were obliged to lodge very sociably in the same apartment with the family where, reckoning women and children, we mustered in all no less than nine persons, who all pigged lovingly together."[2]

Byrd's descriptions hardly bring to mind images of the Virginia gentry culture typified by his own life at Westover, or of Robert Carter's Nomini Hall or even of western Piedmont estates like Edgehill or Shadwell, belonging to the Randolph and Jefferson families. He believed that he was traveling in a remote wilderness, a region lacking even rudimentary forms of social and political organization, an untamed, frontier area in the classic sense. Yet by his investments and his visits to the area, Byrd signaled his intention to bring some degree of order to the region, a form of order that would no doubt reflect some of the values and patterns of authority of his own place of residence in Charles City County. And a little more than a decade after Byrd's visit, in its act incorporating Lunenburg as a separate county in 1746, the Virginia

General Assembly signified its intention to bring the county within the political and cultural umbrella of that traditional gentry society in which men like William Byrd played such an important role.

The social and physical characteristics of the vast expanse of wilderness comprising the early Virginia Southside would pose striking contrasts and formidable challenges to those men who, like Byrd, sought to extend to the region the institutions and cultural values of traditional Virginia society. Indeed, the principal forces for order and stability in the communities of the eastern Chesapeake—the economic power of the planter class, the legal power of the county court, and the moral authority of the established church—were all nearly invisible on the early-eighteenth-century Southside frontier.[3] The "community" of that region throughout most of the first half of the century, before the official creation of Lunenburg as a separate entity, can be conceived as a nearly blank map, with only the faintest tracings of the social, economic, and political interaction that characterized the more settled areas of Virginia.

The physical character of the landscape that Byrd encountered was a pleasing one. The terrain, gently sloping hills intersected by countless small rivers and streams, more closely resembled that of the Tidewater than it did the flatter and less densely forested portions of the central Piedmont. Indeed, moving from the central Piedmont into the Southside, one is struck most by the lushness of the forests of pine, oak, and hickory trees that cover the land even today. The soil, varying from red clay in some regions to a gray, sandy mixture in others, was generally well-drained and more than adequate for intensive agricultural production. The only ingredient differentiating the Southside of the 1730s from the Tidewater region from which Byrd had come was a transportation system that made travel from the Southside to the eastern coastal plain arduous in the extreme. The river system of the Southside, though pleasing to the eye, was nearly useless as a means of transport, a fact which would work to hinder the full integration of the Southside into the better-settled parts of the Virginia colony.

The human population of the early-eighteenth-century Southside tended to be both transient and thinly spread across the landscape. The Indian population, linguistically part of the Iroquois, did not constitute much of a threat even at the time of Byrd's initial visit to the area in 1733. The only hint of concern on that trip came when Byrd and his party discovered that a small body of Indians had recently been encamped in the area in which they were traveling. Some of the men were apprehensive about the danger of attack, but Byrd assured his "fellow travellers" that

The Northern Indians were at peace with us, and although one or two of them may now commit a robbery or a murder (as other rogues do), yet nationally and avowedly they would not venture to hurt us. And in the case they were Catawbas, the danger would be as little from them, because they are too fond of our trade to lose it for the pleasure of shedding a little English blood.[4]

For their part, the Indians were concerned less about aggressive military action on the part of the white intruders than about the gradual encroachments on their land. In 1723 the Meherrins, one of the tributary Indian groups of the region, presented

to the most onrable Govner of Vergeny a petsen from the Mehren Engens to your most onrable hiness and exelenc we pore engens have kneed for to complain to your most onrable hiness for our land is all taken from us and the English do say that thay will come and take our corn from us that we have made in our corn fields and wee cannot live at rest except your most onrable hiness do order sum thing to the contrary. . . ."[5]

While the government in Williamsburg did seek to minimize Indian-white conflict of this sort by authorizing the patenting of land only in those areas where the Indian presence was least significant, both the number and military power of Indian groups like the Meherrins were sufficiently slight that by the time of the official creation of Lunenburg County in 1746 the Indians had either been pushed out of the area, to the south and west, or incorporated into the local white population.

The few white men and women living in the Southside in the first three decades of the eighteenth century were still predominantly English and had tended to move to the region from eastern portions of the Chesapeake. While a few of the settlers came to the Southside directly from affluent, well-established counties in

Virginia's Northern Neck, most migrated westward from closer by, either from the less-promising lower peninsula, around Surry and Isle of Wight counties, or from middle Piedmont counties like Henrico, Goochland, and Hanover. With the rare exception of a few speculators like Byrd himself, those who purchased or patented land in the region in the earliest years were not members of Virginia's great families but men and women of humble fortunes, moving westward small distances at a time in search of enhanced opportunity farther out on the Virginia frontier.[6]

Although some of these humble folk may have had fleeting contact with the standards and ideals of the gentry world in their previous places of residence, whatever predispositions they may have had toward recreating the grand style of life of a Byrd or Randolph were apparently thwarted by the paucity of their numbers and of their economic resources. The houses in which they lived, earthfast structures built on posts buried in the ground and walled with turf, earth, or logs, were indicative not only of a people whose supply of capital was small but also of settlers who were often not committed to staying in any one spot long enough to justify investment of scarce resources in more permanent structures. Byrd himself noted the slothful character of all the "plantations" of the region, a condition he blamed on the "common case [that] in this part of the country the people live worst upon good land, and the more they are befriended by the soil and the climate, the less they will do for themselves." Byrd was probably unjust in his judgment. However fertile the soil may have been, the combination of scarce capital and wholly inadequate access to markets made it impossible for anyone in the early Southside to approach a standard of material life that would have been acceptable to eastern gentry like himself.[7]

The very names of the settlements that these earliest pioneers established suggest something different from the nucleated English village or the well-ordered eastern Chesapeake county; Terrible, Difficult, Panther, Wolf Trap, and Wild Cat creeks give some impression of the dangers and hardships faced by the settlers of those localities, and the Tickle Cunt Branch and Fucking Creek, along which several of Lunenburg County's families patented land, suggest something of the coarseness of their existence.[8] And these

Englishmen and women, possessing only modest economic resources and an impermanent attachment to their humble plantations, were unlikely to be able to afford an investment in slaves, so
in the early eighteenth century the presence of Africans in the
Southside wilderness was an exceptional rather than a common
occurrence.

The bonds of social and political organization tying these few
Englishmen, and even smaller numbers of Africans and Indians,
together were stretched thin. The total land area of the Southside
(which today includes seventeen counties ranging from Prince
George and Dinwiddie in the east to Grayson and Franklin counties
at the base of the Blue Ridge Mountains) amounted to nearly nine
thousand square miles. In 1740, as Map 1 indicates, that vast
territory was organized into just two counties—Prince George and
Brunswick—governing a population of about two thousand tithe-
payers spread across that landscape. The line of actual settlement
at that time probably extended to the south and west to the point
where the Roanoke River leaves Virginia, about one hundred miles
from Williamsburg, with the lands west of that point, stretching
another 150 miles to the Blue Ridge, still virtually vacant. The
two courthouses serving the region, located at what were approximately the geographic centers of Prince George and Brunswick
counties, were still more than a day's ride for the residents living
on the edge of settlement in each county, and the impediments
posed by those great distances, the modest qualifications of the
justices and constables charged with the job of enforcing the law,
and the highly aggressive behavior of those citizens who had made
the decision to inhabit that wilderness made maintaining even the
most rudimentary order problematic in the extreme. Indeed, while
the records of virtually every Virginia county are replete with
examples of disrespect for the established forces of law and order,
the records from the courts of the early-eighteenth-century Southside suggest that the forces of law and order were absent so frequently that there was rarely anything toward which to show
disrespect in the first place.[9]

The Anglican ministers assigned to the three parishes of the
region (John Betty of St. Andrew's Parish, Alexander Finney of
Martin's Brandon Parish, and George Robertson of Bristol Parish)

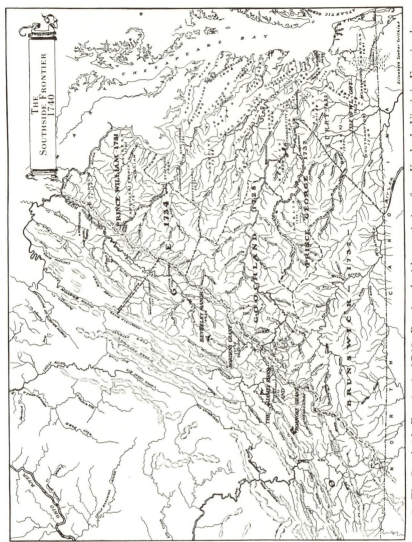

MAP 1. *The Southside Frontier in 1740. Reprinted with permission from Kegley's Virginia Frontier by F. B. Kegley, published by The Southwest Virginia Historical Society, Roanoke, Va.*

had the nearly impossible task of overseeing the moral and spiritual well-being of their far-flung flocks. When queried by the Bishop of London about the state of his parish in 1724, Robertson reported that it included 430 households, whose attendance at church was "pretty strong in good weather" but not nearly as impressive when conditions made travel difficult. Robertson himself had not had any previous experience in the ministry, and indeed had never been formally ordained. The lay vestries of the Southside parishes, recognizing that it was unlikely that the settlers would travel the vast distances necessary for weekly attendance at the parish church, generally instructed the ministers to preach in different parts of the parish on a rotating basis. This practice extended the reach of the established church, but it also undermined still further the authority of the church, for the diffusion of both the minister's energies and the parish's meager resources made it impossible to create a single physical setting in which the lessons and rituals of the established Church of England could be presented in imposing fashion.[10]

If the church, the county court, and the plantation house served as the three principal centers of social activity in the settled communities of Virginia, then the state of community life in the Southside wilderness represented nearly the antithesis of that traditional order. Yet if a half-century before one had been traveling through Hanover County, seventy miles to the northeast of Lunenburg, or, a full century before, through Surry County, eighty miles to the east, the economic, political, and religious institutions of those societies would have appeared equally tenuous. In that sense the history of the Southside frontier represents just one more chapter in the larger story of the transmission of English culture to Virginia. In another, more fundamental sense, however, the subsequent history of the Southside would contain elements altogether different from those that shaped the histories of other Virginia communities a century or even a half-century before.

• THE SETTLEMENT OF LUNENBURG

The process by which this early-eighteenth-century region moved from a series of frontier outposts to a group of settled communities—the process by which the "map" of the communities gained definition—was sufficiently different from that by which English culture was transmitted to the Tidewater and Northern Neck that it was highly unlikely that a county like Lunenburg could ever replicate the patterns of the traditional Virginia culture. Whereas the overwhelming majority of the white settlers of the eastern Chesapeake had been English, the constituent parts of the population of the area that would become Lunenburg came to be more varied. The migration of Englishmen and women from eastern Virginia into Lunenburg continued after 1730, with a large influx of settlers from the "Hanover migration," a movement of predominantly English settlers south and west from Hanover County and its environs, individuals of much the same humble background as those pioneers who first settled in the region in the earliest decades of the century.[11] But those Virginia-born Englishmen were increasingly joined by settlers from Ireland and Scotland who had traveled southward from Pennsylvania, swarming down, in the words of William Byrd, "like the Goths and Vandals of old" and forming a part of the great migration that would change the face of the Southern backcountry by the time of the Revolution. Scottish in nationality, most of those settlers came from families that had migrated to northern Ireland a century before as part of a resettlement policy encouraged by James I. By the second quarter of the eighteenth century, economic discrimination and agricultural depression combined to cause increasing numbers of them to look to America for an improvement in their fortunes. Many of those moving south in the 1730s had already faced the obstacles posed by entrenched white landowners and Indians on the Pennsylvania frontier, and thus their migration into the Southern backcountry was often the second, or even third or fourth, chapter in their search for a better life.[12]

Before 1750 the Scots-Irish migration into Virginia had been confined largely to the Great Valley, but by mid-century many of those settlers had begun to come south through the Staunton River and Maggoty Creek gaps in the Blue Ridge Mountains and to move into the Southside from west to east, thus reversing the traditional flow of settlement on the Virginia frontier.[13] Not everyone (and one suspects that William Byrd would be included in this category) looked on their migration as desirable. It was one thing for those people to congregate in their own relatively isolated and homogeneous communities west of the Blue Ridge, but it was quite another thing for them to mingle, and compete, with those who clung to a definition of civilization that was "English."

To many, the failure of the Scots-Irish to adhere to the traditional forms of the Anglican church was only a signal of a more general cultural deficiency. Charles Woodmason, an Anglican minister who traveled through the backcountry of South Carolina in an effort to convert those Scots-Irish settlers to traditional English religious and social mores, gives us a dramatic picture of the extent to which ethnic antagonisms could be carried. Referring to the "5 or 6000 Ignorant, mean, worthless, beggarly Irish Presbyterians, the Scum of the Earth and Refuse of Mankind" who settled in the Carolina backcountry, he went on to characterize them as

very Poor—owing to their extreme Indolence. . . . They delight in their present low, lazy, sluttish, heathenish, hellish Life, and seem not desirous of changing it. Both men and women will do anything to come at Liquor, Cloaths, furniture, &c, &c rather than work for it—Hence their many vices—their Gross Licentiousness, Wantonness, Lasciviousness, Rudeness, Lewdness, and Profligacy. They will commit the grossest Enormities before my face, and laugh at all Admonition.[14]

Woodmason's assessment was the product of an anguished spirit caused by his obsessive efforts to make the Scots-Irish Presbyterians and Baptists conform to traditional Anglican precepts of decorum and gentility, but if his assessment was more extreme than most, it was nevertheless an extremism born of his inability to reconcile the values of his own, English world with the cultural differences with which the Scots-Irish presented him. And those differences, exacerbated by the natural frictions produced by economic competition, would give to the mid-eighteenth-century Lunenburg landscape a texture very different from that of either the Tidewater or Northern Neck.

The Scots-Irish constituted the largest group of non-English peoples to make their way to the Southside backcountry in search of new opportunity, but the cultural diversity of the region did not end there. In Lunenburg increasing numbers of Swiss and Scottish, and to a lesser extent French Huguenot and German settlers, would be attracted by the combination of cheap land and relatively slight Indian competition for that land, and with their settlement the chances of an exact replication of English culture in the traditional Virginia gentry world would become still more remote.[15]

• THE EARLY ECONOMIC DEVELOPMENT OF LUNENBURG

The settlers who came to shape Lunenburg's social order—diverse in economic position, ethnic and religious background, and often in social aspirations—established their homesteads in a geographic setting that, though ultimately adaptable to the tobacco economy of the eastern Chesapeake, was substantially different in the type of economic development it initially encouraged.

Expansion into the Virginia Southside occurred at a slower rate than expansion into other areas of the Piedmont during the first third of the eighteenth century—which can be explained by a royal land patent policy that encouraged such expansion less actively than in other areas and, perhaps more important, by the impediments to commercial farming posed by the topography of the region. Most notably, the Southside always lacked the advantageous river systems that were such a boon to the growth of the tobacco economy elsewhere in Virginia. The area in and around Lunenburg does have rivers (the Meherrin, the Appomattox, the Nottoway, and the Staunton) but all except the Appomattox flow in the wrong direction, toward Albemarle Sound in North Carolina rather than toward the Chesapeake. Moreover, most of the Southside rivers were unnavigable most of the year; while periodic attempts were made to clear the Appomattox River for navigation, most transportation in that river never went beyond Petersburg.[16]

The impediments that an imperfect river system posed for the transportation of crops to market retarded investment in the region by large-scale eastern planters, who had always taken for granted the advantages they enjoyed with their plantations located at strategic points along the broad banks of the Rappahannock, Potomac, or James rivers. Those planters, who preferred to grow the sweet-scented variety of tobacco that was more highly prized by English smokers, were also no doubt put off by the fact that the soil of the Southside seemed better suited to the cheaper grade, Orinoco tobacco.[17]

In the long run there were many settlers, possessing neither favorable tracts along Virginia's many navigable rivers nor land with the most fertile soil, who found the land of the Southside more than adequate for their needs. Indeed, although the thick forests around Lunenburg may have delayed the process by which the land was cleared for planting, those forests and rolling hills bespoke a countryside that was more promising than the flat, thinly forested lands of much of the Virginia Piedmont. During his 1733 trip, William Byrd found the abundance of hardwood trees to be "certain proofs of a fruitful soil," and as the subsequent growth of the tobacco economy of the Southside attested, the absence of an ideal river system was not an insurmountable obstacle to economic growth.[18]

Throughout most of the late seventeenth and early eighteenth centuries, the royal government in Virginia had discouraged settlement in the Southside both in order to avoid the expense and disruption that Indian warfare might create and to avoid contention over conflicting border claims between Virginia and North Carolina. By 1720, however, the Indian presence no longer posed a threat to European settlement, and the political barriers to settlement had been removed by the royal governor. In fact, in that year Governor Alexander Spotswood agreed to allow individuals to take up free land in the area up to one thousand acres without securing treasury rights or proving head rights.[19]

Settlement proceeded slowly, however, and in 1738 the Virginia General Assembly attempted to provide additional encouragements. In "an act to encourage settlements on the Southern Boundary of this Colony," the assembly noted that the lands in the Southside remained "for the most part unseated and uncultivated" and expressed the belief that "a considerable number of persons, as well of his majesty's natural born subjects as foreign Protestants," would be willing to settle in those lands if the proper incentive could be offered. Accordingly, the 1738 act allowed anyone who settled within the region within the next two years to be exempt from payment of all public, county, and parish levies for a ten-year period and provided for a discount on those levies after that date. In order to attract greater numbers of foreign settlers, the assembly authorized the governor to grant instant letters of naturalization to any alien settlers in the area, provided those individuals subscribed to the customary oaths of allegiance before a clerk of the county court.[20]

The inducements offered by the 1738 act, together with the natural demands created by growing populations both to the north and east, resulted in a quickening of the pace of settlement, as shown by the dramatic increase in the number of land patents issued by the government, by the increase in tithe-payers, and by the speed with which new counties were being created. Of the 3,813 land patents issued between 1703 and 1754, some 1,625 (or 42.6 percent), constituting 44.1 percent of the total acreage, were issued in the ten-year period from 1739 to 1748. The tithe-paying population of the area, which had taken nearly forty years to progress from 1,000 at the beginning of the century to 4,642 in 1739, had jumped to 9,542 by the year 1749.[21]

The pace at which land was being taken up, and the consequent population increase, created the need for new counties capable of providing judicial and administrative services to the new inhabitants of that vast nine-thousand-square-mile region, and this need first brought that portion of the Southside wilderness more decisively within the institutional domain of the colony of Virginia. While the Virginia Southside may have lacked many of the social attributes of the more settled parts of the colony, the willingness of Virginia's provincial leaders to grant full political equality to these newly opened areas stands in marked contrast to the behavior of the established political elites in the Carolinas, where social cleavages between east and west were exacerbated by the determination of the provincial leaders to withhold political rights from the west. In Virginia there was at least an institutional mechanism by which the political culture of the established order extended to newer areas, and though the political decision to create a new county was hardly a guarantee that the citizens of that county would automatically adopt the values and styles of the traditional culture, it did at least provide an institutional framework in which that process of assimilation could begin. In this institutional sense at least, the early history of Lunenburg was shaped by influences that owed less to a common Southern backcountry experience than to the distinctive political traditions of eastern Virginia.[22]

Lunenburg County came into existence on May 1, 1746, the result of an act of the General Assembly of the previous year. It was created by the division of Brunswick County, which had been created fifteen years earlier by the division of the first Southside county, Prince George.[23] As in virtually all cases where a division of a single county into two or more counties was contemplated, the decision to divide Brunswick and create Lunenburg was not reached without opposition. The petitioners in favor of the division, who generally lived farthest from the services provided by the existing county government, based their claims on the necessity of making the judicial and administrative services of the court more readily available to all citizens of the colony. And since the creation of a new Anglican parish with boundaries coinciding with the political lines of the new county was also part of the scheme, the petitioners argued that the maintenance of religion and public virtue would also be enhanced by such a division. The opponents of the division, both in this case and in the numerous subsequent divisions of Lunenburg itself, tended to feel that the advantages to be gained by an expanded government and religious establishment were simply not worth the additional costs that would be incurred in setting up those new agencies. Among those who supported the elevation of Lunenburg to the status of a separate county, many favored that plan only if the exemptions granted by the 1738 act for the encouragement of settlement were repealed, so that the new county would be able to raise revenue sufficient to support the additional costs of a new civil and religious establishment.[24]

This ambivalence toward the creation of institutions that had traditionally symbolized the twin pillars of power and authority in most Virginia communities was indicative of the ambiguity of the character of the Southside social order itself. Lunenburg, for example, encompassed nearly five thousand square miles of land at its creation, over half the total land area of the Southside. That sparsely settled territory was inhabited by 1,270 tithables, indicating a total population of perhaps 3,000. While there are no surviving lists that enable us to calculate precisely the proportion

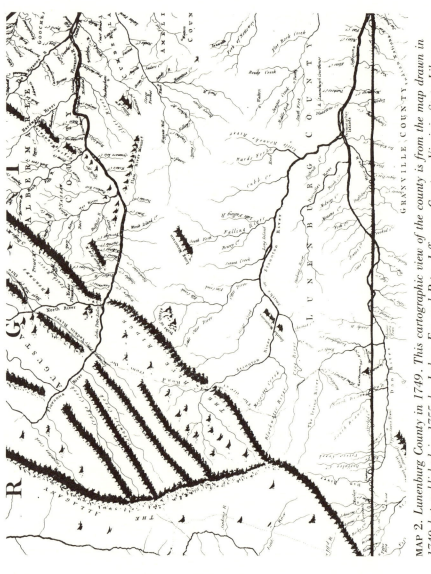

MAP 2. Lunenburg County in 1749. This cartographic view of the county is from the map drawn in 1749 but published in 1755 by Joshua Fry and Peter Jefferson. Courtesy Virginia State Library,

of heads of households, white dependents, and slaves among the tithable population, calculations from subsequent years would indicate that probably half the tithable population were heads of households, one-third were slaves, and the remainder were white dependents.[25] Although settlers tended to congregate in the eastern portion of the county (a predictable pattern given the east-to-west flow of migration into the region before 1750), the dominant impulse among the county's settlers was toward dispersion. In early New England, or perhaps even in a Tidewater Virginia county, a population amounting to 650 households may have constituted a substantial settlement, but when those households were spread out over five thousand square miles of wilderness, the resulting mode of social organization was markedly different from either the New England town or the traditional Virginia county.

With few exceptions the ordinary citizens who found themselves living in Lunenburg at the time of its creation were men and women on the move. Although it is possible to identify a handful of individuals with attachments to the Southside dating back a decade or more, the majority of Lunenburg's first citizens were men like Lewis Deloney, Abraham Cook, or John Edloe, who had arrived there recently from older counties in eastern Virginia.[26] Moreover, most of those new arrivals were not likely to stay put in Lunenburg once they arrived. During the two years separating the assessment of the tithable population in 1748 and 1750, for example, nearly 37 percent of the county's citizens disappeared from the lists. A search of the wills and inventories of the period accounts for 2 percent of that 37 percent, but we are still left with an out-migration averaging perhaps as much as 17.5 percent of the population each year.[27]

The values, motives, and life-styles of these transient residents are almost entirely lost to us. We do know that they owned the least land and the fewest slaves and that the number of tenants and overseers in their ranks was proportionately much higher than that for the population of the county as a whole. But we can only guess at the actual condition of their lives. Among the tenants, some must have lived in crude outbuildings on the farmsteads of others, and among those householders who were listed by the tithe-taker as independent, most no doubt lived in the same impermanent earthfast houses that typified settlements everywhere in the back-country. Some of those structures were most likely erected by the householders themselves, but given the high rate of out-migration from the county, others were probably vacated frequently enough to serve as shelters for successive waves of new settlers.

Transients who found themselves in positions of dependence, working for others, may have been better protected against extreme adversity than those who could claim an independent freehold yet lacked the capital to make that freehold productive. But whatever protections dependence may have offered were plainly not suffi-cient to cause many people to wish to remain in that position long. Independence was the goal, and dependents in Lunenburg who failed to join the ranks of the county's freeholders almost invariably left the county in search of that opportunity elsewhere.

The destinations of transients moving out of the county were so diverse that any consistent tracking of their subsequent careers is impossible, but there is enough scattered information on a few families to suggest that they continued to push south and west, into North and South Carolina, Georgia, Kentucky, and Tennessee, continuing their quest for an improvement in their economic prospects and, with that improvement, the cherished goal of independence.[28]

Those who left in such large numbers for greener pastures were replaced by even larger numbers of newcomers. The total popula-tion of Lunenburg increased at an average rate of 16 percent during the period 1746–51, indicating a migration of new settlers into the county amounting to over 30 percent of the existing population each year.[29] The astonishing mobility—running both in and out of the county—nearly eliminated the hope of creating a stable and all-encompassing locally based community life. The differences in ethnic backgrounds, life-styles, and values even among the estab-lished citizens of the county made the task of community-building difficult, but the extraordinary influx of strangers into that popu-lation strained the bonds of community still further.

The economic structure of early Lunenburg displayed a lack of differentiation characteristic of a frontier region that had not yet become engaged in an extensive world-market-oriented economy. With the exception of a small group of nonresident landowners, most of whom were more intent on speculation than on enhancing their social and political power within the county, there existed in Lunenburg no group that could boast of vastly disproportionate holdings in either land or slaves.

There were essentially two avenues by which one could acquire legal title to land in Lunenburg. The most straightforward (and ultimately most common) form of transaction was outright purchase. In the initial years of the county's history, however, the colonial government in Williamsburg usually granted patents— parcels of free land—to those willing and able to negotiate the various legal and bureaucratic hurdles necessary to secure the patent. Both methods resulted in a generally equitable distribution of land. Table 1 shows that more than 93 percent of the 292 land sales within the county during the period 1746–51 involved tracts of up to six hundred acres, and less than 2 percent dealt with parcels larger than a thousand acres. Some individuals were able to amass larger holdings by means of land patents, but of seventeen men who received land patents in excess of two thousand acres, fifteen resided outside the county. The vast majority of the 447 patents issued during the first five years of the county's existence (82 percent) involved tracts of less than six hundred acres.[30]

The modest character of most individual holdings seems all the more striking when one considers both the quantity of land in the county which remained unoccupied and how cheaply land could be obtained. The cost of the patenting process was roughly £1 for every ninety-three acres of land, and although many people seemed to consider the process too troublesome to undertake, the cost of securing a land patent was not a serious deterrent to ownership. While a few individuals living outside the county (most notably William Byrd, Richard Randolph, and Richard Kennon) used their superior political influence to secure patents far in excess of the four-hundred-acre maximum considered customary, the device of the land patent, particularly during the early years of the county's development, worked toward greater equality rather than inequality in the distribution of landownership.[31]

Patenting was initially the most common method of acquiring land, but Lunenburg's settlers gradually turned toward direct purchase as the preferred way of securing legal title to land. This

TABLE 1 DISTRIBUTION OF LAND PATENTS, LAND SALES,
AND LAND PRICES, LUNENBURG COUNTY, 1746–1751

Distribution of Land Patents

Acres	No. of Patents	% of Patents	Total Acres	% of Acres
0–100	18	4.0	841	0.3
101–200	63	14.1	10,756	4.1
201–300	79	17.7	20,436	7.8
301–404[a]	167	37.4	63,175	24.2
405–600	39	8.7	18,259	7.0
601–1,000	39	8.7	31,382	12.0
1001–2,000	25	5.6	36,981	14.3
2,001 and over	17	3.8	78,868	30.3
	447	100.0	260,698	100.0

Average acreage per patent—583
Median acreage per patent—392

Distribution of Land Sales

Acres	No. of Sales	% of Sales	Total Acres	% of Acres
0–100	37	12.7	2,693	2.8
101–200	65	22.3	10,570	11.0
201–300	61	20.9	15,751	16.3
301–400	63	21.6	22,729	23.6
401–600	46	15.7	23,041	23.9
601–1,000	11	3.7	8,399	8.7
1,001 and over	9	3.1	13,247	13.7
	292	100.0	96,430	100.0

Average acreage per sale—330
Median acreage per sale—270

Distribution of Land Prices

Acres per £	No. of Sales	% of Sales	Total Acres	% of Acres
0–5.0	73	25.9	16,294	17.6
5.1–10.0	76	27.0	23,002	24.8
10.1–15.0	40	14.2	13,880	15.0
15.1–20.0	57	20.2	22,676	24.4
20.1–25.0	19	6.7	9,417	10.2
25.1 and over	17	6.0	7,394	8.0
	282[b]	100.0	92,663	100.0

SOURCE: Lunenburg County Deed Books, no. 1 (1746–51) and no. 2 (1750–52), Virginia State Library, Richmond, Va.

[a]The customary number of acres that an individual could patent and still remain under the technical legal limit of 400 acres per transaction was 404.

[b]This total omits ten transactions that involved only token payments.

development in part reflected the fact that much of the best land had already been taken up through the patenting process, and indeed many land sales involved the subdivision of portions of larger tracts that had initially been acquired by patent. However, the trend toward direct purchase was not necessarily a sign of rigid stratification within the economic order; many people used that method simply because it was easier than the time-consuming method of going to Williamsburg and proving one's claim to a patent.[32]

Because the variation in the purchase prices involving unimproved lands on the edges of the frontier and improved lands in the more settled portions of the county near good roads was so great, the average costs of land purchases during the first two decades of the county's existence are not reliable as guides to the cost of setting up a farm. The most common kind of purchase during the 1740s and 1750s was a parcel of land between two hundred and four hundred acres, most often at a price of around two or three shillings an acre. The range was considerable, with at least one individual picking up 468 acres for only £7 10s. At the other extreme, a 100-acre tract with house and outbuildings was purchased for £100. In general, however, while the move toward land purchase rather than patent did involve some modest increase in the cost per acre of unimproved land, it was not likely to be the determining factor in an individual's ability to become an independent freeholder. The costs of improving the property, building a house, and buying the tools and livestock necessary to make the land productive were much more significant than the £10 or £20 necessary to purchase a tract of one or two hundred acres.[33]

Labor was a much more precious commodity than land in the spacious landscape of the Virginia Southside, and an individual's ability to control a sizable labor force was more important than his land both as a sign of wealth and as a means to wealth. In 1750 only 22 percent of Lunenburg's households could afford slaves, and a mere 2 percent of the households owned more than five tithable slaves. What is more telling, only two men owned more than fifteen tithable slaves—nonresidents William Byrd with sixty-two and William Ruffin with sixteen.[34]

Black slaves were not the only source of dependent labor. In the traditional Virginia society white servants, though on the decline, had often played an important part in the labor force. In Lunenburg in 1750 the number of white males age sixteen and above living with (and presumably working for) another householder was 311, or 15 percent of the tithable population and approximately 5 percent of the total population. Among those 311, only 131 (or 2 percent of the population) were not the sons or other relatives of the head of the household in which they lived.[35] Indeed, while it is possible that many nonlandowning heads of households may have worked for other, landowning householders, it is clear that the number of dependent white laborers who actually lived as servants with the householders for whom they worked constituted an insignificant percentage of the county's labor force at all points in the county's history. The indentured servant, so important to the growth of the economy in the seventeenth-century Chesapeake, would never be an important factor and would gradually fade from existence in the more spacious and open-ended landscape of the eighteenth-century Virginia frontier.

Some of the county's residents, particularly those who owned slaves, were growing tobacco for the export market, but in this county of modest landholdings, scarce supplies of capital with which to purchase labor, and a still-underdeveloped transportation system, most farmers devoted their labors to the production of locally consumed foodstuffs. The bulk of those foodstuffs were no doubt consumed by the families who raised them, but given the extraordinarily rapid demographic expansion of the Southside during the 1740s and 1750s, it is also likely that newcomers to the area constituted a significant market for the corn, wheat, and livestock raised by those established residents capable of producing agricultural surpluses.

Among the grain crops, corn remained the most important part of the settlers' diet, but a substantial amount of the settlers' investment went into livestock. Of the forty-seven estates inventoried in Lunenburg during the period 1746–53, thirty-nine (83 percent) listed cattle in herds ranging from three to fifty-three. Some 57 percent of the farms inventoried raised hogs in herds of one to seventy-four, and roughly one-quarter of the farms raised sheep.[36] The raising of livestock was a sensible solution to the problem of subsistence in a land-rich, labor- and transportation-deprived frontier area. Cattle, hogs, and sheep required relatively little attention, and for those who wished to sell them rather than consume them on the premises, they had a distinct advantage over the grain crops in their ability to provide much of their own locomotion in getting to market.

The cultivation of tobacco would ultimately provide the base on which the Southside Virginia economy would rest, and even in the 1740s and 1750s many settlers did try to set aside some land and some labor to grow the crop. The tobacco most commonly grown in the Southside was of the Orinoco variety, growing on short stems from the stalk, with a narrow, smooth leaf pointed like a fox's ear. When mature, the stalks reached a height of five to six feet, producing tobacco of a dark green color. Though generally not as highly prized as the milder, sweet-scented tobacco, Orinoco was nevertheless the standard type of tobacco exported and sold to European smokers. The tobacco plants themselves were cultivated in a series of small closely clustered hills, usually numbering between four or five thousand per acre. Since a single adult laborer could tend only about six thousand plants of tobacco per year (and a child about three thousand plants), the size of the early Southside tobacco "plantations" was limited by scarce supplies of labor. As a result, few of Lunenburg's early residents could claim extensive involvement in the world tobacco economy.[37]

The other major impediment to easy riches in the tobacco trade was the region's primitive transportation system. And because the nearest tobacco inspection stations were located east of the Fall Line (some fifty or seventy-five miles away), the effects of poor transportation were felt even more severely. Virtually all the rivers in the area were unnavigable by ordinary craft, and few of the roads were wide enough or smooth enough to accommodate wagons, so tobacco planters had to devise alternative means to get their crops to market. The most common means of transport was the simple rolling of hogsheads. As William Tatham, eighteenth-century expert on tobacco cultivation, described it, Southside planters added extra hickory hoops to their hogsheads for reinforcement, turned them on their sides, "drove pegs into the headings, and attached hickory limbs as shafts, and the horse or oxen

FIGURE 1. *These highly stylized drawings depict the four most common ways of transporting tobacco to market. In early Lunenburg the settlers relied primarily on rolling the hogsheads or, less frequently, floating the hogsheads downriver on canoes. Courtesy of The Tobacco Institute*

was attached to this oddity."[38] It was an inexpensive method in the short run, but the hogsheads took a beating on the rough-hewn roads, and a planter might discover at the end of a long journey that the hogsheads were cracked and his tobacco was contaminated with sand or mud.[39]

If a planter wished to negotiate one of the rivers in the region, he might rig two canoes together with crossbeams on which two hogsheads were placed for the trip downstream. This was not an ideal method, for there was always the danger that the tobacco would end up at the bottom of the river; in Lunenburg, where many of the rivers ran in the wrong direction, this mode seemed to hold even less appeal.[40] The important fact about all these options is that they tended to be suited only to planters engaged in a relatively modest production of the crop.

The only individuals in the county who did not conform to this pattern of small landholdings and slaveholdings and primary reliance on the production of foodstuffs were those few whose primary residences were outside the county but who had sizable investments in Lunenburg as well. At the time of Lunenburg's creation, William Byrd (who had holdings of 125,000 acres and sixty-two tithable slaves) and Richard Randolph (with 20,477 acres and thirteen tithable slaves) were the most prominent representatives of a small group set dramatically apart from the rest of Lunenburg's taxpayers by their wealth, political power, and social authority outside the county. It is conceivable that these wealthy nonresidents played an important role in transmitting to the frontier the styles and values of the gentry tradition, and it is certain that by their economic power within the county alone they set a standard for the aspirations of others, occasionally affecting directly the economic life of the county. For example, William Byrd II was listed as the grantor in no less than twenty-nine land transactions during the period October 1750 to October 1751. In Byrd's case the economic power of a large-scale land speculator also carried over into the political arena; he served in the House of Burgesses as a representative from Lunenburg for four consecutive sessions during the years 1752–54, relinquishing his seat only after he was elevated to the Governor's Council in 1755.[41]

It is tempting to regard a man like Byrd as the ranking member of Lunenburg's elite, as a man who by his power and personal authority set and enforced the standards for the rest of the community. But when we look at the infrequency with which Byrd visited Lunenburg, or even at the relative inactivity of Byrd's agents in the overall economic life of what remained a subsistence economy, it is difficult to sustain the belief that Byrd or any of his wealthy co-speculators in Lunenburg managed to exert any appreciable influence on the cultural mores of the county.[42]

When one excludes this small group of wealthy, nonresident landholders and slaveholders from calculations of wealth distribution in early Lunenburg, the distinctly wealthy "economic elite" of the county disappears, leaving behind a cluster of residents at the top possessing only modest holdings. A few longtime residents of the region (men like Clement Read, Henry Embry, and John Twitty) had managed to accumulate landholdings of a thousand acres or more, but even they lacked at this early stage the labor forces required to make their lands anything more than modestly productive in the present and potentially valuable as objects of speculation in the future.

As a consequence, the economic power of the great slave plantation in Lunenburg, both as a source of wealth and as a symbol of other forms of power and authority, remained only a shadow of its counterparts in the traditional culture. That this was a readily observable reality as well as a statistical reality is revealed by the few surviving descriptions of early Lunenburg plantations. We have already read William Byrd's scornful observations on the dismal state of accommodations in Lunenburg in the early 1730s, where the prevailing mode of architecture seemed to be dirty, delapidated, one-room dwellings. Things had improved by the early 1750s, but not to the point that Lunenburg was producing significant rivals to Westover or Nomini Hall. The one resident of Lunenburg who seems to have been consistently building his estate from his arrival in the region in 1733 to the elevation of Lunenburg to separate county status was Clement Read. His plantation was considered by all to be the finest in the area, but its principal distinction, at least at the time it was initially built sometime in the 1730s, was that it was the first framed house in the county.[43] When contrasted to the simple one- and two-room earth or log houses that dominated the landscape, Read's plantation home may have commanded for him a respect that no other resident landowner in the county received, yet Read himself, who had spent his youth in the Tidewater world of William Byrd and John Robinson, must have been acutely aware of how far short of the gentry ideal his estate fell. And Read's house was unquestionably the exception. Although the simple dwellings of Read's neighbors were too unexceptional to warrant description in official or personal records of the county, the accounts of personal belongings in the estate inventories of the period (so detailed that they often include every used bottle, scrap of cloth, or piece of iron) bespeak a life not only of austerity but also of hardship and travail.

William Howard, an original justice of the Lunenburg court until his death in 1750 and one of the most prosperous men in the county, had managed to accumulate most of the essential ingredients of farm production—a slave, thirty-five cattle, ten horses, thirty-seven sheep, thirty-nine hogs, a cart, and a few rudimentary farm implements—but aside from a few knives and forks and some earthenware pots (still luxury items in the Southside, even in the mid-eighteenth century), Howard's household possessions were those of a pioneer and not a grandee.[44] At the other end of the scale, there were men like Charles Simmons, whose estate, valued at £6 18*s*. 1*d*., was meticulously examined after his death in 1751 and then sold to pay his debts. That examination serves to highlight the poverty in which he lived. An iron pot, two bowls, two bottles, an old mug, and some spoons constituted the extent of his kitchen supplies; a hoe, a calf and a yearling, an "old horse" worth less than a pound, a gun, and an old file and drawing knife comprised the goods and tools with which he made his living.[45] The only possessions that separated those among the middling ranks (those with estate valuations between £40 and £75) from unfortunates like Simmons were a few horses of higher value, an axe, a spade, a few cattle, some simple carpenter's tools, a bed (but probably not a feather bed or a bedstead), and a few more plates and pots for the kitchen.

Taken together, all the quantitative measures of economic endeavor and attainment suggest that the manner of economic life experienced by virtually everyone in the county, save a few nonresidents like William Byrd or the exceptional Clement Read, was not markedly different from the upper to the lower end of the economic spectrum. On most farms, no matter what the total acreage, it would have been unusual for a family to have more than three or four acres under active cultivation in tobacco—about the minimum sufficient for a marketable crop—with perhaps another few acres set aside for foodstuffs. Ownership of a slave might permit the household to expand its plantings by a few acres, but that additional harvest was not likely to change either the style or the rhythm of the family's life dramatically. The result was likely to be only a modest crop. With the nearest tobacco inspection stations located far away, and a crude system of transport requiring the rolling of hogsheads to market, the head of the household could hardly expect magnificent profits at the end of the process.

The time not devoted to the cultivation of crops was spent tending and marketing the livestock, which at least in the early years of Lunenburg's existence may have been a more bountiful and dependable source of income than either tobacco or grain crops. Even in the relatively temperate climate of the Virginia Southside, it was necessary to provide a source of heat for the winter months. The primitive technology of harvesting wood—confined to a bow saw and perhaps a sledgehammer and a few wedges—dictated that those 90 percent of Lunenburg's households possessing fewer than two slaves would have to spend about 40 percent of their laboring hours between the months of October and April on the tasks of sawing, hauling, and splitting the wood necessary to provide even minimal comfort during the winter. Even then, with open fireplaces and drafty log and frame houses, the result was likely to be a household environment that was alternately too hot or too cold. And though the meager resources of most Lunenburg planters made it financially burdensome to construct a dwelling separate from the main house for use as a kitchen, failure to take that step exposed one to the altogether too common hazard of burning one's house to the ground in the dead of the winter.[46]

The farmsteads these Southside pioneers constructed were not particularly pretty places—a crude house, a relatively small parcel of cultivated land, slightly larger parcels of grazing land in which the stumps of those trees cut for firewood still jutted from the ground, and all around, more "partially improved" land which, though the trees from the thick forests were starting to come down, was at this early stage exploited only as a source of fuel and left barren and scarred until the labor necessary for further clearing and cultivation could be mobilized.

It must have been a frustrating existence. The abundance of land seemed to offer economic opportunities unimagined in the Old World, but the shortage of labor, an insufficient accumulation of capital which made it difficult even to purchase the equipment to allow a household to maximize the efficiency of its labor force, and the distance of markets from the plantations made agricultural life in the Virginia Southside nearly as arduous and precarious as it had been in Europe. There was, to be sure, an independence in being a freeholder, a fundamental "liberty" that one enjoyed, but that liberty was all too often accompanied by the burdens of carving out an existence in what was still a rude wilderness.

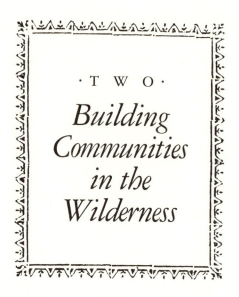

·T W O·

*Building
Communities
in the
Wilderness*

The contrast between the humble way of life in Lunenburg and the styles of the gentry world to the east was dramatic. In the eastern Chesapeake, those who made it to the top of the economic ladder established and reinforced their hegemony by impressive displays of economic power. Their plantations, imposing in their design— with ballrooms, large and ornate dining rooms, wide hallways, glittering crystal and silver plate—were powerful symbols not only of their good fortune in the economic arena but also of their superior claims to political power and personal authority. No one living in Lunenburg could match the economic attainments of the Chesapeake gentry, but once the Virginia provincial government had extended the formal legal institutions of the traditional culture to the newly created county, some could at least aspire to some of the political power and religious authority enjoyed by their counterparts to the east. They would discover, however, that though some small measure of the formal power inherent in Virginia's secular and religious establishments might be transplanted to the west, the personal authority that made Virginia's burgesses, gentleman justices, and vestrymen such imposing figures was not something that could be created by an act of a legislature or the proclamation of a royal governor.

• THE BEGINNINGS OF A FRONTIER RULING CLASS

If the plantation was the seat of economic power in the traditional culture, then the county courthouse and all those establishments and activities near the courthouse served as the settings in which that economic power was most visibly integrated with personal and political authority. Once a month at the courthouse, people assembled to observe the gentlemen justices, bewigged and in their fine waistcoats, adjudicate the disputed issues of the community through jury trial. Bearing the king's commission and sworn "to do equal Right to the Poor and to the Rich . . . according to the Law," the justices usually sat on a raised bench at the center of the gathering. Their power was manifested visibly in the ability to manage the mechanisms of county government, which in turn influenced the distribution of resources in their communities. This could be seen in their control over the legal process of land distribution, the arbitration of debtor-creditor disputes, the process of tobacco inspection, the construction of internal improvements, and the regulation of the commercial life of their counties generally. Moreover, their formal legal power was augmented by their own wealth and economic power, which often gave them a special interest and influence in the outcome of the legal proceedings over which they presided. Not all the business on court days was transacted inside the courthouse, for the monthly meeting of the court was also the occasion for the more informal arranging of deals, the settling of debts, and the enjoyment of conviviality at the tavern or ordinary, of which there was always at least one by the courthouse. In most counties the courthouse served as a fairground on court days.[1]

In early Lunenburg the relatively meager economic power of local resident leaders, together with the impediments to the forceful exercise of power and authority that such a spacious and unevenly settled landscape imposed, created a frailty of institutional power and personal authority that made the court and those more informal institutions surrounding it only pale reflections of those on which they had been modeled.

The Lunenburg court seems not to have played much of a role in the lives of the citizens whose conduct and interests it was charged with overseeing. The volume of the court's official business during the early years of the county's existence was remarkably slight. The Lunenburg justices tried only one-third as many cases during the 1740s and early 1750s as they would in the 1760s and 1770s, even though the population of the county, as a result of frequent subdivisions, remained roughly constant during those decades. One reason for the light caseload was the sporadic character of the court's calendar. During the period from June 1746 to October 1751, for example, the court missed thirty-two monthly meetings, or nearly half its stipulated meetings each year.[2]

Even in later years, when the court met more consistently, the range of concerns of the Lunenburg justices was never as broad as that of their eastern contemporaries. For example, the Lunenburg justices rarely proceeded against individuals for swearing, for drunkenness, for violation of the sabbath, or for bastardy, all of which were common subjects of the court's attention in older counties. Though it is obvious that the gentlemen justices of the Tidewater and Northern Neck were not uniformly committed to a vigilant defense of a strict moral code, the maintenance of that code was at least in the ideal an important responsibility of those entrusted with setting standards of virtue and gentility in their communities.[3]

In Richmond County, in the Northern Neck, where the presence of Landon Carter on the county bench served to alert the court to nearly all breaches of civil peace and decorum, the justices continually sought to serve as the conscience of the public at large. John Penny, presented before the grand jury for being a "common drunkard and notorious swearer," faced heavy fines for his transgressions. All the fines collected from "common swearers" (there were dozens of such violations each year, with the fines usually set at ten shillings) went for the care of the poor in the parish, another area that occupied the attentions of the justices in Richmond much more consistently than in Lunenburg. When Edmund Norton and Edward Goodeby engaged in "fighting and quarreling in the courtyard," the Richmond justices ordered them to suffer the indignity of a half-hour in the stocks. The list of civil and criminal concerns of the Richmond court could be extended nearly indefinitely—fining ordinary keepers for overcharging their customers, keeping a close watch on those who absented themselves from church for more than a month at a time, the disciplining of masters for mistreating their servants, a constant attempt to sort truth from falsehood in assault and battery cases. The dominant impression that emerges from the Richmond County court records during the 1740s and 1750s is of an agrarian society where social relations were sufficiently coarse so as to promote numerous breaches in the legal code, but where the justices bearing the responsibility for upholding that code appear to have been wholly committed to the standards of gentility and decorum which formed the basis of the gentry ideal.[4]

In Lunenburg, by contrast, the lack of attention to matters of decorum seemed to extend into the sphere of criminal law as well. There is a startling absence of activity in the court on such routine criminal matters as disturbances of the peace, minor theft, and even assault and battery. The conditions of life in frontier counties like Lunenburg made it hardly likely that the absence of such routine civil and criminal business before the court was a reflection of the chastity, sobriety, piety, and law-abiding character of the citizens of the area. Rather, the justices were either unable to exert their discipline in such matters or were unconcerned with them altogether. At least in areas involving the maintenance of the public morality, the private behavior of a justice such as Cornelius Cargill, who was noted for his liberality in matters involving both liquor and sexual conduct, suggests that unconcern may have been the prevailing attitude.[5]

The few areas in which the Lunenburg justices did take an active hand suggest the more pressing demands imposed by the unsettled society in which they were operating. The shortage of labor and the vastness of the landscape made the problem of runaway white servants, whose social station and place of origin was vague and often unimportant in this more loosely structured world, an exceptionally difficult one. The Lunenburg records chronicle the attempts of masters to recover their servants, but one suspects that for every servant who was recaptured and punished by the standard formula of extending his or her term of service by twice the number of days the servant was absent, there were many more who were never recovered and therefore do not appear in the court records at all.

Just as the Lunenburg justices were responsible for seeing that

their own servile white labor force did not run away, so too were
they forced to deal with the more numerous instances of those who
had fled from other counties to Lunenburg in search of freedom
and expanded opportunity. In some cases the individual was captured in Lunenburg, identified as a runaway servant, and ordered
back to his or her master. In other cases, such as that involving
Margaret Smith, the problem was one of simple vagrancy. Although
not wanted by any specific individual elsewhere, she was considered a burden on the county's meager public resources and therefore warned out of the county and ordered to return to her last
place of residence in Prince William County.[6]

The most pressing aspect of the court's early business related
not so much to the maintenance of law, civil order, and the public
morality as to the establishment of those rudimentary services and
facilities that were essential to the economic and social life of the
region. The overwhelming portion of the early administrative business of the court was related to the laying out and clearing of
roads, a responsibility that initially fell on the several men in the
county who were deemed competent as surveyors, but which was
then shifted to all "male laboring tithables" in each of the areas
where the clearing actually had to be done. In the first year alone
the court ordered the clearing of no less than thirty-four roads (or
at least stretches of roads), a formidable task that nevertheless
probably still left substantial portions of the five-thousand-square-
mile county unconnected with either the court or the mainstream
of economic activity.[7]

Indeed, during the first year of the county's existence it was
difficult for anyone to be certain of their access to the courthouse,
for that edifice did not yet exist in any permanent way. It is not
known where the initial session of the court met in May 1746, but
the June session was held at the house of Thomas Bouldin, sheriff
of the county, and the July session at "Burwell's Quarter on Butch-
er's Creek," apparently one of the cultivated tracts of the nonresident planter and speculator Lewis Burwell.[8] At the July session
the court ordered the county surveyors, John Hall and Peter Fon-
taine, to make the surveys necessary to locate the geographic
center of the county, the standard means of determining the location of the courthouse, but in August it was determined that the
geographic center was located in a spot which "is Barren and . . .

there is no spring convenient." At that point Lewis Deloney, a carpenter who had migrated west to Lunenburg from Williamsburg, and James Murray offered "to build a Courthouse, stocks and pillory" on Murray's land about a mile away from the center point. Deloney's plans proposed a "sufficient and necessary Prison" and an "office in the Courthouse and a Press for the safekeeping and preservation of the Law Books, Papers and Records which shall or may from time to time be left there . . . and also a Table for the clerk to write on."[9]

The court apparently went ahead with those plans, although by September 1747, a time when Deloney's and Murray's courthouse should have been completed, the justices noted

the many Grievances that attend the present situation of this Courthouse, which are as follows to wit: that the water near and convenient and which is now made use of is unclean, unwholesome, very bad and not fit to drink. That the place where the Courthouse is situate is not Centrical but Inconvenient to the majority of the Inhabitants of the County . . . and is so illy situated that it is Impracticable to have Convenient and necessary Roads to lead to it from hardly any part of the County.

The court then appointed John Hall, David Stokes, and Clement Read to ask the governor's permission to have the site moved, but the records of neither the colony nor the county indicate whether anything ever came of the request.[10]

Next to the laying-out of roads and the construction of the courthouse itself, the licensing of ordinaries was the area of endeavor which probably most affected the lives of the largest number of Lunenburg's citizens. In 1746 alone the court granted nine licenses for ordinaries, most of those to be kept in private homes, but one of them—that granted to John Cooper in December 1746—to be kept at the courthouse itself, thus perpetuating a tradition long in practice in many Virginia counties and at least providing a first step toward the merging of the legal and social functions of the court.[11] Nevertheless, the sheer physical size of the county, which still required more than a day's ride to the court for those on the outskirts of the county, would make a meaningful merging of those functions impossible as far as most of Lunenburg's citizens were concerned.

The sum and substance of the court was dependent on more

than roads, courthouse buildings, and specifically designated legal functions, and in most parts of the Chesapeake the gentlemen justices used their considerable personal authority to enhance the formal political power of the court. In that fashion it was often possible for a single justice to dispense advice, adjudicate disputes, and oversee the administration of county business on an informal basis within his own residential area, where his personal influence was sufficiently great to make it unnecessary for people to travel all the way to the courthouse to present their business. Given the extraordinary difficulty involved for some in traveling fifty miles or more from the outskirts of the county to the court, this would have been a practical way to transact business in Lunenburg. It was at least theoretically possible to do so, for the governor, in making his initial appointments to the court, did make some effort to provide for a relatively even distribution of justices throughout the geographic expanse of the county. [12]

The system of informal justice that prevailed in other parts of the Chesapeake depended on the economic power and personal authority of those individuals entrusted with dispensing that justice, and the ruling elite of Lunenburg could not lay a clear claim to these attributes. [13] One of the most important factors contributing to political stability in an eastern county like Richmond was the presence of men like Landon Carter, who were visibly recognized, if not universally admired, as the *leaders* of their society. Both in its early history and in its later history as well, Lunenburg would remain *leaderless*, lacking individuals capable of embodying in any dominant way the values and aspirations of their fellow citizens.

Lunenburg's early civil leaders had little previous political experience with which to legitimize their authority. For example, in the years preceding Lunenburg's creation from Brunswick County in 1746 only one justice, Matthew Talbot, had previous court experience in the parent county before moving on to serve in Lunenburg. [14] In addition, the original twelve justices of Lunenburg lacked substantial wealth. Only one, Lewis Deloney, could be counted among the twenty-nine largest land patentees of the area, and he ranked close to the bottom of that list. [15] In the five years after 1746, the justices increased their holdings, but not dramatically. Seven bought or patented land in amounts of five hundred acres or more, but only two acquired more than a thousand acres, and none was among the nineteen men who recorded grants in excess of two thousand acres.[16] The justices' slaveholdings were similarly modest; in 1750 only three of the twelve were listed as owning five or more adult slaves, none possessed more than ten, and five held no slaves at all.[17] Finally, the conduct of the justices may well have reinforced popular skepticism about their authority. Not only did the court meet intermittently, but the turnover in office among its early members was exceptionally high. Thirty-nine men occupied the court's twelve seats during its first decade.[18]

All these factors prevented Lunenburg's "gentlemen justices" from meeting the criteria that made that appellation one of such distinction elsewhere in Virginia. Their formal powers were attenuated, and they lacked virtually all the attributes of gentility that enhanced the sway of their counterparts in the older counties. Moreover, those same conditions combined to weaken the centripetal forces that pulled people toward the courthouse site for more informal pastimes. Although Lunenburg did move almost immediately to establish an ordinary at the courthouse site, there is virtually nothing in either the public record or the newspapers or private correspondence of the period to indicate that the county seat served much of an extraofficial public function at all.

The one area in which the county seat served as the center of political life in all counties was in the election of representatives to the House of Burgesses on or near the courthouse green. While in future years Lunenburg would be involved in several excited contests that have added to this particularly colorful aspect of the Old Dominion's political lore, the role of the county seat in the selection of representatives, and the nature of political representation in the provincial legislature itself, remain an ambiguous part of the county's history.

As might be expected, the earliest representatives from Lunenburg were drawn from among those whose previous public service and social connections within the region went back the furthest and whose wealth, relative to that of their constituents, was the most impressive. Major Henry Embry, who as we have seen played host in his less-than-palatial dwelling to William Byrd during the colonel's 1733 trip to the region, had previously served as a sheriff and burgess from Brunswick County before his election to the House of Burgesses from Lunenburg.[19] Clement Read, who in time would become the only resident of the county to acquire virtually all the trappings of the Virginia planter aristocracy, had already by 1746 served as a vestryman of the Anglican parish in Brunswick County, begun a career as a militia officer which would give him a reputation beyond the borders of his own county, and acquired over one thousand acres of land. Moreover, Read was one of the Southside's few permanent residents who also possessed impressive ties to the ruling gentry of the east. Read's family had evidently settled in Williamsburg after immigrating to Virginia from Yorkshire, but sometime after the death of his father, Thomas, Clement Read was made the ward of the soon-to-be Speaker of the House of Burgesses, John Robinson. Robinson apparently sent him for a brief time to the College of William and Mary, after which he moved to King and Queen County. During his stay there he met and married Mary Hill, a young woman of considerable means. Armed with wealth, education, and social connections, Read's ascendancy in the political life of the Southside was rapid. He was apparently appointed king's attorney for Brunswick County a few montths before he actually settled there, and to that position he would add other honors both in the county militia and in the church vestry.[20]

Read's connections notwithstanding, his initial certificate of election was declared null and void because the county sheriff had failed to hold the election within the period ordered in the writ of election. To make matters worse, the frailty of community identity in early Lunenburg was such that Henry Embry had continued to serve as sheriff of Brunswick County for almost a full year after he was elected a burgess to represent Lunenburg, a violation that caused the Committee of Privileges and Elections of the House of Burgesses to void his election as well. As a consequence, Lunenburg would go without representation in the Burgesses until 1748, when both men took their seats.[21] Read and Embry would serve in the House sporadically over the course of the next decade, but neither played a prominent role in the committee work or legislative business of the House, and it is significant that Read soon resigned as burgess in order to accept what was probably to him the more important post of surveyor of the county.[22] As in most

Southside counties, the economic power of a land surveyor seemed more meaningful than the political power or social prestige of a burgess.

For one period from 1752 to 1754, there was a notable exception to the undistinguished character of Lunenburg's representatives to the colonial legislature. William Byrd III, though his father had already sold much of the family's speculative holdings in the county before 1752 and though he himself was a resident of Charles City County, was the sitting burgess from Lunenburg for four sessions beginning in 1752, giving up his seat only when he moved up to the Governor's Council in 1755.[23]

Neither Byrd's correspondence nor the county records give us any clue to the motivation of Byrd in deciding to secure a seat as burgess from Lunenburg or of the county's residents in electing him. It is once again tempting to use Byrd's Lunenburg service as an example of the way the lines of community organization and values extended beyond the bounds of the county toward the larger, gentry-dominated society around it. One can imagine that the citizens of Lunenburg, anxious to give greater standing and weight to their delegation to that body in which the political and social values of traditional society were so visibly embodied, selected Byrd as the exemplar of their hopes and aspirations, as one who could serve their interests far better than they themselves were able to do. There is a logic to that point of view, but however substantial that logic, it proved not to be grounded in reality. Byrd did not appear to be any more active in representing Lunenburg's interests than his less prestigious predecessors. He served on none of the standing committees of the House and, judging from the legislative journals, seems not to have involved himself in any business whatsoever during his three years in the House.[24] It appears that Byrd's service was undertaken more for his convenience and self-interest than for that of his Lunenburg constituents. That this could be the case is further testimony to the frailty of the bonds that tied the citizens of Lunenburg County together. Having little sense of common interest and possessing scant faith in one of their own to exemplify the values a burgess was intended to represent, they turned almost by default to someone outside the geographic bounds of their tenuously constructed community.

• THE ESTABLISHMENT OF SPIRITUAL
  AUTHORITY ON THE FRONTIER

In the settled communities of both England and the eastern Chesapeake, the parish church served as an important complement to secular institutions of government in sustaining the overarching higher culture of which Divinity and Law were twin pillars. At the weekly assemblies of the community for Divine Service—which all Virginians were required to attend once a month—occurred the best and most frequent opportunities for the display of the social authority of the gentry. In the parish churches, built with increasingly secularized grandeur in the eastern Chesapeake, the foremost pews were possessed by men of family and fortune. The fact of the legal establishment of the church—indeed, of its inseparability from the state—was frequently symbolized by the reservation of a great pew for justices and vestrymen, who were usually the same persons.

The individual charged principally with the task of maintaining the legitimacy of the moral and social order symbolized by the established church was the minister—a gentleman by definition—who, having been examined, ordained, and licensed by a bishop and acting therein as a successor to the apostles, could mount the steps of the great pulpit of the church and expound from a selected text the mysteries of the revealed Word of God. The form and tone of the liturgy over which that minister presided reinforced the demonstrations of hierarchy and ranking which were such integral parts of the social organization of the traditional communities.[25]

The Church of England in Lunenburg, however, in spite of the fact of its legal establishment, suffered perhaps even more severely than the court from the diffuse and unsettled nature of the religious community whose spiritual and ethical values it was charged with overseeing. The bounds of Cumberland Parish were identical to those of the county itself. It was difficult enough to persuade the residents of the county to travel long distances once a month for the meeting of the court; the problems involved in persuading the same people to travel those distances every week in order to come together for worship were probably greater. The authority of the lay vestry of the church was not likely to be too intimidating, since the members of the vestry tended to possess the same modest attainments of wealth and prestige as the members of the court.

One other striking fact about the vestry is the absence of significant overlap in its membership and that of the county court. In many settled counties, and in Lunenburg itself in subsequent decades, the overlap between court and vestry was nearly total, but in 1746 only two of the vestrymen, Lewis Deloney and Matthew Talbot, were also gentlemen justices.[26] This diffusion of power between the court and vestry could hardly have strengthened either institution, and it reflected in particular the lack of authority of the court justices. The vestry members, who were elected by the residents when the parish was first formed, may have had at least some claim to authority among the settlers who bothered to turn out to vote for them. That the membership of the court was so dissimilar to that of the elected vestry seems to be testimony to their failure to develop a base of respect and authority among the citizenry.

The ministry of the early Lunenburg Anglican church was hardly in a position to exercise either spiritual or secular leadership. The parish went without a minister for nearly two years and then finally employed the Rev. Mr. John Brunskill, who took up his duties in February 1749. Brunskill, later accused of being "a notorious evil-liver, being given to intemperance and other vices," lasted only a year; he was replaced in February 1750 by George Purdie, who in turn left Lunenburg in less than a year.[27] The Rev. William Kay came next to Lunenburg from Richmond County, where he had previously been turned out by discontented members of that parish.[28] Kay died in 1755, and for the next several years the parish seems to have been dependent on visiting ministers. Finally, in May 1759 the vestry managed to find a minister who could provide the parish with stable leadership. James Craig would serve as minister of Cumberland Parish continuously until his death in 1795, becoming over that period not only one of the pillars of the Anglican establishment but also one of the substantial landowners and slaveowners of the county.[29] Indeed, Craig's arrival in Lunenburg coincided with the beginnings of the process by which the secular and religious elites in the county acquired a stability and legitimacy previously lacking in the earliest, frontier stages of settlement.

Craig has left us with the most striking testimony on the sorry state of affairs in the parish before his arrival. Citing the difficulties imposed by distance as a primary cause, he claimed that there were whole settlements of people who "had never, or seldom been at Church since they were Baptized." Moreover, even those who did manage to attend "were ignorant of the very first principles of Christianity" It was not distance alone that had led to this sad state of affairs. Referring to the "Negligence and immoral lives of those [ministers] who formerly, from time to time, had the [rectorship] of this Parish," Craig believed that the authority of the established church before his arrival might have been better served had there been no ministers in the parish at all.[30]

The church edifices in which Lunenburg's earliest ministers conducted services have disappeared from the landscape. It seems likely that the principal "Chappel" of the parish was a 48-by-24-foot rectangular wooden structure near Reedy Creek, fairly near the courthouse. If it looked like other Southside churches of the era (see Figure 2), it probably resembled a tobacco warehouse more than an English house of worship. There was probably only a simple pulpit, raised before a row of perhaps a dozen pews, and the church almost certainly lacked those ornamental items that made the rituals of wealthier Anglican congregations such sumptuous ones. The vestry also ordered construction of several smaller chapels at strategic points around the county, and while some of these were in fact erected, the minutes of the vestry leave doubt about whether all the orders for construction were completed.[31]

An English-educated minister like James Craig, when confronted with those modest church structures and a far-flung, largely inattentive flock, was surely tempted to echo William Byrd's earlier conclusion that the region was "quite out of Christendom." On the other hand, Byrd and his fellow gentrymen to the east, by supporting legislation that brought to the Virginia frontier the formal institutions both of the provincial government and of the established church, had done much more than their counterparts in any other Southern colony to bring counties like Lunenburg within their own cultural orbit. That they failed to effect a wholesale transfer of their culture to Lunenburg was, as we have already seen, due in part to factors of physical distance, scarce economic resources, and less-than-imposing stewardship from local leaders

FIGURE 2. *Saponey Church, Dinwiddie County, Virginia. The only surviving church from the mid-eighteenth-century Southside, this Anglican church was constructed in 1728. Photo by author.*

FIGURE 3. *Abingdon Church, Gloucester County, Virginia. This Anglican church, constructed in 1754, is a typical though unusually well preserved example of church architecture in the Tidewater. Photo courtesy of Virginia State Library, Richmond, Va.*

entrusted with the institutions of government and of the established church. Just as important, though, there existed in Lunenburg from the very outset influences from sources outside the gentry culture which made the unchallenged acceptance of Byrd's or James Craig's definition of community life impossible.

• ALTERNATIVE MODES OF COMMUNITY ORGANIZATION

The great southward migration of Scots-Irish from Pennsylvania had its first impact on Lunenburg in 1739, seven years before the county's official creation. In that year John Caldwell led a group of some two hundred Presbyterian settlers into the area around Cub Creek, near what is today Charlotte County. Most of Caldwell's group had immigrated to Pennsylvania from Ulster in 1726 and, after a little more than a decade there, moved South to Virginia sometime around 1739. Richard Kennon, perhaps the most active land speculator in the region, sold the group a parcel of land intersected by Wallace, Cub, and Turnip creeks, bounded in the south by the Staunton River, and from that initial purchase was to emerge one of the few cohesive communities in the Southside, at least for a time.[32]

This kind of mass migration, displaying an intention of maintaining the group values and goals of their ancestors, appears to have been the exception in the more diffuse and fluid landscape of the Southside. Like most of those Scots-Irish Presbyterians who settled in the Great Valley of Virginia during the years 1730–50, the settlers seemed to shun "enthusiasm" for an Old Light theological and dramaturgical orientation. Their congregation was served by several visiting ministers during the years between 1739 and 1754 and did not succeed in attracting or supporting a regular minister until 1755. At that time, Robert Henry, a Scotsman educated at the intellectual center of Presbyterianism in America, the College of New Jersey, took over the congregation on a permanent basis. The Cub Creek settlement did not seem to be substantially damaged in its faith by the absence of a regular minister before Henry's arrival. When Samuel Davies passed through the area in 1755, he was impressed by the progress of Caldwell's community.

He noted: "In thirteen days I preached eleven or twelve sermons, with encouraging appearances of success. At the sacrament
in the wilderness there were 2,000 hearers and about 200
communicants."[33]

Caldwell's Presbyterians, unlike many more enthusiastic and
less formally structured religious groups that would appear in the
Southside in the 1760s and 1770s, had a number of advantages
that those more aggressively evangelical sects would not enjoy.
Their cultural style—Old Light, with college-educated ministers
and no driving ambition to extend their influence substantially
beyond the bounds of the Cub Creek settlement—did not appear
to threaten the leaders of the religious establishment in the county,
and thus Governor William Gooch's grant of toleration to the settlement was generally respected.[34] Although the county's spaciousness was undoubtedly frustrating to those wishing to extend eastern
Anglican institutions to all the citizens of the region, that same
spaciousness offered a measure of protection to those Cub Creek
Presbyterians wishing to practice their religion without interference from others. Because the Cub Creek settlers established
themselves at a relatively early stage in the development of the
Southside, they were able to achieve a substantial economic base
with which to bolster their claims to legitimacy. The thirty-three
heads of families among the original group of settlers who purchased land from Richard Kennon bought farmsteads averaging
575 acres, slightly above the average for such deed purchases in
the Southside during that period. While their control over a labor
force other than that provided by the members of their own families
was generally as slight as that of most planters in the land-rich
and labor-poor Southside, there were a few individuals in the
Caldwell settlement who owned five or more slaves by 1750.[35]

The Anglican gentry who controlled the politics of the Virginia
colony had long before passed legislation restricting public office
to members of the established church, but that law, like so many
others, was easily evaded on the frontier. Following the example of
those Scots-Irish leaders who had been successful in making Presbyterianism something close to the "established" religion in the
Great Valley of Virginia, John Caldwell and his brother William
officially joined the Anglican church while at the same time retain-

ing their Presbyterian faith. When Lunenburg was formally organized as a county, both John and William Caldwell were appointed members of the first county court, not because they were accepted members of a well-established ruling elite but because they were known to be the most prominent members of their own particular geographical subdivision within the county. In fact, it seems certain that few in the county even realized that the Caldwells were Presbyterians, for when the election for the first vestry of Cumberland Parish was held, John Caldwell was among those chosen. He immediately declined the post, but the very fact of his election is indicative of the frail identity of the county's Anglican elite.[36]

The Cub Creek Presbyterian Church would live on for most of the remainder of the eighteenth century, but the residential community founded by the Caldwells had been altered drastically by the lure of the frontier beyond Lunenburg by at least 1760. John and William Caldwell died in 1751, and it does not appear that their heirs were capable of holding the remaining Cub Creek settlers together in a community of shared hopes and values. Many of the residents, including several members of the Caldwell family, moved on to South Carolina, and still others traveled west to Kentucky in search of still greater opportunity.[37] By 1760 the character of the Cub Creek settlement had changed completely. No longer an exclusive community of Scots-Irish Presbyterians, its residents began to display a diversity of background and purpose that rendered them indistinguishable from other newcomers pouring into Lunenburg.

It was a spacious, unformed, changing, and occasionally disorderly landscape that presented itself to a new settler in Lunenburg. The government in Williamsburg had brought the services of local government and the church closer to many households in the region when it created Lunenburg County and Cumberland Parish, and the subsequent actions of the court in laying out roads and licensing ferries, mills, and ordinaries would facilitate the kinds of communication essential to the development of a sense of locally based community. And some, like the settlers of Cub Creek, had created their own communities outside the traditional institutional structure of the county. Still others, seeking to combat the loneliness and isolation of the frontier, had patented their lands in the county adjacent to the holdings of relatives or their neighbors in their previous places of residence.[38] By and large, however, Lunenburg remained a place where uncertainty and transiency, rather than social cohesion, were the most striking community attributes. The flow of people in and out of the community, people with an ever-increasing variety of regional and ethnic accents, bound together often only by their common desire to improve their economic prospects, made continuity with the past—whether that past be rooted in the culture of England, Ireland, Tidewater Virginia, or Pennsylvania—uncertain in the extreme.

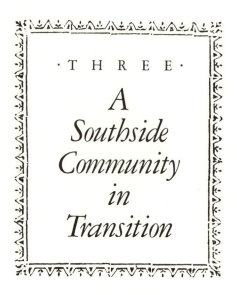

·T H R E E·

A Southside Community in Transition

While Lunenburg's earliest residents and its subsequent immigrants brought with them to the county a great diversity of cultural traditions, the same settlers would, if they stayed in the county long enough, increasingly devote their energies to a common economic endeavor—the cultivation of tobacco. The lines of influence of the Virginia tobacco economy, like the lines of political influence within the county, ran from east to west. Following the dictates of a parliament far to the east, the legislature in Williamsburg framed the laws governing the tobacco trade; tobacco inspectors, operating in warehouses many miles to the east of a frontier outpost like Lunenburg, passed judgment on the quality and therefore the price of the crop; and at least until the 1760s, the tobacco merchants to whom Southsiders consigned their crop also lived in the east. However, the *cultural* process, by which Lunenburg became integrated into the tobacco economy of the Old Dominion and by which Lunenburg's citizens consequently adopted many of the manners, styles, and institutions which that tobacco economy had helped create, differed significantly from that occurring in the eastern parts of Virginia a century, or even a half-century, before. Contradictory forces were also at work pulling Lunenburg toward a cultural and demographic configuration that would undermine and in some instances directly challenge the hegemony of the Anglican-gentry code of values. By the eve of the Revolution, Lunenburg would become a hybrid culture, a society where the traditional values of the gentry coexisted in uneasy partnership with a different set of conditions imposed by the frontier, by immigration, and by political change.

• THE ECONOMIC DEVELOPMENT OF LUNENBURG, 1750–1770

The most visible indicator of Lunenburg's transition from a frontier wilderness to a settled society was the rate at which its population increased. By 1751, only five years after its founding, the county's population had nearly doubled, a rate of increase that would abate only slightly during the next two decades. Along with that increase came demands not only for additional representation in the House of Burgesses but also for easier access to the services provided by court and church. As a consequence, both the county and the parish underwent a series of divisions in 1752, 1754, 1756, 1757, 1761, and 1764, creating nine new counties in the process, until that portion of what remained as Lunenburg had reached a size and population comparable to most Tidewater counties and parishes. Thus, in 1770 Lunenburg's tithable population stood at 1,683, roughly equal to the average population of the county during the twenty-five-year period since its founding. Those residents were now living in an area encompassing approximately 480 rather than 5,000 square miles (see Map 3).[1]

These years of political subdivision were years in which the familiar centers of community life inevitably underwent constant shifts of focus, with the citizens of all but the northeastern portion of the original county being forced to build and staff anew those secular and religious institutions meant to bring order to their societies. Given the distance of the initial court site from most citizens of the original county, it is unlikely that either the Lunenburg court or Cumberland Parish ever served as much of a focus of identification for many residents in the first place, but the frequent shifts in political and religious jurisdiction undoubtedly served

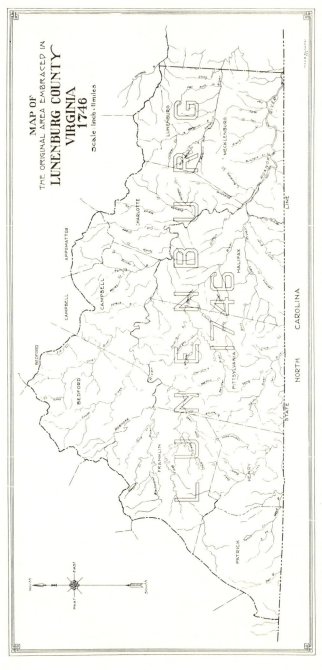

MAP 3. *Lunenburg County, 1746 and 1764. As the map indicates, eleven counties were eventually carved out of the area comprising Lunenburg in 1746. Reprinted by permission from Landon C. Bell, The Old Free State: A Contribution to the History of Lunenburg County and Southside Virginia, 2 vols. (Richmond, 1927), vol. 1.*

only to accentuate the uncertainty of those identifications.

The process of division, like that which caused Lunenburg's initial creation, drew a mixed reaction from the residents of the county. Realizing that distance was hampering both administrative efficiency and social cohesion within the region, some consistently supported division. It is clear too, though, that a substantial minority cared little about increasing either efficiency or group cohesion, preferring instead to accept the diffuseness and institutional weakness of their county rather than pay the additional taxes involved in establishing multiple agencies of court and parish.[2]

Whatever the advantages and disadvantages involved in the division of counties, the areas that remained identified with the original county of Lunenburg had by the mid-1760s achieved both a size and a continuity of economic, political, and religious leadership that brought them more closely into the economic and political mainstream of the colony as a whole. That northeastern section of the original county which would by 1764 retain the name of Lunenburg had a head start on its neighbors in the other parts of the original county. The greatest concentration of the initial county's population had resided in that portion and, however humble their status, so too had most of the county's initial political and religious leaders. Similarly, although the economic base of that northeastern portion of the original county was still modest by the standards of many eastern counties, it did, even as early as 1750, have slightly greater concentrations of wealth in both land and slaves than the rest of the county.[3]

By the mid-1760s, community life in the more densely populated and compactly organized county was gaining definition, as Lunenburg itself was beginning to move toward a more complete integration with both the staple crop economy and the cultural style of the gentry world. The changes were manifest in almost every area of the county's public life—in the status and behavior of its political officials, in the increased authority of the parish ministry and lay vestry, and in the growing importance of the court and parish as centers of activity apart from their official functions. All these developments were dependent on yet another development: the movement of the Lunenburg economy out of the realm of subsistence agriculture toward the cultivation of tobacco for the world market.

The shift in economic direction is verified dramatically in the shift in labor patterns within the county.[4] In 1750 nearly 80 percent of the heads of households in Lunenburg owned no slaves at all, and the holdings of just a few nonresidents accounted for a substantial portion of the total slave population. By the 1760s, Lunenburg's economy was supporting many more slaves, and those slaves were in turn distributed more widely among the residents of the county. The number of slaves in the population had increased from roughly 22 percent in 1750 to 44 percent in 1764 and 53 percent in 1769 (see Table 2). The percentage of slaveowners among heads of households in the county had moved from 23 percent in 1750 to 45 percent in 1764 and 53 percent by 1769. Moreover, the relative importance of the nonresident elite had tended to decline by the mid-1760s, with the holdings of both the most affluent and the average resident slaveowners increasing correspondingly. In contrast to the situation in 1750, when the holdings of a man like William Byrd overshadowed those of everyone else in the county, one can see by the late 1760s the emergence of a local economic elite, whose members held between seven and fifteen tithable slaves each, and a substantial class of slaveowners (approximately 65 percent of the slaveowning population) who had between one and three tithable slaves.[5]

Land prices, though subject to enormous variations (reflecting the different valuations of improved versus unimproved lands) at the extreme ends of the scale, also seem to indicate the changing economic base of the county. The average size of each parcel of land sold during the 1740s and early 1750s was about 330 acres, and the average price paid ranged from between two and three shillings per acre. By the early 1760s the average amount involved in land transactions had decreased slightly, to 260 acres, and the average price paid per acre had increased to about four and a half shillings per acre. This trend accelerated into the 1770s, with the size of transactions continuing to decrease, to 201 acres, and the price rising to almost nine shillings per acre.[6]

The steady increase in the average price paid for an acre of land is not so much indicative of skyrocketing prices for unimproved land as it is a reflection of the steadily increasing number of land transactions involving the purchase of *improved* land, with

TABLE 2 DISTRIBUTION OF SLAVE AND LAND OWNERSHIP, LUNENBURG COUNTY, 1750–1769

	1750[a]		1764		1769[b]	
Tithable Slaves	No. of Households	% of Households	No. of Households	% of Households	No. of Households	% of Households
0	834	77.2	241	55.2	186	46.7
1–2	158	14.6	94	21.7	93	23.4
3–5	68	6.3	69	15.9	81	20.4
6–15	18	1.7	29	6.7	38	9.5
16–30	1	0.1	1	0.2	0	0.0
31 or more	1	0.1	0	0.0	0	0.0
	1,080	100.0	434	100.0	398	100.0
ACRES						
0	(Not available for 1750)		102	23.5	78	19.6
1–49			2	0.5	0	0.0
50–99			7	1.6	10	2.5
100–199			58	13.3	74	18.6
200–299			71	16.4	74	18.6
300–399			49	11.3	44	11.0
400–499			52	12.0	42	10.6
500–999			60	13.8	52	13.1
1,000–1,999			27	6.2	22	5.5
2,000 or more			6	1.4	2	0.5
			434	100.0	398	100.0

SOURCE: Landon C. Bell, *Sunlight on the Southside: Lists of Tithes, Lunenburg County, Virginia, 1748–1783* (Philadelphia, 1931), pp. 58–86, 122–61, 228–46, 269–85.

[a] The tithable population of Lunenburg in 1750 was more than twice that in 1764 and 1769 because the county's boundaries initially encompassed a much larger territory. By 1764, after successive divisions of the county, Lunenburg was only one-tenth the geographic size it had been in 1750.

[b] The number of independent householders on the 1769 tithable list is less than that for 1764 because the returns for two of the county's tithable districts are missing for that year.

finished houses and outbuildings included in the transactions. While the deeds themselves are not specific about what is being conveyed to the purchaser, it is clear from the wide range of prices being paid that some were simply buying empty land and others were buying working plantations. At the lower end of the price scale, transactions involving the purchase of land at no more than a shilling or two per acre, though less common than in the 1740s and 1750s, were still occurring frequently. At the other end of the scale, the increasing frequency of purchases where the price paid was fifteen shillings or even a pound per acre is indicative not of scarce supplies of land but rather of an expanding housing stock within the county.

Much of this evidence—the increase in land values and the growth of a slaveowning class—suggests that some individuals in Lunenburg were becoming distinctly wealthier, but it does not suggest that the poor within the county were necessarily becoming poorer. It is impossible to make precise calculation with respect to changes either in the percentage of people owning land or in the average size of landholdings in the mid-1740s and mid-1760s, because the sources available for each of those periods are not comparable. Moreover, both the land deed books and the tithable lists underestimate the number of individuals possessing independent landholdings.[7] However, the average and median landholdings per household in 1769 (321 and 205 acres respectively) are higher than the calculations for most other parts of colonial America during this period.[8] Similarly, although 20 percent of the people appearing on the 1769 tithable list are shown as owning no land, that number (which probably also includes those who had not yet secured legal title to their land claims) is much lower than the percentage of those who in 1750 had not patented or legally purchased land.[9] In absolute terms the number of people purchasing land, obtaining the goal of an independent sufficiency, was increasing by leaps and bounds, from 60 or 70 per year in the late 1740s to 166 by the early 1760s.[10]

The distribution of wealth as embodied in estate inventories also suggests that those at the lower and middle portions of the scale were not necessarily suffering because of the increasing affluence of those at the top. While in the mid-1760s there was a marked increase in the number of people leaving estates valued at £200 or more, the value of the median estate at that time (adjusted for inflation) stood at nearly twice the size (£73 to £42) of estate valuations in the late 1740s and early 1750s.[11]

Although the percentage of households in Lunenburg owning slaves was approaching that of even the most affluent eastern counties (and therefore departing significantly from the economic and demographic configuration of the Carolina and Georgia backcountry, where slaves were a negligible part of the population), the pattern of slave ownership within Lunenburg was fundamentally different from that in the east. While the members of Lunenburg's "economic elite" may have owned ten or fifteen slaves, their counterparts in the east owned one hundred or more, and the class of "middling" slaveowners (those owning one or two or three slaves) was much larger in Lunenburg than in the east, or perhaps anywhere in the world at any time before or since. In that tragic sense, Lunenburg County provides a dramatic embodiment of the proposition that American slavery did indeed pave the way for American freedom. Lunenburg's *white* residents, blessed with an abundance of inexpensive and generally fertile land and finding themselves increasingly capable of raising the capital to purchase at least a few slaves in a legally sanctioned system of chattel slavery, enjoyed unprecedented freedom to pursue their goal of an independent existence.[12]

The most striking aspect of the economic and social structure of Lunenburg during the 1760s—closely linked with the impact of economic opportunity at various levels in the society—was the continuation of the phenomenal movement of people both in and out of the county. Only 20 percent of the heads of households living in the county in 1769 appear to have been living there in 1750; indeed, in the five years between 1764 and 1769 nearly 40 percent of the heads of households disappeared.[13]

Those who left the county at this time also tended to be those at the bottom of the economic scale, but there are enough examples of relatively prosperous households moving on that an explanation turning simply on economic deprivation is not adequate. For some white settlers who failed to gain or sustain a freehold in Lunenburg, the stigma of dependence in a region like the Southside, where the great majority had gained independence, was perhaps more onerous than it was elsewhere, and the need to push on in the quest for independence was more compelling. Not only did the overwhelming preponderance of their neighbors possess independent freeholds, but the condition of the one sizable class of dependent laborers in the county—the slave population—must have made the less fortunate white settlers despise the notion of dependency even more intensely. For those more fortunate, like the members of John Caldwell's Cub Creek settlement, economic conditions in Lunenburg had almost certainly been better than the conditions under which they had lived before, but for those restless enough to uproot their families for a move from Pennsylvania to the Southside, the challenge of yet another move, at the end of which lay perhaps superior opportunity, was not so daunting.

Among those citizens who chose to stay in Lunenburg, economic prospects were generally improving rather than worsening. Only a handful of individuals seemed to experience a decline in wealth, and in all cases this never amounted to more than the loss of a single slave or the selling of a hundred acres here and there. At the other extreme, a few individuals appearing on all four tithable lists from 1748 to 1769 enjoyed dramatic increases in their holdings. These were individuals like Lydall Bacon who, beginning with his first purchase of 297 acres of land in 1747 and his two tithable slaves, had by 1769 increased his holdings to 1,060 acres, nine tithable slaves, and one white laborer.[14] It is interesting to note, though, that the preponderance of those people who moved to Lunenburg in the 1740s and then stayed there for the next twenty years or more were not people involved in the steady accumulation of land and slaves but rather were individuals who managed to acquire modest holdings early in the game and remained content with those holdings, adding small improvements as the years went by, for the rest of their lives.

James Amoss, for example, purchased 391 acres of land for £20 in 1747, turned around that same day and sold 194 of those acres back to another individual for £10, and then remained content with the balance of his landholdings for the rest of his life. At his death in 1786 he divided his land equally among his two sons and daughter. Amoss remained unable even to sign his name to his will at that time, but his estate, which included three feather beds, a large walnut chest, a large pine chest, the usual kitchen utensils, and a quantity of cattle, hogs, and geese, placed him solidly among Lunenburg's middling planter class.[15] Similarly, Charles Parish patented 400 acres of land on both sides of Allen's Creek near the Banister River in 1751; added to the 215 acres he owned previously, this ended his land activity for the next thirty years. Parish would, however, gradually add to the labor force working that land, beginning with one tithable slave in 1748 and accumulating three more tithable slaves and one white dependent laborer by 1769.[16]

Parish's pattern was probably most typical. While a few individuals, such as David Garland and Matthew Marrable, made at least a part of their livelihood by the purchase and sale of land (Garland, for example, was involved as the purchaser in thirteen land transactions between 1756 and 1774 and as the seller in twenty-three), most individuals had more than enough to handle with their tracts of two hundred or four hundred acres.[17] The crucial problem in Lunenburg, as elsewhere, was acquiring an adequate supply of labor to work even that modest acreage. Thus, at least among that perhaps atypical minority that remained in Lunenburg during the twenty-year period after its founding, the tendency was not to attempt to expand or exchange land but rather to increase the labor force available to exploit that land.

It is one thing to follow the paths of those people who had long-standing attachments to property in the county, and quite another to follow the courses of those who started with very little. If the firmly rooted minority of Lunenburg's population presents us with a picture of relative stability and a relatively low level of acquisitiveness, the white dependent population of the county presents us with nearly the opposite, for that population was mobile in almost every sense of the word. Of the 265 white dependents who could be identified on any of the county's published tithable lists for 1748, 1750, 1764, and 1769, some 130 (nearly half) fail to appear either as dependents or as independent landowners on any of the subsequent lists. This sort of mobility out of the county is not surprising in the cases of white dependents who were unrelated to the heads of households for whom they worked, but even among dependents who were the sons or relatives of the heads of households, more than half could not be traced beyond their initial appearance on the tithe lists, which is once again indicative of the powerful impulse to escape dependence in a land widely heralded for its independence.[18]

The patterns of activity among white dependents who did remain in the county varied enormously. Nonrelated white dependents who stayed in Lunenburg tended not to work for the same household, moving from one employer to another in what was no doubt a highly fluid labor market. Slightly over one-third of the white dependents themselves became independent heads of households in the county. Among this group, the most common phenomenon was for the younger sons of established landowners to acquire land and houses of their own, and it is not surprising that, given the expansive character of the Lunenburg economy, their economic standing in the county tended to be equal or superior to that of their parents once they had achieved independent status. A much smaller group (less than 20 percent) of the nonrelated dependents acquired independent householder status within the county as well. Fully three-quarters of these men never came to own more than one hundred acres or any slaves whatever. In that sense an individual like John Hix, who in 1748 had worked for a middling planter named Henry Cockerham but who by 1769 had acquired 395 acres and two slaves of his own, was an exception. Even among that top quarter who managed to establish at least modest holdings, the more typical experience was that of an individual like George McLaughlin, a dependent laborer for Thomas Winn in 1748 who by 1769 had become an independent landowner with 250 acres of his own.[19]

In general, people who made it to the top of the economic order of Lunenburg by the late 1760s were neither those whose interests dated back before the founding nor those atypical laborers who managed to establish a solid foothold in the Lunenburg economy after their terms of service had been completed. What most often set Lunenburg's wealthiest citizens apart from the rest of the county's population was not the land they owned but the labor and capital they could marshal to work the lands that were still so abundant in the area.

The changing character of Lunenburg's economic elite at various points in the county's history tells part of the story. Perhaps the most striking contrast between the twenty wealthiest men in the 1760s and their counterparts at the beginning of the county's history is that the overwhelming portion of the 1760s elite (eighteen of the twenty) were permanent residents of the county and not absentee planters or speculators. Their landholdings were impressive enough, averaging 1,481 acres; fifteen of the twenty owned between one and two thousand acres, and only three men held in excess of two thousand acres. None of the twenty men, however, was using ownership of large tracts of land as a speculative lever with which to increase his fortune; although some possessed more than one landholding in the county, and while a few used those landholdings to run multiple plantations, no one was engaged in the buying and selling of land in any active and purposeful way.[20] (Appendix 1 details the land and slaveholdings of Lunenburg's wealthiest citizens at various points in the county's history.)

What gave the members of the economic elite their power was their ability to raise tobacco and (to a lesser extent) foodstuffs, and what gave them their ability to accomplish those things was slave labor. The average number of tithable slaves (i.e., slaves sixteen years or older) held by the elite was nine, indicating a total of slaves of all ages at around eighteen). The range of tithable slaveholdings ran from one to sixteen. The most dramatic aspect of these figures is their striking contrast with the slaveholdings of the resident economic elite two decades earlier. Not only did the wealthiest residents in the county own nearly twice as many slaves as their counterparts in 1750, but eleven of the twenty men in 1769 held slaves at or above the average for the elite group as a whole, whereas in 1750 the holdings of William Byrd greatly inflated the average; only seven men in 1750 held more than ten tithable slaves.[21]

When we move beyond the simple facts of land and slaveholdings, however, we find that a composite description of the economic elite is more difficult to assemble. Although we do not have complete information on the age structure of the group, it appears that there was a substantial age spread, from Lodowick Farmer, who was probably no more than thirty or thirty-five, to Lydall Bacon and Richard Claiborne, who were in their late fifties or early sixties at the very least. Because of the range of ages among the economic elite, an "average" figure for the value of their estates at their deaths is not very useful, since inflationary pressures between the first death, in 1777, and the last, in 1816, caused the real value of those estates to vary considerably. Thus, for example, Charles Hamlin's estate, valued at £1,593 in 1787, was in many ways superior to that of Lodowick Farmer, valued at £2,931 in 1816. The best way to determine the "real value" of the estates of those men—and therefore the path their fortunes took after 1769—is to compare the number of slaves they owned in 1769 with the number they owned at their death, as slaves generally constituted nearly three-quarters of the value of the inventories of those men possessing five or more slaves. In virtually every case the variation in the slaveholdings of those men in 1769—when they had reached the peak of the county's economic hierarchy—and their holdings at the time of their death, was slight, with only a few cases of a slight aggrandizement of their fortunes and a slightly greater tendency toward a decrease in the size of their slaveholdings, a natural tendency among men at the high end of the age scale.[22]

Perhaps the most significant variation among the group was the length of time they had lived in the county before 1769, in part a reflection of their different ages. Several of the men—Lodowick Farmer, Thomas Tabb, and Thomas Hardy—had made their first land acquisitions in the county within the past few years, and it does not appear that any of them were inheriting estates from relatives who had lived in the county previously. Rather, these men—most of them young—had moved into the county possessing the capital to start their plantations in a fairly impressive way at the outset.[23] Thomas Tabb, for example, seems to have come from a prominent family in Amelia County and in the late 1750s set out to build his estate in Lunenburg. At the other extreme was William Embry, nephew of Henry Embry, one of Lunenburg's first elected burgesses and an individual whose family connections in the area dated back to at least the early 1730s. Embry began his own land purchases in 1748, but then inherited additional acreage in 1759 on the death of his father. His slaveholdings, which stood at five in 1750, had grown to sixteen in 1769.[24] Lydall Bacon provides a variation on that theme. His family evidently came to Lunenburg from Charles City County sometime shortly before 1746, and through modest land and slave acquisitions he had managed to build his estate to nearly three hundred acres and two slaves by 1750. The intervening years were ones of gradual enhancement of that estate; he would buy and sell land more than a dozen times over the next twenty years, but the expenditures and receipts were always modest and the trend was toward ever-larger holdings. By the time the tithe-taker visited him in 1769, his estate had grown to 1,060 acres and eight tithable slaves, close to the average for the members of the elite as a whole.[25]

The one man on the list who best combined longtime residence in the county, large landholdings and slaveholdings, and a history of continued estate growth after 1769 was Henry Blagrave, whose life seems to intersect with all phases of the county's economic, political, and religious history in the prerevolutionary period. Blagrave arrived in Lunenburg from Caroline County in July 1750 and began to build his holdings immediately. His first purchase of a 180-acre tract was a piece of improved land that included buildings sufficient to begin a working plantation, as the £150 he paid for it was a huge sum of money by 1750 standards. Between 1750 and his death in 1781, Blagrave steadily built his estate until its lands totaled over two thousand acres and his slaveholdings, spread over more than a single plantation site, numbered thirty-three. The total valuation of Blagrave's estate, £3,800, made it one of the most impressive estates of the period.[26]

The most unusual personal history among the group of Lunenburg's wealthiest men belongs to Tscharner DeGraffenreid, the grandson of Baron Christopher DeGraffenreid, "honorary citizen of London, Governor of Yverton, Lord of Worb, member of the Order of Sunshine, Knight of the Purple Ribbon, Master of Arts, Doctor of Laws, and Landgrave of North Carolina." Behind all those fancy titles lies a tale of romance, intrigue, and disappointment, stretching from Bern, Switzerland, to London, and finally to the backcountry of Virginia and North Carolina. The Baron DeGraffenreid, a young Swiss whose taste for the high society in London both interfered with his duties back home and exceeded his family's financial resources, decided in the late 1680s to leave

Switzerland permanently, a plan he carried out so as "not to be detained by creditors and my own people." Arriving in England, he applied to Queen Mary for a grant of money and land to settle a group of Swiss and Palatine Germans on lands in Virginia, an application which was evidently immediately approved. The baron then sent an advance expedition to Virginia while he waited in London for another group of settlers from Bern to join him. That expedition was attacked and plundered by a French privateer at the mouth of the James River, and the survivors were taken ashore and resettled in North Carolina on a point between the Neuse and Trent rivers at the site of the present-day town of New Bern. In the fall of the same year, the baron came over himself with other settlers. When he landed, he was incensed about the location, complaining that Virginia's surveyor general had settled them there because the lands were his own and that he hoped therefore to make a profit on them—an interesting attitude, since the baron's "colony" was no doubt itself a speculative enterprise designed to allow the baron to recoup his sagging fortunes.[27]

After DeGraffenreid's arrival in North Carolina, the story gains in excitement and adventure, with periods of great hunger, danger from Indians, an eventual relocation of the colony at Germanna in the northwestern Piedmont of Virginia, further escapes from angry creditors, a timely intercession by Governor Alexander Spotswood, and finally a voyage back to England from whence he never returned. But the baron's son Christopher stayed behind, and by 1734 he had secured a patent for 1,843 acres in Brunswick County, Virginia; his only son, Tscharner, was to take up residence in that part of Brunswick which became Lunenburg. The debts of his grandfather notwithstanding, Tscharner DeGraffenreid had a sufficient store of political connections and capital to make a fast start in Lunenburg, and by 1752 he had acquired over a thousand acres of land and fifteen tithable slaves. During the next forty years, he does not appear to have added much in the way of material goods to his estate, and his holdings remained roughly the same on virtually all the surviving tax lists of eighteenth-century Lunenburg. He did, however, acquire an impressive number of wives and children during that period—four of the former and fourteen of the latter—and more than any other single man in the county promoted the slowly developing trend toward marriage within the elite.[28]

A mere listing of landholdings and slaveholdings and a description of the varying paths that a Blagrave or a DeGraffenreid took to amass his estate does not tell us much about the quality of the lives that these "first gentlemen" of Lunenburg actually led. A satisfactory description of those qualitative aspects of those wealthy planters' lives lies beyond our grasp. Descriptions of the plantation houses of the period—the most visible indicators of their wealth and the style in which they wished to display that wealth—have not survived, just as most of the plantation houses themselves, still constructed of logs or frame rather than brick, have long since passed from the landscape. An architectural survey undertaken some fifteen years ago lists four surviving houses that might have been built before the Revolution. Two of them— Samuel Garland's Pleasant Hill, and Whitehall, the home of the Hardy family—were built by individuals who were among the most prominent in the county, yet even they are modest structures of only five or six rooms. One of the others—Prospect Hill—was the residence of the Rev. James Craig (see Figure 4). Although it too was built of pine weatherboarding, it was thought to be the most impressive house in the county.[29]

Our only other source for reconstructing the Lunenburg version of the "gentry style" is the inventories left by these wealthy men at their death, but even here, in spite of the extraordinary detail of the inventories, the picture that emerges is puzzling. Henry Blagrave best demonstrates the nature of the puzzle, precisely because he was the wealthiest of the group. It is clear that Blagrave's economic standing was dwarfed by that of a "real" Virginia gentryman. Even with an estate valued at £3,952, Blagrave's plantation could hardly have taken on the appearance of a Westover or a Nomini Hall; there would be no imposing porticoes overlooking the James or the Potomac, no crystal chandeliers in spacious ballrooms, and no villages of two or three hundred bondsmen and bondswomen tending the gristmills, bakeries, dairies, and warehouses on the plantation grounds. Yet one might expect that a man

FIGURE 4. *The Craig Plantation. The plantation home of the Rev. James Craig, minister of Cumberland Parish, Lunenburg County, from 1759 to 1795. Craig's plantation, perhaps the finest in the county at the time of the Revolution, included a profitable mill. Photo by the author.*

who could afford thirty-three slaves (an investment of about £3,300 at the prevailing market price of the day) would have a few luxury items—some pieces of silver plate, or a silver watch, or a portrait or even a picture. Yet these things are missing from Blagrave's inventory. We can find cattle, horses, sheep, hogs, pails, tubs, saws, hoes, files, planes, harnesses, reaphooks, several jugs, and a hogshead of rum, but aside from a set of silver teaspoons, a fiddle, and one wine glass, we find little that evokes the habits of a Virginia gentleman.[30]

Blagrave was not the exception; virtually all the members of the "elite" in prerevolutionary Lunenburg passed up the opportunity to purchase consumer items that might have enhanced their claims to gentility, preferring instead to invest their excess capital in additional slaves. The reasons underlying those decisions were no doubt complex, relating as much to the financial constraints imposed by the still-infant Southside tobacco economy as to a personal preference for the accumulation of black laborers over luxury goods. The consequence of those decisions, however, was a pattern of economic and social behavior that was a long way removed from the genteel, paternalistic, and occasionally hedonistic styles so frequently cited as the defining characteristics of the "Southern patriarchy."

Both Rhys Isaac, in his provocative study *The Transformation of Virginia, 1740–1790*, and Eugene Genovese, in his analyses of antebellum Southern society, present persuasive evidence that those Southern partriarchs did in fact exist.[31] William Byrd II, who was so instrumental in the early settlement of Lunenburg, seemed to fit that image. He wrote in 1726:

I have a large Family of my own, and my Doors are open to Every Body, yet I have no Bills to pay, and half a Crown will rest undisturbed in my Pocket for many Moons together. Like one of the Patriarchs I have my flocks and my Herds, my Bond-men and Bond-women, and every soart of trade amongst my own Servants, so that I live in a kind of Independence on every one but Providence.

As Isaac notes, Byrd explicitly opposed "money" to "patriarchy" in his idyll. Although nearly all the trappings of a patriarch—the elaborate refinements of dress, furnishings, and diet and the imposing facades of the plantation house and its surrounding outbuildings—owed their existence to a form of money, namely, credit, Byrd regarded matters of money and markets only as means to his patriarchal ends.[32]

Looking ahead to the mid-nineteenth century, it is plain that Byrd had his counterparts in individuals like James Henry Hammond of South Carolina and Louis Manigault of Georgia, who provide us with excellent archetypes of planters who believed that patriarchy, and not profits, was the essence of what the Southern, slave-based agricultural system was all about.[33] But to the planters of eighteenth-century Lunenburg, still on the outer margins of the world tobacco economy and certainly on the periphery of "genteel culture," the concern for profit took precedence over the desire to create the illusion of a patriarchy, for profit was essential if one was to expand one's supply of labor and therefore one's productive capacity.

Nor was it simply in material possessions and styles of life that the leading tobacco planters of Lunenburg failed to replicate the standards and the values of their counterparts to the east. Perhaps most crucial, they failed to acquire the influence over the local tobacco economy enjoyed by those who had made their fortunes in the eastern counties earlier in the century. By the time the South-side tobacco economy was first reaching a truly productive phase (the 1760s and 1770s), control over the tobacco trade was being transferred from resident planters and merchants to large Scottish merchant houses based in Glasgow. Those merchant firms had been involved in some form or other with the tobacco trade since the mid-seventeenth century, but beginning in the 1740s and 1750s the Glaswegian role expanded remarkably. Taking advantage of the shorter sailing time between Scotland and Virginia, the lower operating costs out of Scottish ports, and most important, an organizational structure that consolidated the trade in the hands of a few large firms, those Scottish merchant houses began to set up stores in nearly every tobacco-producing area in Virginia, advancing short-term credit in cash and merchandise on the collateral of future tobacco consignments. The factors who ran those stores, instead of being independent resident merchant-planters, as their predecessors had most often been, were salaried employees on temporary assignment in Virginia.[34]

These developments were felt everywhere in Virginia, but no-where with greater force than in the Southside, where the need for additional credit was greatest and where the local economic elite was least capable of supplying it. As a consequence, control in the Southside of virtually all those aspects of the tobacco economy other than the actual cultivation of the leaf itself—the inspection, pricing, and purchase of tobacco, the advancing of credit, and the provision of a store of imported, manufactured goods—fell not to the resident economic elite but to a group of salaried outsiders.

By the eve of the Revolution, the Scottish share of the tobacco trade throughout the whole of Virginia was just under 50 percent, but in the Upper James District, the greatest part of which was the Southside, the Scottish share of the market was closer to two-thirds. Twenty-six Scottish firms did business in the region, with six especially prominent, and two, Alexander Speirs and Company and William Cuninghame and Company, towering over the others in importance. Those two firms, which between them set up stores at the courthouse site in every Southside county as well as in other strategic points in those counties, together accounted for nearly half the Upper James District's shipments to Scotland and about a third of the district's trade with the whole of the British Empire.[35] Beyond providing Southside planters with short-term credit which could not have been acquired elsewhere, the effect of this was to alter fundamentally the traditional character of both economic and social relations in the Southside. The Southside economy was regulated in relatively impersonal fashion by salaried employees of firms based three thousand miles away, not by resident planter-gentry capable of riding through their county to oversee personally their economic interests and interconnections, in the fashion of William Byrd or Robert Carter.

Nearly all those in Lunenburg who grew tobacco—tenants, "middling" planters, or members of the economic elite—found themselves enmeshed in an economic system which, though it often increased their personal wealth, decreased their personal "independence." Lunenburg's planters may not have had the same habits of conspicuous consumption as their wealthier and more self-indulgent counterparts to the east, but they seemed no less reticent about accepting credit in order to expand their plantations. This aspect of their entry into the market economy was vital to the growth of the Southside, but it also brought Lunenburg's citizens, as we shall see, into the courtroom as defendants in a burgeoning number of debt cases. Similarly, the swings in tobacco prices during the 1760s and 1770s and occasional sharp curtailments of British credit (as in 1762 and 1772, when financial crises in England forced English merchants to press their Virginia clients for payment of back debts) all made Lunenburg planters increasingly dependent on market forces well beyond their control.[36] Still, it is plain that just when many planters in eastern Virginia were contemplating diversification, most of Lunenburg's planters were moving wholeheartedly into the tobacco economy.

Even if they lacked the fancy paraphernalia and economic influence of the traditional Chesapeake gentry class, the people who constituted the elite of this emergent Southside economy had come a long way from their humble, even primitive, condition at the time of the founding of the county. They were showing themselves to be people of substantial productive capacity, and the region in which they lived was fast becoming a vital part of the economy of the colony as a whole. And, as both the county at large and the local elite acquired more substantial economic power, those institutions of civil and religious power and authority which were themselves heavily dependent on the character of the individuals who controlled them began to acquire a stability and legitimacy they had not previously demonstrated.

• THE EVOLUTION OF A RULING ELITE, 1750–1770

The individuals charged with managing the civil affairs of their more populous and productive Southside county were more powerful and wealthy than their predecessors, and as the commercial and legal demands of a burgeoning tobacco economy became more numerous and complex, the duties of the institutions those men dominated expanded accordingly. This enhancement of the power of the Lunenburg political elite did not occur overnight, and the members of that elite would never achieve the level of mastery attained by their counterparts in the older, more settled counties of Virginia, but it is clear that by the late 1750s they had begun to move away from the inchoate cultural style characteristic of the frontier toward a mode of organization and conduct more typical of traditional Virginia culture. By 1770 that fusion of political, religious, and economic power within the county was well advanced, and those Lunenburg residents who bore the title "gentleman justice" were beginning to have at least a partial claim to the formal power and personal authority that the term connoted.

Nine of the seventeen men serving on the county court in 1770 were among the county's twenty wealthiest men, and all but a few held land and slaves in amounts just a shade below that standard. In all, the average landholding among the justices was 1,015 acres, and none of the justices had holdings that fell below the county average of 275 acres. The justices' slaveholdings indicate even more dramatically their accumulation of economic power. Only fifty-three people in Lunenburg had the capital to support five or more tithable slaves, yet sixteen of the seventeen justices held at least five, and seven of the justices were among the eleven men in the county owning ten or more tithable slaves.[37]

The established church had traditionally operated in concert with the civil government in maintaining civic virtue and the public morality, and to that end there had always been a close connection between the Anglican vestry and the county court in most areas of Virginia. That connection had not been a particularly strong one in the earliest years of Lunenburg's history, but by 1770 sixteen of the seventeen men serving on the court were active Anglicans, nine of them were among the eleven vestrymen of the church, and another would become a vestryman in the near future.[38] (See Appendix 2 for a more detailed presentation of the justices' holdings.)

Among the justices, only Lydall Bacon and Henry Blagrave had landholdings or family connections stretching as far back as 1750, and the great majority of the justices had only begun their economic and political involvement with the county in the past decade. There are some indications, however, that even if the justices were relative newcomers to the region, they would as a group in future years sink their roots more deeply into the county's soil than many of those counted among the county's economic elite. Although many of the justices were just starting their careers on the bench, their service would continue well into the future, with the average length of service amounting to more than fifteen years per justice. Moreover, during the next twenty years the justices would prove capable of consolidating their power, often passing it on to sons and other close relatives.

Another point of contrast between the economic and court elites is that the family names listed in the ranks of the economic elite tended to undergo considerable change over time, whereas once the justices managed to acquire political power they tended to hold on to it. That they did so was undoubtedly related to their ultimate length of residence in the county; the wills and tax lists of the period indicate that at least some among the economic elite were inclined to move on even after they had acquired substantial wealth in Lunenburg, but the justices are a distinct exception in this highly mobile society, demonstrating a marked propensity to live out their days within the confines of the county.[39]

The different persistence rates between the economic and political elites is indicative of the extraordinarily dynamic quality of economic growth within the Southside and the southern frontier more generally. The political structure of the Southside, even though much more loosely arranged than in the east, was nevertheless managed at least in a formal sense in ways that were geared toward stability and continuity. Following the advice of sitting justices, royal governors continued to control access to the bench, and if the county oligarchs of the Southside were not as powerful as they were in more settled counties, and if the roster of potential justices was not quite so closely circumscribed, the very nature of the process itself tended to lead toward concentrations of power. In the burgeoning tobacco economy of the Southside there was ample room for aggressive newcomers who would not only build a substantial estate in the county in a single generation but also be prepared to leave the county and go elsewhere with their fortune before their careers had ended. The whole process was strikingly similar to that described by Wilbur J. Cash in his classic work *The Mind of the South*. In Cash's view, the traditions and ethos of the antebellum South drew heavily on those of the Virginia aristocracy, but the people who built their fortunes and carried those traditions across the South were not the descendants of the Byrds or Carters or Lees. It was people like the Caldwells (lineal antecedents of John Caldwell Calhoun), the Billups, and the Talbots, the aggressive planters and their sons and daughters from Lunenburg, who though they may have started their fortunes in the Virginia Southside, ultimately transplanted their possessions and energies ever southward and westward across the antebellum South.[40]

The increase in the wealth, power, and commitment of the justices to long-term service to the county was accompanied by a simultaneous expansion of activity within the court itself. In the 1740s and early 1750s the court heard an average of seventy-five cases per year; by the mid-1760s, in a county that was one-tenth the physical size but equal in population to the original county, the court was hearing over three hundred cases per year. The court also met more frequently, missing only two or three sessions each year in the decade 1765–75. As the business of the court grew more complex, the justices also became involved in a wider variety of administrative business. Whereas the principal administrative function of the court in the first decade of the county's existence was laying out roads and licensing ordinaries, by the mid-1760s the justices were involved not only in the administration of business relating to the production of tobacco but also in the building of gristmills, bridges, and ferries, the clearing of rivers and streams, and the general business of a rapidly developing economy.[41]

As the court expanded its activity and as the geographic territory for which it was responsible shrunk to one-tenth the original size, it became a more immediate force in the lives of the ordinary citizens whose interests it attempted to serve and whose conduct it was charged with regulating. This meant not only an expansion of the services the court might provide but also an increase in the number of ways the court might intervene in a punitive way. In many instances one's perception of whether the court was expanding services or meting out punishment depended on which side of a civil suit one happened to be on, but whatever the circumstances of individual cases, the most dramatic change in the court's caseload was the heavy increase in the number of debt cases. In the earliest years of the county, the number of debt cases coming before the court each year was about thirty, perhaps a reflection of a more informal (and more violent) way of doing business and of the lack of goods or capital to lend in the first place. By the mid-1760s the volume of debt cases before the court reached 150 per year, the sums at stake in those cases ranging from a few shillings to several hundred pounds.

The eagerness with which most of Lunenburg's citizens used the court—be it for the repayment of a few pounds lent to a neighbor or a few shillings for a job not completed according to specifications—was apparently one trait that they shared with citizens throughout Virginia and most of America.[42] Perhaps it was because the court was such a familiar institution, presided over by friends and neighbors and serving as an important gathering point even for those who had no immediate business before it. Whatever the reasons, Lunenburg's citizens did not hesitate to use the court to settle even the most trivial financial disagreements. Indeed, there seems to be relatively little difference between the wealthy and the humble in this respect. Although wealthier people appear more often as plaintiffs in a larger number of debt cases, the most striking aspect of the debt proceedings is the extent to which all ranks in the economic order were suing and being sued.

The volume of cases in which differences among the county's citizens on matters relating to money and property were arbitrated constituted the overwhelming portion of the court's judicial activity. As in previous decades, the court on the eve of the Revolution took relatively little responsibility for the civic virtue of those citizens within its jurisdiction, and even then the volume of criminal cases seems to have been slight. Lunenburg residents did appear more willing than in earlier years to lodge formal complaints of assault and battery when one man suffered a beating at the hands of another or, more rare, when a woman was mistreated by a man, but most often, after the heat of the combat had cooled the injured party allowed the charges to be dropped once the case was brought by the court to judgment.[43]

The county sheriff, who most often alternated service in that post with service on the bench, was the one man in the county who bore the brunt of civil conflict, criminal behavior, and occasionally the effects of economic cycles on the county's population at large. As the individual ultimately responsible for the collection of taxes, he was the person who had to harass those citizens—sometimes a significant portion of the population—when they fell in arrears. He was also responsible not only for stopping breaches in the civil and criminal code but also for punishing those convicted of violating those codes. And the increased volume of both criminal and debt cases was straining the resources available to the sheriff. Beginning in 1766, County Sheriff Joseph Williams began a protracted campaign to get the justices to do something about the deplorable state of the county prison, but the justices, reflecting their fellow citizens' parsimonious attitude toward public expenditures, were unimpressed, responding that if one of the houses built for prisoners was insufficient the sheriff should then use another, smaller house built earlier. Williams answered that both houses were insufficient, but then went ahead as best he could, evidently placing criminals and debtors in the same crowded jails. This brought a rebuke from the justices in which Williams was ordered, "Do not make use of the smallest [of the county's two prisons] to put debtors in, it being for to hold criminals." A few months later the court ordered Williams to "pay out . . . so much [money] he hath in his hands" to get the prison repaired, but that sum was obviously insufficient, as the complaints continued until 1771, when the court ordered a thorough repair of the prison.[44]

The courthouse site began to serve not only as the center of formal institutional power for the county but also as one of the principal centers in which the citizens of the emergent Lunenburg community could join together in work and play. It was at those sites, where the citizens voluntarily came together for participation in and enactment of the common rites and rituals of their culture, that Lunenburg's elite had their best opportunity to display and enhance their personal authority.

There is little doubt that the physical locale of the courthouse was serving increasingly as a point of organization for nonlegal functions. At some point (probably after the final division of the county in 1764) another courthouse, along with prison, pillory, and perhaps most important, a tavern, was constructed at an intersection on the main road near the center of the newly limited county. Since most of the activities occurring near the courthouse were private affairs, they went unnoticed in the public records of the county and colony, but through the pages of the *Virginia Gazette* and references in the journals of travelers we can gain a fleeting impression of the kinds of business transacted and diversions enjoyed at the courthouse site. For example, in 1771 Lunenburg resident James Cole inserted an advertisement in the *Virginia Gazette* announcing "a match of cocks to be fought at Lunenburg courthouse on Tuesday the 17th of September between the Dinwiddie and Lunenburg Gentlemen." The "gentlemen" of the county were also induced to put up sizable sums of money on the outcome. There were to be fifteen separate fights, with £5 going in each case to the winning side, and £50 to the overall winner. The public was assured that "there will be good entertainment for all Gentlemen that are disposed to come." The cockfight, in comparison with the thoroughbred horse race, was a slightly less genteel but no less powerful symbol of the proud, competitive, and frequently combative ethic of the gentry world, and it is clear that that ethic had traveled as far as the Virginia Southside.[45]

The horse race—at least races among finely bred thoroughbreds—had evidently not yet reached Lunenburg. None of the principal gentlemen of the period listed stud or racehorses in their inventories, and there is no indication that a racecourse (a common sight in the Tidewater and Northern Neck) was ever constructed in the county. There is, however, increasing evidence of other activities—mercantile fairs, horse sales, auctions, and slave sales— all occurring near the courthouse, transforming that site at least occasionally into a genuine center of community life and not merely a place to come when in trouble or in conflict with a neighbor.[46]

As those agencies and centers of secular power and authority assumed greater importance in the life of the county, so too did the Anglican church, the traditional agency of moral and spiritual authority, enhance its position. The Rev. James Craig would succeed where his predecessors had failed in providing the county with stable religious stewardship. Craig, who was a student at Westminster, London, from 1738 to 1742 and then proceeded to Christ Church, Oxford, where he was a Westminster Scholar and was awarded a bachelor of arts degree in 1746, was one of the few Anglican ministers in the Southside who could plausibly fit the gentry's ideal of a "learned clergyman."[47] With his impressive attainments, signifying not only high educational achievement but also lofty social class and status, Craig was no doubt aghast when he initially encountered the citizens whose souls he was supposed to oversee, and must have at least pondered the providential currents that had moved him from the cloistered halls of Oxford to what was to him a rude wilderness. While he may have satisfied the criteria of a "learned minister," neither the "gentry" nor the common folk who made up his early constituency could qualify as a stable and respectable congregation. Yet Craig must have made a considerable effort to adjust to his new surroundings, for in the thirty-five years of continuing service to the church in the county he would not only bring some degree of order to the spiritual chaos that prevailed on his arrival, but he would also transform himself into an important pillar of the planter-gentry establishment.

Craig's job may have been facilitated by the steady transformation of the vestry into a body of more considerable substance and stature than it had been in the earliest years of the parish. By 1770 the vestrymen displayed much the same characteristics as the members of the court; nine of the eleven were themselves justices of the court, and the two who were not had achieved nearly comparable levels of affluence.[48] When Craig took over his ministry, his principal church was still the original one at Reedy Creek, with subsidiary chapels at Flat Rock Creek, Little Roanoke River, and Otter River. By 1770, however, there was considerable sentiment for improvement of the Reedy Creek church, and in November of that year the vestry agreed to an "addition . . . twenty eight by twenty four feet, with five pews to each side, and three windows, also, with eighteen lights in each, and a gallery with two windows and eight lights to each window, and that the old Church be repaired." This probably would have amounted to a substantial improvement to the old structure, but six months later the vestry decided not to be content with renovation and instead to opt for an entirely new church. That church was to be sixty by twenty-eight feet, eighteen feet in pitch, and it was to be built of thinly cut strips of wood, or "scantling." The vestry solicited bids in an advertisement in the *Virginia Gazette* and a few months later gave the contract to Pines Ingraham, who agreed to complete the structure by October 1773. While construction began without too much delay, events would conspire to hold off final completion of the church until well after the Revolution.[49] Meanwhile, Craig would have to make do with the existing structures, but the very willingness of the vestry to go ahead with the project indicated an improvement in the fortunes of the established church. Of course, no matter what the state of *piety* in the parish, the *fortunes* of the established, tax-supported church were bound to improve as ever-increasing numbers of tithe-paying citizens immigrated to Lunenburg.

In some respects, then, we can see the social organization of prerevolutionary Lunenburg, through a combination of economic and demographic growth and through the formation of a distinctive local elite that combined economic, political, religious, and familial power, beginning to move toward a partial conformity with the wealthier and more established counties of the east. Ultimately, however, those individuals who occupied center stage in the secular and religious affairs of Lunenburg continued to carry with them many of the habits of the frontier, and their behavior often fell strikingly short of the genteel ideal so prized by those leaders of the traditional culture.

• THE ABANDONMENT OF DEFERENCE

The controversy and conflict surrounding the choice of Lunenburg's elected representatives to the House of Burgesses dramatically illustrate the uncertainty and openness of Lunenburg's rank order hierarchy and the tenuous claims to power and authority of those who attempted to carry the cultural and political standards of their county. Those contests are particularly revealing of the values and styles of Lunenburg's citizens. In their legal form they were exactly like those occurring in every other county in Virginia, but their variations in actual conduct and resolution tell us much about the nature of the gap between the formally articulated norms of the established gentry culture and the actual modes of behavior in an emergent frontier culture. Moreover, perhaps more than any other single public ritual in Virginia culture, those contests allow us to see and weigh the relative importance of all those values— economic power, gentility, liberality, conviviality, competitiveness—that both defined the ties that bound the community together and provided the community leaders with their claims to power and authority.[50]

The one literary source most often used by historians to reconstruct the spirit, style, and ethic of elections in the traditional Virginia culture is Robert Munford's play *The Candidates*, written in 1770 but not published until after his death in 1798. Through the play run two themes. One, depicted in scenes of drinking, brawling, and improper electioneering, has served to epitomize the popular and obstreperous side of Virginia elections, but the other presents a more sober and restrained side of the Virginia electorate, which whatever its excess still adhered to a traditional, deferential ethic. The tendency among historians has been to view Munford's descriptions of the disorder surrounding Virginia elections as a deviation from the norm, an amusing sidelight to the story but not representative of the true spirit of the story itself. The genius of Virginia politics was that the wealthy, well-born, and well-educated individuals who monopolized power in the Old Dominion did so both at the behest of a respectful citizenry and out of a sense of duty and independence that set them apart from those ordinary citizens who legitimized their power.[51]

That description may be an accurate portrayal of the political culture of the more stable and settled counties of the Tidewater and Northern Neck, but the world in which Robert Munford lived—that part of the Virginia Southside which until 1764, when the county of Mecklenburg was given separate status, comprised the southwestern portion of Lunenburg—was clearly one in which contentiousness and disorderliness at election time were more often the norm than an amusing sidelight.

The most abundant testimony on the character of political conduct in the Southside comes from the records of election returns that required adjudication before the Committee on Privileges and Elections of the House of Burgesses, a committee of which Munford himself was a member when he began his own long career as a burgess in 1765. No area in eighteenth-century Virginia kept that committee busier than Munford's own home counties.[52]

Munford was no doubt familiar with the details of the 1758 contest for Lunenburg's two seats in the House of Burgesses, involving Clement Read, Matthew Marrable, and Henry Blagrave, particularly since he himself would shortly have extensive public and private dealings with each of those individuals. He certainly knew and respected Read, one of the few Southside residents who personified the gentry ideal. Indeed, Read's background and conduct were so singular in the less genteel Southside that he was probably the only local person other than Munford himself who could have served as Munford's model for the character of Worthy in *The Candidates*.[53]

The report of the committee of the House of Burgesses charged with investigating the 1758 election gives further testimony to Read's unchallenged status in the county, and even more dramatically provides a striking commentary on the less distinguished character and conduct of the other aspirants for office in the election. Indeed, the whole history of the 1758 election—its cast of characters, its eventual outcome, and the ethic underlying the decision relating to it—bears such a close resemblance to many of the scenes in *The Candidates* that one cannot help but think that it served as a direct inspiration to Munford's literary work.

In the parlance of eighteenth-century politics, the principal attachment between voter and candidate was that of "interest," but the very concept of the "joining of interests" was subject to infinite shadings of meaning. To serve the interests of one's constituents and in turn to secure the crucial support of "men of interest" for one's candidacy, was the necessary and proper precondition for election to high office in Virginia, but as both *The Candidates* and the 1758 Lunenburg election demonstrate, the line separating proper and improper joining of interests was often overstepped. On the one hand, the natural alliance of men of stature like Worthy and his slightly less prestigious colleague Wou'dbe was considered an appropriate joining of interests, but on the other hand the combination of men like Sir John Toddy, a gentryman of dissipated habits, and Guzzle, the perennial drunkard, ran contrary to the code of Munford's ideal society. Wou'dbe, on hearing that Guzzle and Sir John had joined forces to oppose him, expressed the view typical of a Virginia gentryman: "Their interest, I believe, has not weight enough among the people, for me to lose anything by making them my enemies."[54]

Ideally, the mutual sets of interests that made up the deferential relationship between representative and voter were so self-evident that they required no overt act of reinforcement, but the very nature of the unspoken arrangements of power and authority that lay at the foundation of that system, particularly in the more loosely structured society of the Southside, made it inevitable that some candidates would seek opportunities to advance their interests at the expense of their rivals. This spirit motivated that much-heralded practice of "treating" in Virginia elections, and because such treats represented a deviation from rather than an affirmation of the traditional system, the Virginia House of Burgesses took steps early in the eighteenth century to outlaw the giving of "money, meat, drink, present, gift, reward, or entertainment . . . in order to be elected, or for being elected to serve in the General Assembly."[55] While "liberality" and hospitality were important virtues that helped define the personal authority of a member of the Virginia gentry, there were countless other attributes—disinterested public service, economic power, an imposing persona—that should have made it unnecessary for the gentry to prove their interest in their constituents' well-being by the practice of "treating" in an ideal deferential social order. Even in the more stable political culture of the Northern Neck, the system of rank order and deference was uncertain enough to cause a gentryman as prominent as George Washington to stage occasional election-day treats, but on the whole the frequency with which candidates resorted to treating, and the degree of disorder attending those treats, was far less than in the more uncertain social hierarchy of the Virginia Southside.

In the contested Lunenburg election of 1758, Clement Read was the only one of the three principal contenders whose own persona was sufficiently distinguished to be able to avoid the necessity of open electioneering. While it was acknowledged that one "Memicum Hunt gave a Treat on Behalf of Mr. Read to a Company of Militia he had formerly commanded," even Henry Blagrave, the candidate who had initiated the protest over the conduct of the election, admitted that Read himself had nothing to do with the treat. Indeed, it appears that Read, like his fictional counterpart Worthy, kept his own personal involvement in the election to a minimum.[56]

Matthew Marrable, who later became involved in a number of acrimonious personal disputes with Munford during the 1760s, was considerably less restrained in his conduct, committing virtually every impropriety that, in Munford's opinion, separated a parvenu from a genuine gentryman. Marrable treated the voters on several occasions before, during, and after the election, "spending seven weathers and thirty gallons of rum on that occasion," and while it is true that he cautioned his supporters "to take care they should not intoxicate themselves, least a Riot might ensue at the Election," the committee examining the election was sufficiently concerned about the improprieties committed in Marrable's name that it voided his election, ruling in favor of Read and Blagrave.[57]

Marrable's greatest indiscretion was to write a letter to

Mr. David Caldwell, a Man of Great Interest in the County, strongly soliciting his Interest, in which is contained the following Words: "This shall be my obligation to be liable and answerable to you, and all who are my Friends, in the Sum of five hundred pounds, if I do not use the Utmost of my Endeavors (in case I should be a Burgess) to divide this our county of Lunenburg in the following manner, to wit, Beginning at Byrd's Mill, running a straight line to the Head of the Nottoway.[58]

Caldwell, a member of the family that had founded the Cub Creek settlement and a man who served as the principal agent for William Byrd III in his land dealings in the area, was indeed an important "man of interest" whose opinion of the rival candidates could affect the outcome of the election, but to attempt to win his support either by pledging to vote a particular way on a specific bill or, worse, by the promise of money was wholly contrary to the deferential code. In this respect Marrable's behavior was more characteristic of Munford's Strutabout, who promised the voters he would repeal their taxes, "make the rivers navigable, and bring the tide over the tops of the hills, for a vote." By contrast, Munford's archetypal gentry statesmen, Wou'dbe and Worthy, disdained making promises to the voters, pledging instead only to use their best judgment in determining the common good. In this respect, Wou'dbe was forthrightly modest in his promises to the voters:

Guzzle: And what the devil good do you do then?
Wou'dbe: As much as I have abilities to do.
Guzzle: Suppose, Mr. Wou'dbe, we were to want you to get the price of rum lower'd—wou'd you do it?
Wou'dbe: I cou'd not.
Guzzle: Huzza for Sir John! He has promised to do it, huzza for Sir John!

Twist: Suppose, Mr. Wou'dbe, we should want this tax taken off—cou'd you do it?

Wou'dbe: I cou'd not.

Twist: Huzza for Mr. Strutabout. He's damned, if he don't. Huzza for Mr. Strutabout.

Prize: Why don't you burgesses do something with the damn'd pickers? If we have a hogshead of tobacco refused, away it goes to them, and after they have twisted up the best of it for their own use, and taken as much as will pay them for their trouble, the poor planter has little for his share.

Wou'dbe: There are great complaints against them, and I believe the assembly will take them under consideration.

Prize: Will you vote against them?

Wou'dbe: I will if they deserve it.[59]

Through the voice of the beleaguered Wou'dbe, Munford made it clear that the irresponsible whims of the citizenry and the challenges of demagogic rivals such as Strutabout and Sir John Toddy made the burdens of public office frequently oppressive. "In order to secure a seat in our august senate," complained Wou'dbe, " 'tis necessary a man should either be a slave or a fool; a slave to the people for the privilege of serving them, and a fool himself for begging a troublesome and expensive employment."[60]

It was a willingness to undertake that "troublesome and expensive employment" that signified the spirit of noblesse oblige which motivated men like Clement Read to serve their county, but as one reviews the contested elections occurring in the Southside region near Munford's home even into the 1770s, it becomes clear that the behavior of Marrable was much closer to the norm than the behavior of a Clement Read. Henry Blagrave, who was elected along with Read in the 1758 contest, was hardly a paragon of gentility himself. In a subsequent election in 1772 he was accused of an assortment of breaches in campaign etiquette. James Johnson, an innkeeper, testified that "before the Poll was opened Mr. Blagrave applied to him, and told him if any person wanted Drams to let them have them," and other reports indicated that Blagrave bribed one voter with a promise of a five-shilling pocketbook. The accumulated effect of the testimony was sufficiently damaging for his election to be declared invalid.[61] Nor did Blagrave's private conduct seem any more decorous than his public conduct. He was censured twice by his church for drunken and "unchristianlike behavior" in 1774, and on the second occasion remained so unrepentant that he was excommunicated from the church altogether.[62]

Matthew Marrable, the guilty party in 1758, on another occasion presented himself before the House of Burgesses as the aggrieved party. Just two years earlier, in spite of his own admission that he had bought the voters a "Tickler and a bottle of Rum," he had protested against the ungentlemanly behavior of Thomas Nash. Although his protest was overruled in that case, he would persist, gaining election to the House of Burgesses in 1769 and several more times in the 1770s.[63] All these charges and countercharges respecting illegal treating, the manipulations of militia companies, and false promises to the voters were indicative of a society where the standards of conduct and the lines of personal authority were not wholly clear.

If Clement Read's conduct represented the genteel ideal to which Munford aspired, and Matthew Marrable's represented the more frequent norm, other occurrences served as a reminder that some of the citizens of the Southside had not yet even begun to make the transition from the disorderly state of the frontier to the well-ordered hierarchy of traditional Virginia society. In that same investigation of the 1758 election involving Read, Blagrave, and Marrable, the committee took special note of

the behavior of one John Hobson, which was very illegal and tumultuous; in offering to lay Wagers the Poll was closed, when it was not; in proclaiming at the Courthouse that the poll was going to be closed, and desiring the Freeholders to come in and vote, and then, violently, and by striking and kicking them, preventing them from so doing, by which Means many Freeholders did not vote at the said election.[64]

The number of disputed elections occurring throughout Virginia generally during the decades before the Revolution is indicative of a society that, whatever its pretensions to traditional modes of social order, was nevertheless far more fluid than the English society on which it had been based, but the situation in Lunenburg exceeded all the bounds of acceptable behavior even in that more loosely structured electoral system. With a few notable exceptions, such as Read and Munford themselves, each of whom had close contact with the traditional gentry code by dint of their upbringing and past experience in eastern Virginia, the aspirants for high political office in Lunenburg retained too many of the vestiges of the frontier—swearing, fighting, excessive drunkenness, and perhaps most telling, striving too aggressively for popular approval—to be able to win an undisputed place at the top of the social hierarchy of their community.

The less genteel character of the members of the Lunenburg elite was also displayed in their continuing unconcern for the manners and morals of the citizens whose conduct they were charged with overseeing. The one aspect of the court's business that did not change appreciably was the justices' concern for enforcing the public virtue in the county. The records of the church vestry, of the court, and of the county grand juries indicate only sporadic activity on matters of discipline relating to swearing, drunkenness, breaking of the Sabbath, and even bastardy.

Those people who laid claim to economic, social, and political leadership in Lunenburg on the eve of the American Revolution were therefore deficient in several important traditional areas. Their economic power, while steadily growing, was not on a scale so grand as to grant them unchallenged primacy in the economic affairs of the county, nor was it sufficient to provide them with the style of life that was the hallmark of those gentrymen with more confident claims to political power and personal authority. It was not only formal power and position that Lunenburg's leaders lacked, for the consequent inability of Lunenburg's leaders to behave like gentry in the traditional meaning of that word—their inability to present a persona of gentility and public and private virtue to their fellow citizens—was both a cause and an effect of their shakier claims to formal power.

Part of the reason for the failure of Lunenburg's leadership class to establish full hegemony over their community lay in the still-incomplete nature of that community itself. The tobacco economy of the region was expanding rapidly, but it had not yet generated enough wealth to allow any single individual or group of individuals to achieve unquestioned dominance. Similarly, while the supporting institutions of the burgeoning economy—county courts, tobacco inspection stations, general stores—were becoming more important in the lives of the county's citizens, that process was still in a relatively early stage. Yet there were more fundamental reasons for the failure of Lunenburg's elite to assume all the characteristics of ruling elites in more settled parts of the colony, and those causes related more to the very nature of the community over which they were expected to rule than to individual failings in leadership. The very population growth that was both a cause and a reflection of Lunenburg's emergence into the mainstream of the economic life of the Chesapeake was at the same time the source of a cultural diversity that would make it impossible for the values of the traditional culture to continue unchallenged. A significant portion of Lunenburg's growing population—no matter how bright their economic prospects might seem—would begin to turn in different directions for their definition of community and thus weaken still further the traditional bases on which community order rested.

·FOUR·

The Evangelical Revolt in the Backcountry

There was considerable stir among the people in the church meeting-houses and parish vestries of the Southside in the 1760s and 1770s. As the Rev. James Craig complained, the enthusiastic, itinerant preachers "gain Proselytes every Day, & unless the Principal Persons concerned in that Delusion are apprehended, or otherwise restrained from proceeding further, the consequences will be fatal." Of course the evangelical perspective on those developments was quite different. In the view of the itinerant preachers whose exhortations were witnessed by crowds numbering in the hundreds and occasionally the thousands, the revival of simple religious faith, uncorrupted by the worldly trappings so typical of the established church, was a clear sign of divine favor.[1]

The rise of enthusiastic, evangelical religion was a movement of profound social as well as theological significance in the history of eighteenth-century Virginia, for it posed a striking challenge to an Anglican-gentry culture that had hitherto paid allegiance to an altogether different set of religious forms. Those forms, which relied on an educated clergy discoursing from learned texts before a congregation often seated in strict observance of the prevailing social hierarchy of the parish, were distinctly at odds with the leveling spirit inherent in the evangelical style, which emphasized the self-abasement of all, clergy and congregation alike.

In a recent book as important for its methodology as for its fresh interpretation of eighteenth-century Virginia history, Rhys Isaac has identified the "evangelical revolt" as the most dramatic and far-reaching event in the "transformation" of Virginia. That transformation was the process by which the hegemony of the gentry culture was weakened in many spheres, but in particular it was a process by which "the vivid culture of the gentry, with their love of magnificent display, [was made] to coexist with the austere culture of the evangelicals, with their burden of guilt." In Isaac's view, the character of the evangelicals' culture was "structured to an important extent by processes of reaction to the dominant culture." Moreover, the "revolt" that was occurring was in large measure indicative of "internal disorder," of inherent weaknesses and contradictions within the Anglican-gentry culture itself. In Isaac's argument, the sources of discontent—revulsion against the ostentation of the gentry and against the increasing worldliness of the gentry's Anglican ceremonies—and the purveyors of that discontent—the evangelical ministers who denounced the Anglican gentry's moral corruption—were all endemic to Virginia, home-grown products of a culture that was not serving the spiritual and worldly needs of all the Old Dominion's citizens.[2]

The evangelical challenge to traditional Anglican norms was to some extent a logical response to many of the failings within the Anglican-gentry culture itself, for many Anglicans of the more humble sort had good cause to question whether the religious institutions and rituals of Anglicanism spoke adequately to their own needs. These "internal" failings may therefore explain some of the attraction to the evangelical cause of English men and women living in eastern counties such as Lancaster, Westmoreland, or Caroline, where Anglicanism had always represented the dominant—indeed, the only—religious and social norm. They are not, however, sufficient explanation for the much more dramatic insurgence of the evangelicals in those counties like Lunenburg, where the hegemony of Anglican leaders was never well established and where the population, which was legally bound to support the Anglican establishment, was much less attached to the values of that culture from the very outset. In this sense the "evangelical revolt" in Lunenburg was a phenomenon tied less to the religious history of Virginia than to a much larger and ultimately more far-reaching cultural development throughout the whole of the Southern backcountry.

• PATTERNS OF RELIGIOUS AFFILIATION IN LUNENBURG

William Byrd had likened the immigration of the Scots-Irish from Pennsylvania in the 1730s to the invasion of the "Goths and Vandals of Old," yet that migration was only a trickle compared with the flood not only of Scots-Irish but also of Germans and Swiss arriving in the Southside in the 1760s and 1770s. Moreover, the rate of turnover in Lunenburg's population continued nearly unabated; while some seventy-five new households were added to the tithable lists each year, approximately fifty picked up stakes and moved on during the same period.[3] Given both the diversity and the exceptionally high mobility of Lunenburg's population, it should not surprise us that Anglican-gentry hegemony would face challenges not only from a few within the ranks of the established church but also from newcomers who had never accepted the social and religious precepts of the Church of England.

The evangelicals—in particular the radical Separate Baptists—in Lunenburg would come to represent the most dramatically distinct, countercultural alternative to the mores and values embodied in the established church, but it would be misleading to depict patterns of community organization in the county as moving toward only two fixed and opposing points. There existed in virtually every county in Virginia a continuum of religious belief (and unbelief), closely correlated to particular cultural styles, which manifested at one extreme a close identification with the values of traditional, Anglican-gentry culture and at the other extreme a set of values that were in considerable measure defined in opposition to those of the dominant culture. Along that continuum, however, were ranged other groups and individuals—those citizens who retained some nominal but not particularly intimate connection to the Anglican church; the great number of people who eschewed attachments to any church whatsoever; the Presbyterians, who in their formal theology resembled evangelical Baptists but in cultural style were more closely aligned with the Anglican-gentry orders; and finally, a widely varying assortment of Baptists, some organized in "regular" Baptist churches, submitting to discipline from a formally organized "association," and others, like Lunenburg's Separate Baptists, guided only by the spirit of the membership of their own congregation.

If the Anglican-gentry style of religious and social organization represented the mode of community organization to which most of Lunenburg's economic and political leaders at least aspired, then these alternative modes of behavior just as often represented the norm to which most of the citizens of the county adhered. Probably the most numerous group in the county, judging from the dismayed observations of Anglican minister James Craig, was that composed of the unchurched, that mass of people who, according to Craig, "had never, or seldom been at Church since they were Baptized" and who "were ignorant of the very first principles of Christianity."[4] Technically the unchurched were Anglicans, for they paid for the support of that church, and since they had not indicated any formal intention to dissent from the precepts of the established religion they were counted among the members of the Church of England. It is difficult to trace the geographic origins, wealth, or length of residence in the county of those who disdained formal religious affiliation, because their refusal to identify with any one religious group has granted them an anonymity that is difficult for the historian to penetrate. It seems likely, however, that these were precisely the sort of folk who not only failed to appear on the membership roles of any of the churches, but also moved in and out of the county with the greatest frequency, regarding Lunenburg as little more than a temporary stopping place on the road to some greater opportunity in the future.

The Rev. Charles Woodmason, that Anglican divine who stalked the Carolina backcountry in search of sinners ready for redemption, gives us a vivid if overwrought impression of the mode of life of some of these men and women. Woodmason was convinced that he was "in the midst of the Heathens, Arians, and Hereticks." He decried "the open profanation of the Lord's

Day. . . . Among the low Class it is abus'd by Hunting, fishing, fowling, and Racing—By the women in frolicing and Wantoness [*sic*]. By others in drinking Bouts and Card Playing."[5] These folk, though unmoved by the desire to travel from their individual farmsteads to church on Sundays, may at least have involved themselves in the convivial pastimes—gambling and cockfighting—that occurred around the site of the courthouse. It is even more certain that the taverns of Lunenburg county, of which there were more than a dozen by 1770, offered another important point of common contact. And as a petition from at least one segment of Lunenburg's citizenry attests, the conduct of some at those taverns was not always the most genteel. The petitioners complained that the tavern located adjacent to the courthouse was infested with "a nest of bad and nefarious characters," including "some persons violently suspected of Horse-Stealing and sundry other Crimes."[6]

Perhaps just as common as those who avoided all contact with organized religion were those who identified at least nominally with the established church, taking their marriage vows from an Anglican minister, having their children baptized in the church, and occasionally attending services, but who departed dramatically from the genteel Anglican ideal in their conduct both in and out of the church. There were no doubt some who required the sort of sermon that Woodmason delivered on at least two occasions in the Carolina backcountry in 1770. He implored his congregants:

Bring no Dogs with You—They are very troublesome. . . . When you are seated—do not whisper, talk, gaze about—shew light Airs or Behaviour—for this argues a wandering Mind and Irreverence towards God, is unbecoming Religion, and may give Scandal and Offence to weak Christians:—Neither sneeze or Cough, if you can avoid it—and do not practice that unseemly, rude, indecent Custom of Chewing or of Spitting, which is very ridiculous and absurd in Public, especially in Women and in God's House.[7]

Those sneezing, coughing, chewing, spitting people, though they may have stopped in at the Anglican meetinghouse from time to time, were hardly the sort of people whom James Craig had in mind when he began his journey from Christ Church, Oxford, to America, nor is it likely that those nominal Anglicans felt the same sense of attachment either to the formal institution of the church or to the men charged with the moral stewardship of the church as did the more pious communicants in the traditional culture. It is likely, however, that both the unchurched and the nominally churched felt they had more in common with the emergent gentry who dominated Lunenburg's Anglican church than they did with those pietistic individuals who would identify themselves with the evangelical movement. If the unchurched were short on gentility, then so to a lesser extent were the wealthier and better-connected lay leaders of Lunenburg's Anglican establishment. Similarly, they shared with those Anglican gentrymen a special fondness for the convivial and competitive aspects—tippling, dancing, cockfighting—which had always been a partial but by no means the *only* defining quality of the traditional culture.[8]

As we have seen, the connection of the unchurched with traditional agencies of power and authority was severely attenuated both by the relatively weak claims to authority of those who served in leadership positions in the church and the court and by their own unconcern for most of the services offered by those individuals and agencies. Undoubtedly their principal concern remained centered on their families and farmsteads, and given what we know about the continuing high rate of out-migration from the county, they were not even uniformly wedded to the idea of their farmsteads as permanent homes. In sum, while a considerable number of Lunenburg's citizens may have adopted the sporting, convivial side of the old cavalier tradition, they remained essentially plain folk, without strong ties to established institutions of power or authority and without deep roots in the soil of Lunenburg itself.

If the unchurched and the nominally churched were connected to the traditional culture by avenues of sport and conviviality, then the Presbyterians, though their formal theology placed them among the ranks of the "dissenters," met as well as any group in the county (including even the members of the Anglican gentry themselves) those standards of decorousness that formed the more genteel side of the cavalier ideal. As in the case of virtually any religious group except the Anglicans—whose parish lines were drawn to be identical to those of the county—the definition of the Presbyterian religious community in Lunenburg was by no means coterminous with that of the county itself. The principal Presbyterian meetinghouses of the eighteenth-century Southside were located either on the fringes of Lunenburg or in adjacent counties, so it is difficult to speak of "Lunenburg Presbyterians" with any precision. The earliest Presbyterian churches at Cub and Buffaloe creeks were composed principally of the Scots-Irish settlers who had moved to Lunenburg and its environs before the county had achieved legal status. One of the earliest spiritual leaders of that settlement was John Thompson, an Old Side Presbyterian who preached there as early as 1739, but judging from the scattered records of subsequent years, the church was alternately under the guidance of both New Side and Old Side ministers. Cub Creek, which seemed to have shared both congregants and ministers with Buffaloe Creek during those early years, had much the same Scots-Irish and predominantly Old Light tendencies. As many of those Scots-Irish moved on, however, and as the Anglican church in Lunenburg gained strength, the locus of Presbyterian influence in the region tended to move northwest to Prince Edward County, where Briery Church was formed in 1755. The first pastor of Briery, Robert Henry, took over the duties as leader of the older Presbyterian congregation at Cub Creek at the same time and was closely identified with Samuel Davies and New Side styles of Presbyterianism. The Briery congregants, in contrast to those at Cub Creek, seem to have been mainly English rather than Scots-Irish until the late 1770s.[9]

Although the conflicting styles of evangelical New Lights and more traditional Old Lights would create schisms within the Presbyterian church in other parts of America, Henry seemed able to serve the needs of the predominantly Old Light congregation at Cub Creek just as effectively as he administered to the New Lights at Briery, and even more striking, he and his congregants seemed able to live in perfect harmony with the members of the established church. While the incompleteness of the Presbyterian church records and the significant overlap between Lunenburg and Prince Edward County residents in those records that do exist make it impossible to trace precisely the character of all Lunenburg's prerevolutionary Presbyterians, those we can trace appear to have been at least equal to the Anglican church members in both wealth and permanence in the county. As we have already seen, John Caldwell, the leading spirit of the Buffaloe and Cub Creek settlements, was one of the original justices of the county and was even appointed to the original vestry of the Anglican church until he informed the other vestry members of his disinclination to serve. A decade later, at a time when the Anglican church itself was beginning to accumulate some greater institutional and moral authority, the Presbyterians continued to be represented among the most prominent and powerful citizens in the county. While Anglicans continued to dominate most of the important positions in county government, Lunenburg families like the Cragheads, Pettuses, Venables, Billupses, and Waltons were prominent in both the economic life and the political life of Lunenburg, while at the same time playing important roles in the Briery Presbyterian Church in Prince Edward County.[10] The similarities between those Presbyterians and their Anglican neighbors are also borne out by the extent to which members of each religious group seemed to move back and forth between the churches of the other. In many cases, members would be carried on the rolls of both churches for several years, and judging from contemporary testimony, neither church felt unduly threatened by the other. Indeed, the Anglican minister James Craig saw the Presbyterians as fellow sufferers from and allies against the evil of "enthusiasm" emanating from the camp of the Baptists.[11] This relationship between Anglicans and Presbyterians was typical of the way in which the standard-bearers of cavalier society were more interested in style than theological substance; the letter of the Calvinist doctrine to which Southside Presbyterians subscribed was not dramatically different from that of the Baptists, but their ministry—often well educated and disdainful of lay preaching and emotional displays of religious enthusiasm—was quite in keeping with the standards and styles of Craig and his Anglican vestry.[12]

The process of evangelization is often as much dependent on organization as on theological awakening, and it was the Baptists of Lunenburg who in their style of life, in their theological doctrine, and in the organizational vigor of their leaders represented the most dramatic challenge to the mores and values of Anglican-gentry society.[13] Had the wave of evangelicalism appeared in the earliest phase of the county's history, at a time when the social and economic order was less defined and the dominant cultural style of the county still inchoate, conflict between Anglicans and dissenters almost certainly would have occurred, but it may have been considerably more diffuse. Appearing when it did, however, at a time when an increasingly assertive Anglican elite was beginning to strengthen its control over a set of traditionally important secular and religious institutions, the result was a dramatic disjunction between the values, life-styles, and patterns of social interaction of those identifying with the dominant culture and of those adhering to the pietistic system of evangelical religion. In most Tidewater and Northern Neck counties the Anglican elite was at least strong enough to contain the evangelical challenge for several decades, but in Lunenburg the conflict between established and dissenting religion would shake the social structure of the county almost immediately.

• THE BAPTIST INSURGENCE

The emerging evangelical community of Lunenburg, even though it would come together in tangible form in just a few meetinghouses within the bounds of the county, had its origin in many far-flung lines of itinerant activity reaching out into New England, the middle colonies, and the rest of the Southern backcountry. As early as 1754, Shubal Stearns, a former Presbyterian born in Boston and converted to the Baptist faith in Connecticut in 1751, founded a church at Sandy Creek, Guilford County, North Carolina. The Baptists seem to have launched their itinerancy from that location. Stearns, along with his brother-in-law Daniel Marshall, had within a few years acquired active converts in southwestern Virginia in the persons of Dutton Lane, William and Joseph Murphey, and perhaps most important, Samuel Harriss.[14] All those men preached in and around Lunenburg in the mid to late 1750s, and judging from James Craig's comments, they constituted a considerable threat to Anglican hegemony as early as 1759.

Craig complained of the growing numbers of "ignorant en[thusiastic anti]paedobaptists" in the county, blaming their emergence both on the ignorance of the people in his parish and on the moral laxity of the Anglican clergymen who had preceded him. Both Samuel Harriss and William Murphey had been sufficiently active in the area to cause Craig to disparage them for disseminating "the most shocking delusions." Carrying with him the prevailing stereotype of the Baptist preacher as unlearned and uncultured, the Anglican divine noted that William Murphey was "so ignorant that he cannot read or write his name."[15] However, he would have had a more difficult time pinning that stereotype on Harriss, for at the time of Craig's letter that Southside Virginia resident was a burgess from Halifax County and a colonel in the local militia, one of the few Baptist leaders of the prerevolutionary period to have attained substantial status in traditional agencies of governmental and social power.[16]

Whatever the attainments of the itinerants who circulated in and around Lunenburg, it is clear that their message—which ran contrary to all the symbol and substance of Anglican ritual—was being heard by increasing numbers of frontier residents. Craig lamented, "They gain Proselytes every Day, and unless the Principal Persons concerned in this Delusion are apprehended or otherwise restrained from proceeding further, the consequences will be fatal."[17]

At the time Craig wrote those words, the Baptists had not yet become sufficiently organized within Lunenburg itself to erect their own church meetinghouse, but they had constituted themselves into one of the most interesting and conceivably most threatening Baptist church groups in Virginia history near Bluestone Creek, in what would later become part of Mecklenburg County. The Bluestone church, which seems to have received its inspiration initially from the preachings of William Murphey and Philip Mulkey, was composed of several whites and a substantial number of blacks belonging to the estate of William Byrd. It lost its cohesion when Byrd's estate was sold and many of his slaves dispersed, but during its brief existence the church was said to have awakened "many . . . bright and shining Christians" among the blacks of the region and was generally credited with laying the groundwork for the later establishment of other congregations in the county.[18]

In 1771, radical evangelical religion achieved its first permanent institutional form in Lunenburg with the establishment of Meherrin Separate Baptist Church in the central western portion of the county. Its origins dated back well before that year, however, for as early as 1757 or 1758 Dutton Lane had attracted attention with his preachings in that neighborhood. At that time Joseph Williams, one of the magistrates of Lunenburg, interrupted one of Lane's exhortations with the charge that he was disturbing the peace and instructed him never to preach in the area again. Lane did move on to other neighborhoods, but Williams, although the knowledge would have shocked him at the time, would ultimately become an active member and deacon of the Meherrin church at the time of its founding.[19] His son, John Williams, would become converted at the same time and go on to become Lunenburg's and the Southside's most venerated evangelical preacher.

The principal institutional inspiration for the Meherrin congregation was Nottoway Church, founded just a few miles to the north in the county of the same name in 1769. Sometime in 1770 it was determined that there were sufficient numbers in Lunenburg itself to support a church, and on December 13, 1770, the dissenters petitioned the Lunenburg court to allow them to establish a place for "publick and divine worship." By that time Joseph Williams, the earlier persecutor of the dissenters, not only signed the petition but was one of the sitting justices who ruled favorably on it.[20] Samuel Harriss continued preaching in the area, and along with Jeremiah Walker, Elijah Baker, John Williams, and James Shelburne he took the lead in laying the groundwork for the eventual establishment of the Meherrin congregation on November 27, 1771. The 108 adult members who became a part of the original Meherrin congregation, and the 170 who joined it over the course of the next decade, together with those who joined the four additional Baptist churches founded in Lunenburg in the 1770s and the early 1780s, would indeed, at least in the perceptions of the members of the Anglican establishment, "threaten the subversion of True Religion."[21]

While the absence of institutional records before 1771 makes it difficult to draw any firm conclusions about the character of those who were attracted to evangelical religion before that date, we can, with the founding of the Meherrin church, begin to identify more precisely the attitudes and attributes that distinguished the Baptists from those who adhered to the value system of established religion.

The most dramatic difference between Baptists and Anglicans was one of style. At the root of this different style was the distinct way in which the Baptists sought to prepare themselves for salvation, that final goal which conditioned their behavior in the meetinghouse. A substantial portion of the meeting was given over to the enforcement of church discipline, and the most common disciplinary actions were aimed at behavior that was an integral part of the dominant culture—fighting, drunkenness, playing cards, betting on horse races, ostentatious dress, and breaking the Sabbath.[22]

The church members were not concerned only with those obvious examples of sinful behavior. Their disciplinary proceedings were aimed at promoting a "Christian community," and to that end the congregation also acted decisively to promote mutual cooperation and punish "unchristian behavior." Gossiping about one's neighbors, engaging in sharp business practices, defaulting on a loan—all these were considered unchristian.[23]

In many cases the congregation acted as a substitute for and supplement to the legal agency of the county court. One of the persistent debates within the meeting revolved around the question of whether "civil suits at law are not allowable in some cases against members in fellowship." Many brethren felt that resort to the court should be banned in all cases, while others believed that some contact with the court was necessary. The ultimate decision, which came only after lengthy debate, was that appeal to the court was "lawful in some extraordinary and particular cases." This was no idle debate, for the Baptists tended to turn to the meeting rather than to the court for settling secular conflicts. Settlements of secular conflicts within the meetinghouse usually took the form of disciplinary decisions regarding the default of debts, "unchristian behavior" in business affairs, or mistreatment of a wife, servant, or slave. In many of these cases the church was clearly acting as a substitute for the court. In the suspension of Charles Cook for burning the arm of one of his slaves as punishment, or in its consideration of the complaint of two black members respecting the "unchristian behavior of Rebecca Johnson" for separating husband and wife by selling the husband, the church assumed responsibility in areas where the court had not dared to tread.[24]

The concern of the church for "Christian" behavior was not confined to these quasijudicial proceedings. On an almost weekly basis the members of the church collectively legislated on all manner of conduct, posed in a series of "queries" in the minutes of the meetings. Roughly half the questions related specifically to church doctrine: "Is it censurable to hold to the principle of Infant Baptism? [Yes—unanimously]"; or "Is there such an office as lay elder or elders distinct from that of a Deacon? [Unresolved]." Just as frequently, though, the church members attempted to define good conduct in a host of practical questions: "Is it lawful to keep an ordinary? [It may be, but suffering drunkenness is unlawful]"; "Is it lawful to beat or whip servants or children . . . before the method that Christ has laid down in the 18th Matthew [No—by majority vote]"; or even, "Is it lawful to follow the trade of oyster selling? [Not in itself, simply considered]."[25]

The space in the Baptist minute books given over to judicial or legislative matters of discipline is substantial, but it would be a mistake to overemphasize the punitive aspects of the Baptists' community organization. The members of the Meherrin church had succeeded in establishing a close-knit Christian community sharing common and deeply felt values to an extent never before achieved by any other institution or association of individuals in the county. Moreover, within the limits of a slaveholding society that community operated in an egalitarian fashion. Questions of church doctrine were determined by the vote of all the free male members of the congregation, and matters relating to discipline and secular policy were decided by the vote of the entire congregation, male and female alike. Even slaves were admitted as full members of the Meherrin church, and while it is clear that their white brothers and sisters were vigorous in imposing their own standards of conduct on them, it is nevertheless equally clear that the church provided to the thirteen slaves who joined the Meherrin meeting from 1771 to 1776 important avenues for consolation and self-expression.[26]

The history of the black community in Lunenburg—a community that by the time of the Revolution comprised nearly half the total population of the county—is virtually invisible in most of the surviving records of the county, but the Baptist records, which display a concern for the conduct of all church members, white and black, at least give us a glimpse into the character of the Afro-American experience in the Virginia Southside. In the prerevolutionary period, most Southside blacks lived on relatively small plantations in which white masters worked in close concert with and supervision of just a few other slaves, and thus the slaves' opportunity to create anything resembling an autonomous black community in their workday lives was severely constrained. For at least a few slaves the Baptist meetinghouse provided a place for congregation and communal participation that was lacking in the lives of most of their counterparts. The experiential, participatory form of Christianity offered by the Baptists was much more inviting than the austere, passive Calvinism of other denominations, and it is plain that the African slaves used the forms of white Christianity to their own cultural ends. The white leaders of Lunenburg's Baptist church may have used church discipline to enforce their view of "proper" social behavior on their black slaves, but blacks were deriving reciprocal benefit from their religious experience as well, securing for themselves an identity connected both to the sacred worlds of their masters and to their own secular experience in slavery.[27]

The disciplinary records of the Meherrin church reveal the reciprocal character of that experience. On the one hand, blacks appear much more frequently than their white counterparts as the objects of punishment at the hands of the congregation. The rebukes ministered to Johnson's Dick and Williams's Sam for "disorderly walking" and "misbehavior to elders," to Clay's James for "lying and whoring," and to Williams's Charles and Walton's Amy for committing adultery with one another all served not only to uphold strict Baptist codes of "Christian behavior" but also to enforce submission of those slaves to the will of their masters. On the other hand, Baptist discipline could work in the other direction, as in the case of the suspension of membership of one Charles Cook for the sin of "burning one of his negroes."[28] Similarly, the Baptists' concern for the sanctity of marriage vows worked both to uphold the views of the white Baptist majority and to provide some security for slave families. While the Baptists never went so far as to demand legal recognition of slave marriages, they did, within their own religious communities, both honor the reality of those unions and punish those slaves who transgressed against them.[29] This sort of ameliorative action, though hardly constituting a direct challenge to the institution of slavery itself, was nevertheless not without meaning in a society where most masters were free to mete out punishment to slaves or break up slave families without interference from others within their community.

Evangelical religion did serve to shift some of the focus of the slaves' concerns to the world beyond, to help them accommodate themselves to their condition on earth, but it is a mistake to depict the slave religious experience in Lunenburg or elsewhere in the South as being merely otherworldly. As Albert Raboteau has noted,

The conversion experience equipped the slave with a sense of individual value and personal vocation which contradicted the devaluing and dehumanizing forces of slavery. In the prayer meetings, the sermons, prayers and songs, when the Spirit started moving the congregation to shout, clap, and dance, the slaves enjoyed community and fellowship which transformed their individual sorrows. That some slaves maintained their identity as persons, despite a system bent on reducing them to a subhuman level, was certainly due in part to their religious life. In the midst of slavery, religion was for slaves a space of meaning, freedom, and transcendence.[30]

Most of the debates among Baptists over church doctrine and discipline occurred in "private places," behind the walls of the meetinghouse or in a private home, where church congregants drew together out of the range of unbelievers and scoffers to nourish their faith. But it was in their public mode of worship, in the great comings together for exhortation and baptismal ceremonies, that the Baptists in Lunenburg presented the most visible challenge to the decorous styles of traditional religion. Prior to the emergence of the Baptist revivals, public life in colonial Virginia had revolved around ceremonies over which the acknowledged leaders of the secular and religious spheres of the colony could exercise control. The Baptist revivalist preachers broke through this hierarchical and elaborately staged ceremonial mode by holding meetings on the spur of the moment wherever they might gather a crowd.[31] For a region with no major market towns and few natural centers for coming together, the crowds they gathered were enormous. In his journal for May 12, 1771, Lunenburg's John Williams recorded that he preached to "4 or 5,000 souls," and the average crowd to which Williams and other Baptist ministers preached at their great public meetings was nearly five hundred.[32]

Perhaps no public gathering was more resonant of the values and aspirations that bound the Baptists together than the ritual of adult baptism, for in this powerful and intensely emotional ritual they entered into a fellowship of believers and set themselves apart from most other members of their society, who were usually open in their derision of such practices. In this ritual in particular, where the communicants laid themselves open to frequent public ridicule, the Baptists departed not only from the norms of traditional Anglican ritual but also from the norms of the Presbyterians and the unchurched as well. Meherrin's John Williams captured some of the emotional fervor of the baptismal experience in 1771:

We broke up that night and met next morning by nine o'clock and took experience until about eleven. Then I preached to a number of people from 23d Matt., 33d verse. Bro. Stratton exhorted, then took experience till about two o'clock, then Bro. Harriss preached from 5th chapter 2d Corinthians, 20th verse. Bro. Hall exhorted, a great exercise among the people. Then proceeded to baptism, and oh, such a baptism I never saw, not only with water, but in a great measure by the Holy Ghost. The Christians fell to shouting, sinners trembling, and falling down convulsed, the devil a raging and blaspheming, which kindled the flame of the Christians and the Lord, we hope and trust, plucked a soul in that time out of the jaws of death, hell and eternal destruction. Glory to his great name. I was [carried] away in the time of exercise.[33]

The Baptists at Meherrin, in "taking experience" in the mode described so vividly by Williams, had created an alternative mode of community organization, excluding as much as possible the dominant county institutions of court and Anglican church and substituting in their place the intense communalism of the public meeting and the meetinghouse. Moreover, it was a mode which, at least in the highly emotive ritual of the baptismal experience, joined blacks and whites together in a common quest for religious salvation. In some important respects the folk-based culture of the Lunenburg evangelicals was similar to that of the Puritans of early-seventeenth-century New England. Although the Lunenburg evangelicals would never succeed completely in establishing a "Christian, utopian, closed corporate community" (the very nature of the landscape and the economy of the Virginia Southside rendered that kind of settlement unthinkable) it is clear that they were inclined toward a mode of community organization and conduct that emphasized an intensity of shared experience and an exclusivity that stood in contrast to the dispersed and often disorderly world around them.[34]

• COMMUNITIES IN CONFLICT

The different modes of religious organization and behavior of the Anglicans and the Separate Baptists were mirrored in their social circumstances. For example, the contrast between the two groups in terms of economic and political power could hardly have been more striking. Anglicans dominated county government at nearly every point; Baptists, with only two exceptions, were not represented in the ranks of the politically powerful.[35] The Baptists' lack of political influence was accompanied by paucity of economic power. The wealth and influence of the *leaders* of the Baptist and Anglican churches are not fully amenable to comparison, because the Baptists explicitly rejected elaborate hierarchies of vestrymen, churchwardens, and sextons, but the radically different economic status of the two ministers at this stage in their careers and at roughly similar ages seems symbolic of the differences in the congregations at large. Anglican minister James Craig owned more than 1,000 acres and thirteen tithable slaves in 1772; by 1782 his holdings had increased to 1,599 acres and included a gristmill and forty-two slaves, making him one of the two or three wealthiest citizens in the county.[36] The two early leaders of the Meherrin Baptist congregation, John Williams and Elijah Baker, were hardly in the same league. Neither man can be identified as owning land or slaves on the tithable lists of the late 1760s and early 1770s, although there is some evidence that Williams did own some slaves by 1771. By 1782, after Baker had moved out of the county, Williams possessed a modest holding of two hundred acres, and while the tax lists again indicate that he owned no slaves, he may have possessed at least a few.[37]

It is impossible to calculate the total wealth of the original Meherrin congregation, since many of the members do not appear on Lunenburg's tithable lists and some of them lived in adjoining counties for which no lists survive. Among adult male members who can be traced, however, the average landholding was only 135 acres, less than half the county average of 275 acres. About a third of them owned no land at all, and only the exceptional Henry Blagrave, a recent convert who had been an Anglican vestryman just two years earlier, could be counted among the affluent with his holdings of 2,170 acres and twelve tithable slaves.[38]

For the Baptist congregants who joined the church in the next decade and who appear on the first complete tax list compiled for the county in 1782, the pattern of wealth remained much the same. Among the Meherrin taxpayers in 1782 (a sample that probably inflates Baptist wealth since it excludes those who were too poor to appear on the lists in the first place), the average landholding was 220 acres and the average slaveholding slightly more than two per household. The county average in 1782 was 267 acres and four slaves, and even more noteworthy, the average holding of Anglicans at that time was 481 acres and nine slaves per household.[39]

The Anglicans and Baptists differed not only in their present circumstances but also in their previous life histories. The ethnic backgrounds and previous places of residence of members of the two groups were markedly dissimilar. In 1770 the Anglican members of the court and vestry were relatively firmly rooted in the county, at least by the standards of a highly fluid, frontier society. Most of them had lived in Lunenburg for more than a decade, and nearly all would continue to live out their days there. And although almost all the members of the court and vestry had immigrated to Lunenburg within their own lifetime, they tended to come either from older Piedmont counties or from the Tidewater and Northern

Neck. Most significant, virtually all the leaders of the Anglican-gentry establishment, as well as the rank and file of the Anglican church, identified with a cultural tradition that was English.[40]

It is more difficult to trace the life histories of the Baptists. More recently arrived, less likely to remain, and less prominent in the economic or public life of the county than their Anglican counterparts, the facts of their lives both before and after their arrival in Lunenburg are more elusive. However, a small number of Baptist leaders attained enough prominence—often notoriety from the perspective of the Anglican public officials of the region—to have left some mark on the record of the county. John Williams, one of the founders and longtime leaders of the Meherrin church, was born in Hanover County and probably moved to Lunenburg with his family as a youth in 1749. His father, Joseph Williams, was himself the son of a Welshman who had immigrated to Hanover and was the only member of the original church who had enjoyed both economic and political power in the area. Although the Anglican minister, James Craig, would no doubt have looked on Williams as just one more intruder into the ranks of what he believed should be a "learned clergy" (it is not clear, for example, whether Williams ever secured a license to preach from the civil authorities), by the standards of most Southside evangelical preachers Williams was an intellectual paragon, playing an important role, usually as a mediator, in resolving the doctrinal disputes between Arminians and strict Calvinists within the church during the 1770s and 1780s.[41]

Another leading Baptist, Elijah Baker, was born in Lunenburg and spent his early years as "a man of low parentage and small learning." By his own account he was initially "a lover of pleasure more than a lover of God," but falling under the influence of Samuel Harriss he engaged in a long and difficult battle with his conscience. While "he became at first the subject of partial reformation and an attentive hearer of the gospel," he evidently had periods of backsliding, for by his own testimony "the struggle between his own heart and the humbling requisition of the Divine Word was long and desperate."[42] It was precisely this sort of conflict that so many of those drawn to the evangelical movement faced. Down one path lay the temptations and worldly pleasures that were an accepted part of the traditional culture but were given a wildness and roughness in the backcountry that drove an Anglican divine like Charles Woodmason to such despair. Down the other path lay the austere, unyielding code of the Baptists, a code that was unambiguous in its mapping of the true path to righteousness. Those who chose the path of the evangelicals would find it extraordinarily difficult to follow strictly, for they lived in a society where people routinely drank spiritous liquors from morning until retiring, where the legal sanctions against fornication, adultery, and bastardy were virtually nonexistent, and where the prevailing social pastimes were cockfighting and the tavern brawl.

Baptist congregants who were less affluent, more recently arrived in the county, and less likely to stay are more difficult to follow. We have already seen that, collectively, they were much poorer than their Anglican counterparts, and it is not surprising that given the often scanty character of their economic investment in the life of the county they were also less likely to form permanent attachments to Lunenburg. For example, a high proportion of those who joined the Meherrin church during the years 1771–75 were either relative newcomers to the county or so young that they had only recently begun to appear on the tithable lists. Of the fifty-four adult male Baptists who can be identified on the 1769 list, only twenty-four (44 percent) appeared on the list five years earlier; only five (9 percent) appeared on the county's first complete list, compiled in 1750. By contrast, among the sixty-four individuals who can be definitely identified as members of the Anglican church during the years 1771–75, forty-eight (75 percent) appeared on the tithable list five years earlier, and sixteen (25 percent) appeared on the list of 1750. These Baptist and Anglican persistence rates compare with averages of 60 percent and 20 percent respectively for the county at large during the same period.[43]

Given the marked differences between Baptists and Anglicans on such matters as theological substance and style, economic position, and length of residence within the county, one might suspect that this separation of religious cultures might be reflected in the choice of residential location for the congregants of each denomination. If we look at patterns of denominational strength within the region as a whole, that expectation is given some verification. For example, Presbyterian influence seems to have continued to be confined to the northwest corner of the county and beyond, spreading out through Prince Edward and Charlotte counties. And shortly after the Revolution the Methodists would gain a striking number of converts in the area just south and east of Lunenburg, in Brunswick County. But in the prerevolutionary period Baptists and Anglicans were spread fairly evenly throughout Lunenburg. John Williams himself lived near the present-day village of Fort Mitchell, close to the Meherrin meetinghouse, and Williams's many kinfolk, who lived near him, caused some residential clustering in that area. Similarly, James Craig's plantation was located less than a mile from the principal Anglican chapel of Cumberland Parish, and church attendance among the county's Anglicans may have been higher among those who lived close to that chapel. By and large, however, the active adherents to those faiths were not clustered closely together.[44] There were several different Anglican chapels constructed throughout the county at which Craig preached on a rotating basis, and given the casual attitude that most Anglicans took toward their religion, no strong pressures worked toward residential clustering among Anglicans. The communal impulses generated by the Baptists' mode of religious observance seem more likely to have impelled the members of that sect to live more closely together, but the highly mobile nature of the Baptist population itself worked against such residential patterns. Moreover, the very modes of Baptist preaching, which depended heavily on itinerant preachers, meant that the Baptists were able to reach large numbers of communicants in spite of the obstacles imposed by distance.

These striking contrasts between Anglicans and Baptists in such important matters as church ritual, preaching style, geographic and ethnic origin, and earthly condition would ultimately lead to overt conflict, not just in Lunenburg but throughout Virginia and the whole of the Southern backcountry. Although some of the underlying sources of that conflict were no doubt generated by inherent weaknesses in the Anglican-gentry culture itself, the conditions of life in the backcountry exacerbated those weaknesses. In that sense, the lamentations of James Craig had less in common with those of eastern Anglican clerics—who at least were preaching to reasonably full congregations in solidly constructed churches in which the status hierarchy among those in attendance was well settled—than he did with South Carolina's Charles Woodmason, who denounced the Baptists in his backcountry region as "a Gang of frantic Lunatics broke out of Bedlam."[45]

Yet although both Craig and Woodmason would have been among the last to recognize the fact, these two pious Southern backcountry clergymen shared at least one common objective with the Baptist leaders whose practices they found so offensive: the mission of bringing some means of order and cohesion to a severely fragmented citizenry. In Woodmason's case that mission was constantly being thwarted by "lawless Ruffians" telling him "they wanted no Black Gown Sons of Bitches among them," threatening his very safety in much the same way that Baptists were intimidated by Anglicans, who urged their suppression, and by nonbelievers, who scorned their pious rituals. And Craig, though he did not record any instance of purposeful disruption, certainly interpreted the prevailing apathy among the citizenry of Lunenburg toward his Anglican services as a form of disorder in itself.[46]

Craig and Woodmason were engaged in bitter competition with the Baptists, however, not only for souls but also to see which of two drastically opposing views of social order would prevail. Those contests would occur nearly everywhere in Virginia, but in few places with the intensity generated in Lunenburg and the rest of the Southside. James Craig had given some advance warning of the potential for conflict as early as 1759, when he noted his attempts at suppressing the "growing madness" of the religious enthusiasts, but he warned at the same time that "they [the evangelicals] pray for Persecutions, and therefore if you fall upon any severe Method of suppressing them, it will tend to strengthen their cause."[47] That suppression, which had begun as early as 1757 or 1758, when Sheriff Joseph Williams had ordered itinerant Baptist preacher Dutton Lane out of the county, would continue right up to the Revolution. The county magistrates consistently attempted to use their legal powers against the Baptists, prohibiting night meetings and making it difficult for individuals married by Baptist ministers to legalize their vows. By the early 1770s Lunenburg's Baptists were openly protesting the sanctions imposed on them by the

Anglican establishment. They petitioned the House of Burgesses, complaining that they "find themselves restricted in the Exercise of their Religion, their Teachers imprisoned under various Pretenses, and the Benefits of the Toleration Act denied them."[48]

Though it was a consequence of social and ideological currents extending far beyond the borders of Virginia, the conflict between Anglicans and Baptists in Lunenburg would nevertheless be thrust squarely within the jurisdiction of the government of that colony. And the initial response of the Anglican gentry who controlled the business of the Virginia House of Burgesses was to suppress the "evangelical revolt." In 1774 a majority in the Virginia lower house not only succeeded in blocking attempts to liberalize the colony's laws on religious toleration but also came close to passing a bill seeking to limit further the liberties granted to dissenters. Only a decision first to circulate the bill to the public at large—a move which set off a storm of protest from the evangelicals—and the more pressing business of the mobilization against Great Britain prevented the bill's passage.[49]

The conflict therefore between the members of the dominant culture and the dissenters had become embodied in nearly every facet of the social order—in theological style and doctrine, in economic circumstance, and finally in the politics of the colony itself. This political conflict between Anglicans and dissenters was reaching its most critical stage at precisely the moment when the supreme political movement of the century—Virginia's struggle for independence from Great Britain—was reaching its decisive stages of resolution. This convergence of the constitutional revolt against the traditions and policies of the mother country and the evangelicals' revolt against established religious styles and values would open for the first time in the history of eighteenth-century Virginia the opportunity for a thorough reordering of social and political power within the new commonwealth. In Lunenburg, where the claims of the Anglican gentry class to social authority and political power were more tenuous even before the advent of the Revolution, the explosive potential of that convergence would be all the greater.

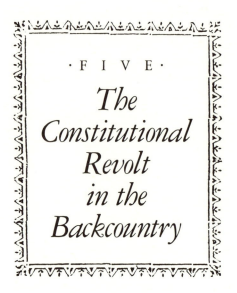

· F I V E ·

The Constitutional Revolt in the Backcountry

Whatever the potential for conflict posed by the "internal disorder" inherent in the evangelical revolt, the Virginia social order managed to display remarkable cohesiveness and unity of purpose in mobilizing itself for the external revolt against Great Britain. The cultural divisions appearing in areas like Lunenburg would ultimately produce profound changes in the way Virginians defined both their civil and religious polity, but in the short run the constitutional conflict provoked by the British—and the hardship produced by the military conflict that would follow—served to submerge the differences between Anglicans and evangelicals and to join virtually all the citizens of Lunenburg in the common cause of the Revolution.

But Lunenburg's citizens did not rise to rebel against the mother country spontaneously, and the success of the Whig leaders of eastern Virginia in mobilizing backcountry counties like Lunenburg in support of the Revolution is testimony to the power of political institutions to resolve conflicts and promote consensus. Throughout much of the Southern backcountry the strains of regional, economic, ethnic, and religious antagonisms, in concert with a corrupt and inequitable system of provincial government, produced civil uprisings against eastern political authorities during the 1760s and early 1770s and, more serious, helped foster bitter and bloody divisions between Whigs and Tories during the Revolution itself. The citizens of the Virginia backcountry, though afflicted by many of the same social divisions as their counterparts to the south, were nevertheless a part of a colonywide political system that, whatever the variations from east to west, did provide them with a sense of connection with the rest of their colony which was notably lacking in other parts of the Southern backcountry.

• THE MOBILIZATION OF REVOLT

Like most of revolutionary America, Lunenburg managed to carry on much of its business during the period from 1763 to 1776 as if the resistance movement against Great Britain—indeed, as if the mother country herself—did not exist. The myth of a constant and unified resistance to British oppression during the years 1763–76 is one which, though congenial to our patriotic instincts, has in recent years given way to a more realistic view of the way political resistance movements build momentum. Prior to 1774 even the most politically conscious activists in the major urban areas of America confined their activities to a generally well-ordered resistance to specific British policies. They did not initially intend their activities to lead to a wholesale denial of British authority, and they certainly did not wish for a severance of their amicable and generally useful attachment to the mother country.[1] Moreover, in areas which were out of the mainstream of commercial or political activity—and that surely included most of America—early resistance to England was sporadic at best. Even the residents of Concord, Massachusetts, located so close to the main center of resistance activity in Boston, remained generally unconcerned with imperial policies until late 1773, when the British government began to tamper with the workings of local government and when local "committees of correspondence" were formed to carry the message of resistance to the hinterlands.[2]

If Concord, the temporary meeting place of the extralegal provincial assembly of Massachusetts and the scene of the initial outbreak of hostilities in the Revolutionary War, was slow to involve itself in the movement for independence, then it should hardly surprise us to discover that Lunenburg—over a hundred miles from the provincial capital in Williamsburg and light-years away from the seat of the empire in both spatial terms and the concerns of her citizens—was not wholly caught up in the early stages of the struggle.

Lunenburg's two burgesses, Henry Blagrave and William Taylor, most likely supported Patrick Henry's resolves denouncing the Stamp Act in the Spring 1765 session of the General Assembly. Contemporary accounts of prerevolutionary Virginia politics refer to a bloc of Southside Piedmont counties that regularly supported Henry's positions, and though the vote on the Stamp Act Resolves was not recorded, Lunenburg's representatives did subsequently tend to side with the Hanover County lawyer. It is clear, though, that even in Henry's home county the intensity of citizen involvement in the imperial dispute was uneven and sporadic, and judging from the nearly total absence of petitions, court actions, or county meeting accounts from Lunenburg on the subject, it seems reasonable to assume that the character of Lunenburg's attention to early disputes relating to the authority of the English parliament over the affairs of the colonies was slight.[3]

By the time of the Townshend Acts in 1767, there was at least sufficient interest in the county to cause Lunenburg burgess Henry Blagrave to communicate his sense of public opinion in his county to the readers of the *Virginia Gazette*. Blagrave made no mention of any formally organized meetings in the county to discuss British policy, instead claiming only that he had personally "made a strict inquiry amongst my constituents concerning the taxes the Parliament of Great Britain insist on." The attitude of the citizenry differed little in substance from the constitutional orthodoxy of the time; "the people do not think they ought to be taxed there [in Parliament], as they may have authority from their most gracious Sovereign to hold Assemblies here, for that purpose, as well as others." Blagrave went on to praise George III as "the best of Kings," but then to lament "that his Majesty has some mischievous subjects, as they understand they are represented in Great Britain to be rebellious, &c, when they declare they have no such intention, but that they intend during life to be faithful and loyal subjects to his Majesty. . . ."[4] This view—that an essentially benevolent king had been misled by a few mischievous or corrupt parliamentary ministers—seems to have been widespread among most Americans at this stage of the conflict. Anxious to defend their rights while at the same time expressing devotion to the empire itself, the colonists were careful to isolate the source of their grievances with the king's advisers rather than the king himself.[5]

Blagrave maintained that his constituents were prepared to make substantial financial sacrifices "to the utmost farthing that they are able to pay," for this support of the dignity and security of the Crown and its possessions, but that the proper device for securing that financial support was to requisition the Virginia Assembly and to allow that body, through its elected representatives, to collect the monies. Although Blagrave's articulation of his constituents' constitutional position was firm and unyielding, he, like most Americans of the time, persisted in narrowing the grounds of his opposition so as to make subsequent reconciliation more easy to achieve. He closed his report to the *Gazette* with the following admonition:

They convinced all his Majesty's liege people, to keep the King's commandment, as it is their indispensable duty, and not to be hasty, or stand in an evil thing, for a wise man's heart discerneth both time and judgment, although the work of God is unsearchable; and Solomon faith, there is a time wherein one man ruleth over another to his own hurt, and that which is far off and exceeding deep, who can find it out; therefore let us do as we would be done by, as God is the author of all things.[6]

However predictable in political substance Blagrave's communication may have been, its style—particularly its concluding spiritual reference—was indicative of the impact of the evangelical movement. Most Virginia remonstrances, while shot through with a moralism that proclaimed the Americans' superior virtue, were nevertheless more secular in tone, leaving out any mention of God's will and certainly not taking the Calvinist view of the "unsearchable" character of that will.

It is perhaps noteworthy that Blagrave was virtually the only member of the ruling elite of Lunenburg who was attracted to evangelical religion. He was one of the original congregants of Meherrin Separate Baptist Church, and although his lapses from grace were both numerous and serious, his formal commitment to the church signified at least an intent that made him unique among the political leaders of his county. It is difficult even to speculate on the character of Blagrave's relationship with Lunenburg's other political leaders or with his constituents. He himself had lived in the county for nearly twenty years by that time, and he had previously had close ties with the Anglican church, serving as a vestryman. It therefore seems likely that Blagrave, in spite of the unorthodox character of his religious belief, enjoyed some acceptance among his peers in the economic and political elite. It is true that he was involved in more election disputes than any man in the county, but this seems more the result of what was by all accounts a flamboyant and exuberant mode of behavior than any attempt by his political opponents to mount a special attack on him because of his religious beliefs.[7]

It is tempting to portray Blagrave as representative of an evangelical, patriotic vanguard in the Virginia backcountry, but if he presents us with an example of a firm, moralistic opponent of British usurpation, then Lunenburg's other representative to the House of Burgesses in 1769 presents us with a different perspective. John Randolph, attorney general of the colony of Virginia, brother of Speaker of the House of Burgesses Peyton Randolph, friend and defender of Virginia's royal governor Lord Dunmore, and, by 1775, a reluctant Loyalist who set sail for England, was elected to serve Lunenburg as a burgess in 1769. Described by one contemporary as "in person and manner, among the most elegant gentlemen in the colony," Randolph had never actually lived in Lunenburg and had not previously involved himself in the political affairs of the county.[8] Yet even as late as 1769 the power and prestige of the Randolph family name was such that he was able to use his landholdings in Lunenburg as a device to secure a forum in the House of Burgesses for his views respecting the conflict with Great Britain. His term of service for Lunenburg would last only a year, after which he would be appointed to sit as a burgess representing the College of William and Mary, a vantage point which he used to keep the governor informed of the burgesses' activities.[9]

We have no information on the actual conduct of the 1769 election in Lunenburg, so it is difficult even to make a conjecture about how Randolph's constituents perceived him. Certainly his eminence, manifested in his extraordinary economic power as well as in his elegant persona, had something to do with his election. Still, as in the case of William Byrd's service to the county some fifteen years earlier, voter apathy was probably the primary determinant in the election of this absentee grandee. Even as the Revolution drew near, Lunenburg's citizens, perhaps even more than the rest of the American populace, were primarily interested in their families and farmsteads.

The county took no public action on any of the imperial issues confronting America during the period from 1769 until July 1774, at which time Lunenburg joined all the other counties in Virginia in sending resolutions to the recently convened Virginia Convention. The set of resolves from Lunenburg was not printed in the *Virginia Gazette* because of lack of space, but they probably did not differ much from those sent to the convention from neighboring Dinwiddie County.[10] Those resolves reaffirmed the citizens' "Cordial and unfeigned Affection and Loyalty for his Majesty's Person and Government," but in phrases that made reconciliation between Parliament and the colonies seem more and more unlikely, they went on to bemoan "the ill Effects which may flow from some recent and dangerous Innovations, imagined and contrived in the House of Commons." What followed was a bill of particulars, with vigorous denunciations of the Tea Act and the punitive measures aimed at Boston in the Coercive Acts. The Dinwiddie residents, like those in most parts of America, made no attempt "to justify the Outrage committed by the People of Boston in destroying the Property of the East India Company," but they could see no justification for "depriving a whole people of their Rights for a Trespass committed by a few." The resolves ended with an avowal of common purpose, toward the end of devising a "firm and prudent Plan of Opposition to every Invasion of our Rights," and though their tone plainly indicated that the citizens were still searching for some basis for reconciliation, such ground for accommodation was narrowing rapidly.[11]

As sporadic resistance turned toward consideration of sustained revolt, the members of Lunenburg's Anglican-gentry elite appear to have been in firm control of events in their locale. Although the county's delegation to first the Burgesses, then the Virginia Convention, and finally the House of Delegates (the postrevolutionary counterpart to the Burgesses) did not remain unchanged between the years 1770 and 1780, the same five prominent Anglicans—Thomas Pettus, Lodowick Farmer, Richard Claiborne, John Garland, and John Glenn—tended to rotate positions in those bodies. None of those individuals ever managed to achieve any real prominence within the revolutionary movement throughout the colony or the independent state as a whole, but within the smaller world of the county their claim to leadership appears to have been quite secure.[12]

In the year preceding independence it became increasingly difficult for anyone to make known his or her opposition, or even ambivalence, toward America's posture toward the mother country. By an act of July 1775, local committees, which were created to replace the now legally dissolved county courts, were charged with the job of organizing the militia for defense and searching out those "enemies of America" who were working against the public interest. The local committee in Lunenburg did not proceed in any formal way against those "enemies of America" during the period before the actual Declaration of Independence, but by December 1775 at least a few citizens in the Southside were feeling considerable pressure from patriot leaders in Lunenburg. On December 16 of that year the county's citizens petitioned the Virginia Convention, affirming their determination "with their lives and fortunes, to defend the liberties of America, and to stand or fall with their Country." The real motivation behind the petition, however, was to complain about a recent act of the convention protecting the legal rights of British merchants living in the area. The Lunenburg petitioners complained that

Experience having proved that the good purposes thereby intended, are not answered, but on the Contrary, jealousies and distinctions, which before might have existed, are thereby greatly increased; and praying the said Resolution may be rescinded, and in lieu thereof a Test established, whereby the Friends of America may be distinguished from those who are inimical to the glorious Cause to which this Country is engaged.[13]

Although there was no explicit anti-Scottish reference either in this petition or in other public proceedings of the county at the time, it appears that a significant portion of the animus in Lunenburg was directed at Scotsmen in particular. At the January 9, 1777, session of the county court, the justices "ordered that the Sheriff give notice to John Patterson, James Burnes, John Graham, and James Mercer . . . to show cause if any why they should not be represented to his excellency the Governor as subjects to the King of Great Britain and ought to be ordered to depart this Commonwealth." The following week, Graham and Mercer acknowledged their continued attachment to the Crown, Patterson and Burnes absented themselves from the court, and all four were ordered to leave the colony.[14] Three of the four men—Patterson, Burnes, and Graham—were of Scottish origin, and their banishment from the county no doubt served only to strengthen the tendency of Southsiders to equate Scottish nationality with Toryism.

It is likely that there were conflicts over questions of allegiance that never reached the level of legal accusations but that must have produced considerable animosity among individuals. Robert Munford, who had used the political foibles of his Lunenburg neighbors as a partial basis for his play *The Candidates* in 1770, was moved to write another drama sometime between 1777 and 1780 on the problem of political allegiance in the revolutionary Southside. This play, *The Patriots*, combined comic satire with a heartfelt indignation at the circumstances that "in times like these, of war and danger, almost every man is suspicious even of his friend."[15] And again, in Munford's view, it was the Scots (and Scots merchants in particular) who were the targets of suspicion. The revolutionary zealots in *The Patriots* are inclined to condemn virtually all Scots for treason out of hand. Colonel Strut, who was probably modeled after Mecklenburg County's Colonel Bennett Goode, proclaimed when he brought a group of Scotsmen before the county committee: "The nature of their offense, gentlemen, is that they are Scotchmen; every Scotchman being an enemy and these men being Scotchmen, they are under the ordinance which directs an oath to be tendered to all those against whom there is just cause to suspect they are enemies." When one of the Scots protested that there was no proof of his disloyalty, another committee member, Brazen, retorted: "Proof, Sir! We have proof enough. We suspect any Scotchman. Suspicious is proof, Sir. I move for the question Mr. President." Munford's own view was no doubt expressed by Meanwell, who ventured:

The ungracious treatment that some Scotchmen have met with, the illiberal reflections cast out against them all, give little hope of their attachment to a country, or to a people, where and with whom they have already tasted the bitter herb of persecution; some there are, who have behaved well, conform'd to the public will, nor given any cause of offense; yet even those have not met with the common offices of civility among us.[16]

The animosity toward the Scots had a specific economic underpinning, buttressed perhaps by a more general distrust of "foreigners," that was the consequence of the rapidly growing importance of Scottish merchant houses in the tobacco trade of Virginia. There is no question that the amount of credit advanced by Scots factors increased alarmingly during the decade preceding the Revolution, and similarly it seems clear that the extension of that credit was most striking in the Southside, where the need for capital to finance an expanding agricultural economy was greatest and where alternative sources of ready capital were most scarce. When the Revolution came and the Southsiders found themselves indebted to just a few "foreign" firms, each represented in relatively impersonal fashion by a group of "hirelings" in Virginia, the result was a xenophobia, fueled by economic interest, that far exceeded previous animosities among other ethnic groups in the region.[17] Indeed, the Scots factors served as an important source of ideological fusion among planters of all economic stations in the Southside, for nearly everyone who grew tobacco fell under the domination of the Glaswegian merchant houses. If "independence" in economic as well as in political life was the primary goal of the Southside settlers, then the extirpation of the Scots merchants was probably as important as the elimination of British political authority.

When we look beyond the particular case of the Scots factors, what is most surprising is that the events surrounding the separation from the mother country caused as little trauma and division among the population as they did. By and large, the record in

Lunenburg points to an impressive unity of commitment to the patriot cause. On May 15, 1776, when Lunenburg's representatives to the Virginia Convention (David Garland and Lodowick Farmer) voted in favor of Edmund Pendleton's resolution ordering Virginia's delegates to the Continental Congress "to propose to that respectable body to declare the United Colonies free and independent states," they were reflecting the nearly unanimous sentiment of their constituents back home.[18] The primary impact of the Revolution in Lunenburg lay not in the ideological or ethnic divisions it generated within the social fabric of the county but in the terrible disruption and dislocation wrought by the participation of the county's residents in the war effort itself.

• THE IMPACT OF WAR

There is scant place in the larger history of the revolutionary war for Lunenburg. The county was not the site of any dramatic or decisive battles, and none of its citizens emerged as a distinctly heroic figure in battles elsewhere in the American states. Yet the county's contribution to the war effort was remarkable.

The citizens of Lunenburg had appeared largely unconcerned about the specifics of the struggle with Great Britain before 1775 or 1776. Moreover, virtually all Lunenburg's citizens—political officials and ordinary settlers alike—had been on the periphery of the political decision-making process in Williamsburg since the time of the county's founding in 1746. In the thirty years before independence, Lunenburg residents had only rarely bothered to petition their legislature on subjects of public concern, and Lunenburg's representatives never attained any special prominence in the legislative affairs of the House of Burgesses. At the moment of independence, however, this politically inactive and apparently leaderless county came to life. Whatever detachment Lunenburg's citizens may have felt from the political events of their colony gave way to an impressive display of commitment to the common cause of the Revolution once the call to arms was sounded. Lunenburg's citizens, leaders and rank and file alike, proved themselves ready to make the kinds of sacrifices—suffering death, destruction, and the disruption of life and property in the process—that caused the revolutionary war to be such a revolutionary experience.[19]

It is in some ways typical of this backcountry Southern county that its militia records, like so many of the other public and personal records relating to its history, have been dispersed and destroyed. Indeed, the haphazard organization of the Virginia militia system as a whole makes it difficult to identify the relationship of any particular county unit to the larger organization of the state or Continental armies. Those records from the Continental army which do exist suggest that the militiamen from Lunenburg, most of whom in previous years had probably not even bothered to venture a few miles from their plantations to the county courthouse to vote on election day, traveled great distances and risked great dangers during the Revolution itself.

The Lunenburg militia companies of Nicholas Hobson, James Johnson, and Peter Garland all participated in the Pennsylvania campaigns and had spent the horrible winter of 1777–78 at Valley Forge. Of the eighty-six men serving in James Johnson's company in 1776 and 1777, a period encompassing the campaigns in both New Jersey and Pennsylvania, thirty-nine were killed in action or died of disease.[20] Nicholas Hobson's company, which also served in those campaigns, lost thirty of its sixty-eight men, twenty-five of those deaths occurring in December 1776 and January 1777. The list for Hobson's company, from which he himself had to retire because of ill health in September 1777, was down to one officer, one sergeant, and five enlisted men by March 1778. The company, which had been suffered to weather the bitter winter at Valley Forge, had only barely endured.[21]

By 1781 the number of able-bodied men in Lunenburg available for militia service had dwindled from its 1776 level of 573 to 382.[22] This decline in recruits was something that plagued Washington's army every year after the initial enthusiasm of 1775 and 1776 had worn off. In Lunenburg, as in so many other areas, hopes for a speedy and glorious victory gave way to the grim reality of a protracted, bloody civil war.

The county's own brush with the fires of battle was relatively insignificant in terms of the larger theater of war, but it has given Lunenburgers their only substantive piece of revolutionary folklore. During Lord Cornwallis's Virginia campaign in the summer of 1781, the British cavalry, under the command of Lieutenant Colonel Benestre Tarleton, carried out a number of raids on selected spots within Virginia, the most famous of which was the nearly successful attempt to capture Governor Thomas Jefferson and the entire Virginia legislature in Charlottesville on June 4, 1781. One of the less spectacular raids was aimed at a supply depot located on the site of the gristmill belonging to Lunenburg's James Craig. On July 23, 1781, Tarleton's forces arrived at the mill, destroying it and virtually all the provisions stored there. Craig's role in the affair has been stoutly defended, indeed applauded, by the county's residents from that time to the present. Craig, possibly under the threat of personal injury from the British troops, signed an oath agreeing "not to take arms, be of council, or commit any other act that might militate against the success of the British army," and for that act he was temporarily deprived of his ministerial office by the revolutionary government of Virginia. Lunenburg's ruling elite immediately rushed to Craig's defense, however. Less than a month after the raid, ninety-nine of the county's citizens, including a number of county court justices and the leading officers in the county militia, petitioned the governor for a restoration of Craig's office. Describing him as "a person eminently distinguished for his zeal and attachment to the cause of American liberty," they claimed that he had signed the oath only "after seeing the cruel vengeance of the enemy in the destruction of a very great part of his property, and himself treated with indignity and insult, tho in a very low and precarious state of health."[23] Craig's fate was not an unhappy one. By the end of the war he had received not only a pardon but also a good measure of celebrity among the members of his parish, and despite the destruction of the mill he remained one of the wealthiest men in the county.

Perhaps more important than the details of Craig's own fate are the glimpses that the correspondence generated by Tarleton's raid gives us of the state of the defenses of the county during the latter months of the war. David Garland, reporting the details of Tarleton's raid to Governor Nelson, was led to complain that "there is not one man in twenty that has a gun &c in this county, they having [been] at three several times impressed into the countries' service and not returned."[24] A day later County Lieutenant Nicholas Hobson reported similar conditions. "They find it impossible," he lamented, "to arm one-seventh of the militia; such has been the drought of arms." He reported that there did not remain even "ten fire-locks fit for use in the County; nor are there as many pounds of ammunition of any kind."[25] The militia force of the county, which technically numbered 382, was down to only 86 in active service. It was impossible, Hobson claimed, to give a completely accurate return of the state of provisions in the county, because "one of the County commissioners who is a prisoner with the enemy refused to take a parole, and the other declined to give information because he is paroled by them."[26]

However serious Lunenburg's problems during those dark days of the Southern campaign may have seemed, the loyalty of the county's residents to the patriot cause remained intact. This fact stands in sharp contrast to the situation prevailing in other parts of the Southern backcountry, where the civil war between England and America had become a guerrilla war pitting neighbor against neighbor. General Nathanael Greene, assessing the situation in the backcountry of South Carolina in December 1780, reported that "the whigs and tories pursue one another with the most relentless fury killing and destroying each other whenever they meet. Indeed, a great part of this country is already laid waste and in the utmost danger of becoming a desert." Even by 1782, after Yorktown, Greene lamented that the backcountry was "still torn to pieces by little parties of disaffected who elude all search and conceal themselves in the thickets and swamps from the most diligent pursuit and issue forth from these hidden recesses committing the most horrid murders and plunder and lay waste the country."[27] In Lunenburg, in spite of declining enlistments and citizen grumbling about the disruption and poverty accompanying the war, the great body of the citizenry remained loyal to the patriot cause.

Still, it was one thing to profess loyalty and quite another to raise the requisite number of recruits to replenish the ranks of the militia, which had been ravaged by a combination of sickness, death, and the economic necessity of returning home to tend to the business of the plantation. By the time of the battle of Yorktown the militia forces of Lunenburg and Mecklenburg counties were so low that the units had to be combined, with Lewis Burwell of Mecklenburg assigned the command and Colonel David Stokes of Lunenburg left without a command altogether.[28] In a bitter complaint to the governor, Stokes protested the indignity. While his letter inspires some sympathy for his wounded honor, and admiration for his determination to stay in the fray, it is most interesting in its unintended commentary on the character of the relationships between officers and enlisted men in the Virginia militia.

By Stokes's testimony it seems that even in frontier Lunenburg the militia, perhaps more than any other institution in Virginia, was an organization where the ruling gentry took its patriarchal prerogatives seriously. He complained:

If the constant reward of officers for spending their fortunes in training the militia at home, collecting them for service, providing for their wants and marching them to different parts where their assistance is required, is that of being dishonorably discharged within sight of the field of action, it is almost certain no men of sense or influence will ever undertake to be a country drudge, or laborer in the field to plant those laurells, which he will forever be forbidden to gather.[29]

It seems plain, at least from Stokes's complaints, that "men of influence" were willing to spend their time and money in providing for the needs of their less esteemed countrymen in public service, but that their expenditures were predicated on some fair return of honor and, perhaps with good fortune, glory.

But even under the best of circumstances those exercises of noblesse oblige among the militiamen were likely to produce frustration. Stokes characterized the normal behavior of the militiamen as being typified by "unruly licentiousness." Some militia officers, he maintained, sought to grovel before the people in order to flatter them into enlisting in their units; "I am, sir," he claimed, "as much above the weakness of fearing to offend as I am above the baseness of desiring to flatter, or the remotest wish to gain myself a temporary influence by the ridiculous daubings of fawning and adulation." Stokes believed that it was probably his refusal to truckle to the ordinary militiamen that accounted for the shrinking numbers in this county unit, but he was convinced that though the force was only at half its requisite numbers, those men had "acquired a confidence in me not easily to be obliterated."[30]

It was probably in the militia forces of Lunenburg that the extremes of the gentry's pretensions to power and authority and the unruliness of the citizenry at large were seen in their clearest display and their most dramatic opposition. Questions of contest, honor, and pride, which were so much a part of the gentry code, were all bound up intimately with the process by which the militia submitted to discipline and ultimately in the way in which it performed in the field of battle. However, those inclinations toward dominance and the manly assertion of honor were in constant tension with the independence and general obstreperousness of the ordinary folk, whose cooperation was essential for reinforcement of gentry authority. Even in settled eastern counties, where the ruling hierarchy was more secure, the polite and deferential behavior that typified court day or election day often gave way to tumult and disorder when those same citizens were made to pay their respects by the considerably more substantial sacrifices involved in military service. For example, an Elizabeth City County militia captain and tavern keeper noted:

For many Years past [he] hath kept an hospitable house, and freely entertained all Persons that came there, as well Strangers as Freeholders. That at the Muster of his Company, after the Exercise was over, he usually treated them with Punch, and they would after that come before his Door and fire Guns in Token of their Gratitude, and then he would give them Punch 'til they dispersed, and that this has been a frequent Practice for several Years.[31]

Even William Byrd, who might be expected to command as much respect from his men as any man in the colony, routinely noted in his diary:

I caused the troop to be exercised by each captain and they performed but indifferently, for which I reproved them. [Massot] . . . was drunk and rude to his captain for which I broke his head in two places. When all was over we went to dine with Captain Jefferson. . . . Most of the company went home with John Bolling and got drunk.[32]

When the sacrifices demanded of ordinary militiamen went beyond merely showing up for a militia muster and were as dangerous and protracted as those required during the revolutionary war itself, the tension between leaders and the rank and file was likely to be increased considerably. The howl of the Virginia soldiery during the Revolution for increases in their rations of rum and whiskey could be heard across the state, and judging from the quickness with which the government responded to those cries, doubling the rations, it is evident that provision of strong drink was one of those obligations that the ruling gentry held to be most sacred.[33] In Lunenburg—which was underpopulated as a consequence of the toll of the war, low on the basic supplies of military subsistence, and possessed of a population diverse in background and belief—the ability of local commanders to fulfill their obligations to their men was even more tightly constrained, so the deference expected from those men must have been even more difficult to enforce.

A statistical profile of the militia forces of revolutionary Lunenburg confirms this picture of an organization predicated along traditional lines of gentry dominance but reflecting the more uncertain character of Lunenburg's authority structure and the strains of war. The officers of the militia forces were predictably both wealthier and more prestigious than the enlisted men. The five revolutionary war colonels from the county (John Glenn, Nicholas Hobson, Abraham Maury, David Stokes, and Benjamin Tomlinson) had average landholdings and slaveholdings of roughly five hundred acres and more than nine slaves. Those averages would have been even higher were it not for the modest holdings of Stokes, who though the son of a prominent and wealthy man in the county had not yet inherited much of that wealth. Those five men also possessed among them considerable political power and social authority; many had already served several terms on the county bench, and Hobson and Glenn would begin their service after the Revolution had ended. Similarly, three men (Tomlinson, Stokes, and Hobson) would also serve on the parish vestry.[34]

The fourteen men who served as captains in Lunenburg's revolutionary militia differed little from their higher ranking compatriots. Their average landholdings and slaveholdings (582 acres and slightly over nine slaves) were nearly identical; half their members would serve on the county court after the Revolution, and a nearly equal number would serve on the vestry. Nor does it appear that simple factors of age and seniority explain why some individuals reached the rank of colonel and some only that of captain. Although it is not possible to calculate the precise ages of all the officer corps, the average date on which the five colonels in the county first acquired land was not any earlier than that for the captains.[35] Rather, it appears that the more elusive quality of "authority"—the ability to command at least a modicum of respect from the often unruly enlisted men—was what separated those who reached the highest militia rank in the county from the lesser-ranking officers.

The wealth and attainments of the lieutenants and ensigns were less imposing but still significantly above the county average. Their average landholdings were just over four hundred acres, their slaveholdings six. Just two of the twenty-one men in this group, however, managed to gain appointment to the county bench, and only four to the parish vestry. Many of the men among the lower-ranking officers, though they may have possessed less land and fewer public offices, were members of the same families that appear so prominently in the history of the county. In many cases, however, they were the younger sons of those families, blessed with substantial economic advantages but still blocked in their paths to the highest offices that the county had to offer.[36]

The profile of the enlisted men of Lunenburg suggests neither the archetype of a "citizens' militia" of independent landowners nor a replication of European armies composed of the dregs of society.[37] The average landholdings and slaveholdings of the forty-one enlisted men whose property could be traced on the county's first complete postrevolutionary tax list of 1782 were 181 acres and 2.4 slaves, but these averages inflate the aggregate wealth of the common soldier in Lunenburg, as there were many in service who owned no taxable property at all. Fully three-quarters of the men whose names appear on the militia lists cannot be located on the 1782 tax list. Certainly not all those men were members of a propertyless proletariat, for the high death toll of the war itself, continuing high rates of out-migration from the county of soldiers whose terms of enlistment had expired, and the increasingly common practice of combining militiamen from several counties into one unit account for a substantial portion of those not appearing on the tax rolls. Still, if the pattern of militia service in Lunenburg resembled that elsewhere in America, at least some of those soldiers were probably young men on the economic margins of their society. And even among those forty-one men who did appear on the tax lists, twelve owned no land and twenty-two apparently owned no slaves. Most of the landholdings fell between fifty and three hundred acres, and if the four enlisted men who owned more than ten slaves are eliminated from the calculations, the aggregate slave ownership falls to just a little over one slave per person.[38]

The demands of war took their toll on those humbler men more noticeably than on their higher-ranking superiors. Perhaps the primary reason for the difficulty in tracing the property holdings of enlisted men is that the first comprehensive tax lists in Virginia were compiled in 1782, and the high death rate among these common soldiers, among other things, served to remove them from the tax rolls in permanent fashion. For example, in the militia companies of James Johnson and Nicholas Hobson, the companies that had to endure the bitter disappointments of the Pennsylvania campaigns of 1776–77, the officers all managed to escape death, while sixty-nine of the enlisted men (47 percent of the unit) lost their lives.[39]

Those who remained at home were hardly immune to the ravages of war. The hardships experienced by those who suffered through the war without husbands and sons (who were sources of emotional support as well as valuable labor) are mostly unrecorded and unremembered, but the plight of those who found themselves in straits so desperate that they had to appeal to the court for aid has been recorded at least cursorily. For example, on May 18, 1777, the court ordered that "Millicent Chambliss, Mary Lightfoot, Mary Mitchell, Ann Connell, Margaret Bohannon, Catherine Booz, and Elizabeth Hightower, having families of small children in distress and their Husbands being in the Continental Army, . . . be supplied at the public expense" portions of corn, pork, beef, and bacon for the sustenance of their families.[40] In June, July, September, and December 1777 and throughout the early months of 1778, the court acted in similar fashion to aid other families.[41] Some, like Mary Mitchell, would encounter further hardships. Although she was probably not aware of it at the time of her petition to the court, her husband Thomas had died just a week earlier in Alexandria. Most of those who had petitioned for relief while their husbands were at war had probably been in straitened circumstances before that time, and their experience once the war was over did not seem to offer much improvement. Joseph Bohannon and his wife did not have enough stake in the county even to appear on the tax lists before the war. In 1782 they were listed on the tax rolls, but were recorded as owning neither land nor slaves; by 1795 they had managed to gain ownership of sixty-two acres of land, and at Joseph's death in 1810 their position could hardly have been much better than it had been a quarter of a century earlier. The total value of the goods in Bohannon's estate was only £24 2*s*. 6*d*. Aside from a "Barren Cow and Bell," a horse, a pine table, and the very minimum of farm and kitchen implements, Bohannon's estate was devoid of virtually anything. Most of the others—John and Catherine Booz, Philip and Mary Lightfoot, and John and Millicent Chambliss—simply never appeared on any of the pre- or postrevolutionary tax lists at all, which indicates their tenuous claims within the county.[42]

By the end of the war the tithable population of Lunenburg stood at 2,022, a figure about equal to the population level at the outbreak of hostilities, but some three hundred households higher than in 1777, when the initial phases of the war took so many away from the county, some never to return. This leveling off of population growth was an unusual phenomenon in a society that had enjoyed steady growth all during its history, and at least in the short term it bespoke a condition of life for some within the county that was truly arduous. Lunenburg's sheriffs, like their counterparts all over Virginia, were among the first to feel the effects of hard times; they fell consistently behind in their tax collections during the revolutionary era and themselves had to petition for relief from the legislature. From the cries for debtor relief emanating from the Southside, it is clear that the difficulty of collecting debts in the public sector carried over to the private sector as well.[43]

These short-term trends of wartime suffering were bound to exacerbate existing tensions between contending cultural and economic groups within the county, and as we shall see, the political turmoil accompanying the Revolution gave groups like the evangelicals an unusual opportunity to press for a redress of grievances. At the same time, however, the common republican ideology of the Revolution, together with long-term trends of economic and demographic growth, would begin to have their effect once the war was over, working to bring about first a legal and then later a cultural accommodation between the contending groups in the Virginia Southside.

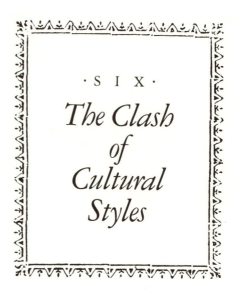

·SIX·

The Clash of Cultural Styles

Given the escalation of social conflict between Anglicans and evangelicals before the Revolution, we might expect that the hardships and disruptions occasioned by the onset of war would serve to heighten those conflicts further. Indeed, in the years immediately preceding independence the evangelicals had more to complain about than they had a decade previously. As late as 1774 the Virginia House of Burgesses, which had spent much of its time during the previous ten years denouncing the arbitrary powers of the British Parliament, was close to passing a bill that sought to limit further the toleration granted to members of dissenting religious sects in the colony. And local officials, acting on the authority of the exceedingly hazy body of English precedent on that subject, were at the same time intensifying their efforts to prohibit itinerant ministers and the holding of night meetings among the evangelicals.[1]

Between 1774 and 1776, however, the internal conflict between gentry and evangelical cultures seemed to be submerged in the general consensus on the necessity of mobilizing against the British. In resolutions passed at the Meherrin meetinghouse and forwarded to the Continental Congress, the Lunenburg Baptists supported the orthodox constitutional position of the period, denouncing "the violent usurpations of a corrupted ministry" and asking "every Christian Patriot" to enlist himself in the struggle. Indeed, the rhetoric of the patriots, the calls for the defense of virtue against corruption and the representation of the struggle against England as an important opportunity for purging American society of luxury and vice, was in accord with the austere doctrines and life-styles of the newly formed Baptist communities.[2]

Rather than widening the rift with the Anglicans, the patriotic fervor of the Baptists worked at least temporarily in the direction of consensus, for there was little difference between Anglicans and Baptists in terms of their ultimate loyalties on the question of independence. Although the militia forces of Lunenburg were predictably commanded by members of the same families that had always dominated the affairs of the county court and Anglican parish, there were sufficient numbers of simple farmers exhibiting a wide variety of religious experience—Anglicans, evangelicals, and unbelievers—to give substance to the assertion that the struggle for independence was truly a common cause. And there were few dissenters from that cause. Neither the Baptists nor the Anglicans were plagued by loyalist dissidents within their congregations.[3]

If we were to attempt to gauge the relationship between the immediate events of the coming of the Revolution and internal conflict and strain within the social order, we would have to conclude that far from unleashing latent social conflict, the Revolution in Lunenburg County actually served to submerge differences between the contending groups. And if we look at the standard indexes of economic, political, and social authority both before and after the Revolution, we again find evidence of stability and continuity, with the same relatively wealthy and prestigious sorts dominating positions of authority after the Revolution as before.[4] There is even superficial evidence indicating that the Baptists themselves experienced a temporary loss in their sense of spiritual commitment and distinctiveness due to their political involvement in the common cause of the Revolution. By August 1776 there was considerable concern expressed at one of the meetings of the District Baptist Association over the decline in piety among church members, a decline that was blamed on the widespread involvement of the congregations in political and military affairs.[5]

Yet in spite of the oscillating level of piety that has tended to affect all enthusiastic religious movements in times of peace and of war, the nature of the authority structure would in the course of the Revolution and its aftermath become transformed by radical changes in the social-religious forms through which that authority could be expressed. More than most revolutions, the American Revolution occasioned an enormous awakening of interest in politics as a mechanism for both good and evil. Because the provincial leaders of the Virginia colony, unlike their counterparts in other Southern colonies, had been so conscientious about extending their own institutions of local and provincial government to the backcountry, it is not surprising that discontented groups in the Old Dominion would at the time of the Revolution begin to use those institutions more aggressively to redress their grievances. At this point of *political* mobilization, the fate of dissenters in Lunenburg would become tied to that of dissenters elsewhere in Virginia, and thus our account of their struggle must leave for a moment the confines of the county and move to the seat of provincial government, where the political outcome of the struggle between the established church and the dissenters was decided.

• THE FIGHT FOR DISESTABLISHMENT IN THE LEGISLATURE

The confrontation between the insurgent separate Baptists and the dominant Anglican gentry had been deadlocked for at least two years when the delegates came to Williamsburg in May 1776 to take the necessary steps to inaugurate independence and create a new, republican frame of government. During this time the Anglican church had seemed to be so determinedly defended by those who sat in the seats of power that the dissenters had not dared to present any petition that might undermine in any way the privileges of the established church. But by the spring of 1776, the republicanizing work of the representatives, coupled with circumstances created by the war, transformed the situation overnight. With independence, the Anglican church in Virginia—supported in the past not only by public taxation but also by the weight of history and the authority of kings—was transformed into the Protestant Episcopal Church, a religious entity with the same rules and rituals as that of the mother country, but with a far less secure institutional foundation. The catalyst for the transformation of that Episcopal Church was the Virginia Convention's Declaration of Rights, drafted in January 1776, shortly after the convention had made its decision for independence. That the vast majority of the framers of the Declaration of Rights had no intention of encouraging the overthrow of established religion made the consequences of their actions no less profound.

George Mason's original draft of the Declaration of Rights contained an article upholding the principle of religious toleration, but James Madison modified that passage so that it not only affirmed the principle of the "free exercise of religion" but also asserted that "no man or class of men ought, on account of religion, to be invested with particular emoluments or privileges, or subjected to any penalties or disabilities." This last assertion, with its implicit attack on the "emoluments or privileges" of the established church, was eventually deleted, but the defense of the "free exercise of religion" was retained in the final draft. Most members of the Virginia Convention, undoubtedly relieved at the decision to soften Madison's version and further persuaded by Patrick Henry's assurances that the article on religion was not a prelude to an attack on the established church, were quite willing to support a vaguely worded statement on religious freedom. Indeed, most convention members probably did not even interpret the article on religious toleration as a renunciation of their right to regulate the activities of the "unlearned," itinerant preachers who had been the object of quasilegal harassment by local officials for more than a decade.[6]

Just a few months later, however, when the first session of the Virginia House of Delegates convened, the delegates were confronted by an unprecedented "Ten Thousand Name petition," circulated largely by the Baptists, demanding an alteration in the prevailing religious establishment. The implication was clear; some accommodation was essential if the dissenters were to join in the "common cause" of the Revolution.[7] Although the final move toward disestablishment in Virginia was not effected until January

1786, the action of the 1776 assembly seems radical when one considers that as recently as 1774 a near majority of the members of the House of Burgesses had actually leaned toward further suppression of the rights of dissenters. The act passed by the 1776 session of the assembly not only institutionalized the general principle of toleration but also struck several blows at the privileged position of the Episcopal church. Most significant, it exempted dissenters from that time forward from contributing to the support of the church. Even more portentous—for it foreshadowed disestablishment altogether—it suspended temporarily the payment of the salaries of the Anglican clergy.[8]

Still, the principal effect of the 1776 legislation was to open, not resolve, the conflict between dissenters and supporters of the established church. The portion of the act exempting dissenters from supporting the Episcopal church specifically stipulated that the question of a general assessment for the support of Protestant religions be made part of the future legislative agenda. Moreover, suspension of the salaries of the Episcopal clergy was considered by many to be a temporary expedient, reflecting the concern that "by the exemptions allowed dissenters, it may be too burthensome in some parishes to members of the established church if they are still compelled to support the clergy by certain fixed salaries."[9]

Although the final outcome of the battle had not yet been decided, it is nevertheless remarkable how much the terms of that struggle had been changed. Whereas the Lunenburg Baptists had found themselves an embattled, countercultural minority in the early 1770s, by 1776 they could draw confidence from their growing numbers everywhere in Virginia and from obvious changes in policy on the part of the highest legal authority in Virginia.

Judging from the grousing of the members of the established church in Lunenburg, the Baptists had forced the issue by displaying a newfound militance, asserting that they expected concessions with respect to religious liberty if they were to support the patriot cause wholeheartedly. The Episcopalians in Lunenburg were particularly bitter about the tactics of the evangelicals, complaining about the success of their appeals to the lower orders. They claimed that the dissenters had mobilized support for their attempt to undermine established religion "by imposing upon the credulity of the vulgar and engaging infants to sign petitions."[10] And the evangelicals did not appear to be willing to rest content with that one legislative victory. By August 1775 the Baptist Association had appointed three of its members, the Rev. John Williams of Lunenburg among them, to serve as active lobbyists for their cause while the Virginia Assembly was in session. Their lobbying efforts produced immediate results, for within a month of their appointment the Baptists had received the assembly's permission to have their ministers preach to members of the Virginia militia.[11] It is unlikely that the assembly's concession on that point was simply a matter of goodwill; rather, with probably half the population falling into the category of "dissenter," the legislature, if it hoped to raise a numerous and loyal army, could do little else.

The religious reforms of 1776 amounted to a significant victory for the dissenters and a major concession on the part of the defenders of the established church, but several issues would remain unresolved during the next decade, with dissenters (especially the Baptists) petitioning for an end to all the established church's privileges, and traditionalists attempting to win acceptance for a general assessment for and plural establishment of all Protestant religions.[12] The issue was brought to a head in the years 1783–85, when in the dark aftermath of General Charles Cornwallis's invasion, with moral and financial bankruptcy appearing imminent in Virginia, the decline of religious observance in the state seemed to many leading citizens to be a forerunner of catastrophe. Under the leadership of Patrick Henry, substantial support was mustered for a religious tax scheme by which citizens would be compelled to make a contribution to the maintenance of religion but free to designate the church to which their contributions would go. In December 1784 the House of Delegates approved a "Bill for establishing a Provision for Teachers of the Christian Religion," but prudently determined to order it published and distributed so that the opinion of the public might be tested. A petition campaign on an unprecedented scale ensued. When it was over and the petitions were before the House in the fall of 1785, it was clear that active sentiment was overwhelmingly against the general assessment. There were about 10,000 signatures against and about 1,500 for it. With this weight behind them, the dissenters, aided immeasurably by liberal, rationalist aristocrats like Thomas Jefferson and James Madison, were able to accomplish a radical disassociation of the state from religious concerns by securing passage of Jefferson's "Act for Establishing the Freedom of Religion" in January 1786.[13]

• THE FIGHT FOR DISESTABLISHMENT IN LUNENBURG

The conflicting values, aspirations, images, and symbols at stake in the prolonged struggle over religious establishment in Virginia were all clearly evident in the local contest over the issue in Lunenburg. Between 1776 and the passage of Jefferson's statute in the winter of 1785–86, six petitions came to the House of Delegates from Lunenburg. Five were in favor of public support for ministers of religion; the remaining one was a radical Christian rejection of any kind of establishment.

Through the five pro-establishment petitions (and the "Bill for Teachers of the Christian Religion" to which the fifth expressly attached itself) there recurred two dominant themes: the importance of religious instruction in the *moral formation* of the members of society, and the necessity for religion to be under the guidance of a *learned clergy*. With variations in the wording, the statement was repeated in all five of the petitions "that . . . the stability of our government, and the preservation of peace and happiness amongst the individuals of it, depend in great measure upon the influence of religion." "The general diffusion of Christian Knowledge," the writers of the bill declared, "hath a natural tendency to correct the morals of men, restrain their vices, and preserve the peace of society."[14] However, it was equally clear to the supporters of establishment that this "cannot be Effected without a competent provision for learned teachers," which necessitated "Support and Encouragement of Persons properly qualified to perform the Offices of public Worship and Instruction." Not only must they exercise this function with the dignity expected of their profession, but experience had proved that voluntary support was "very precarious and inadequate . . . in Consequence of which Men of . . . Genius will be discouraged from engaging in the ministerial office, Religion must languish and decay, and the State be in a great Measure deprived of one of the best Means of promoting its Virtue, Peace, and Prosperity." For the same reason that the authorities within society needed to ensure that support for the dignity of the office was adequate and secure, they should provide

that no Person may intrude into the ministerial Office, who is unqualified . . . [and therefore] every Candidate [should] go through a regular Examination before proper and able Judges, according to the Rules practised by the Church whereof he is a Member; licensing only such as are qualified to discharge the sacred Function with Honour to themselves and Benefit to their People.[15]

These specifications for ministers of religion were essentially enumerations of the attributes of the genteel parson, and behind that stereotype lay a reverse view of the common people who were to fall under the parson's guidance. This view of the relationship between the clergy and their flock was made explicit in the General Assessment Bill to which the Lunenburg establishmentarians later gave unqualified support. The measure indicated the duties that the clergy, relieved by the assessment from the necessity of daily toil, should undertake. These consisted of "instructing such citizens [the pressing problem of the slaves is glossed over] as from their circumstances and want of education, cannot otherwise attain . . . knowledge."[16] The compulsory contribution was justified by pointing out the proven lack of sufficient liberality among the people to make voluntary provision for higher instruction. Behind the stereotype of the credulous vulgar there lurked the more alarming image of the itinerant mechanic, or even slave, preacher. It was to banish this threatening presence that the examination of the eligibility of clergymen was proposed. Indeed, the principal function of a learned, dignified clergy was to defend the fold against such intrusive wolves.

These perceptions of the humble preacher and the genteel parson were completely reversed in the anti-establishment petition circulated in Lunenburg by the Baptists. The wording of the petition reveals the extreme evangelical position on the relationship of religion to authority and the values of traditional society. The petitioners declared that the Christian teacher bill was "contrary to the Spirit of the Gospel," a dogmatic reassertion of their stand against worldly dignity, in a land where the gentry's pride was proverbial. They articulated their renunciation of earthly power in a humbly proud moralization on the fact that

the Blessed Author of the Christian Religion, not only maintained and Supported his Gospel in the World for several Hundred years without the Aid of Civil Power, but against all the Powers of the Earth, [by] the excellent purity of its Precepts and the unblameable behaviour of its Ministers (with the divine blessing) [it] made its way through all opposition. [17]

The character of their ideal pastor, already indicated in their version of early Christian history, was made clearer in the body of the petition, where the probable consequences of a reestablishment of religion were contemplated.

Would it introduce any more useful and faithful Men into the Ministry? Surely not. Those whom divine grace hath called to that work will esteem it their highest honor . . . [but] on the Contrary it [the general assessment] will call in many Hirelings whose Chief motive . . . would be Temporal Interest.

A committee of several Virginia Baptist associations made clear in its petition of November 3, 1785, what it thought of a liberal, genteel, independence for the parsons when it declared "that as Ministers are the Voluntary Servants of the Church, So every Church or Congregation should be left to reward them in such a manner as they shall think their services deserve."[18]

These opposed image-sets—the genteel parson and the vulgar itinerant on the one hand, and the inspired messenger and the worldly hireling on the other—provided the rhetorical staple in the petition campaigns, but even more fundamental were the contrasted forms of congregation implicit in this imagery. For the establishmentarians the valued ministerial style was associated with a rank-ordered gathering ranged in symbolic degrees of deference beneath an elevated pulpit that could be ascended only by a minister licensed by constituted authority. For the evangelicals the evocations were quite different. What governed the ministry was not the higher authority of learning and tradition vested in a bishop or a presbytery, but the individual congregations. It was the people of God who recognized "the gift" of the Holy Spirit and regulated the exercise of it by those "usefull and faithfull Men" whose possession of it elevated them to the rude platforms from which the Word of God was preached. The image in that case was of societies of simple folk gathered around men of their own kind. The number of those in whom "the gift" might be recognized included even the humble slaves.

These contrasting religious contexts were closely linked to conflicting aspirations for society at large. The world to which the parson in his ornate pulpit belonged was the world of the squires and the organic hierarchical community over which they presided. The world of the Baptist preacher moved by the Holy Spirit, whether on a stump or in a barnlike meetinghouse, was an egalitarian world of humble people seeking their own ultimate meanings according to their own lights. In their gathered churches these folk had already constituted an exclusive, nonhierarchical, popular, participatory system of association and authority. The contending forms of the churches thus came to represent important universal symbols, and the struggle over the means of supporting churches—imposed taxation or voluntary contribution—was in reality an intense conflict over profoundly opposed visions of what society should be like.

The nature and meaning of this social conflict become even more apparent when we analyze the signatories on each side of the controversy. Among the signers of the establishmentarian petitions, there was in general a close connection between an individual's conception of the proper character of the social order and his or her place in that social order. At the top of the list of the signers of the Lunenburg petitions supporting the general assessment proposal were the names not only of all the Episcopal vestrymen but also of nearly all the members of the county court. Among those signing the petition whose religious affiliation could be determined, all were Episcopalians. The wealth of both the prominent signers and those without formal political power who supported them was substantially greater than the mean for both the population of the county at large and the signers of the anti-establishmentarian petition. The average landholdings of the entire group of the 140 signers of the general assessment petitions of 1783 and

1784 was 390 acres; the average for the sixteen signers who held high church and civil office was 511 acres, while the average land-holding in the county at large was only 267 acres.[19] See Table 3.

Figures for slave ownership are an even more important indicator of the wealth of the establishmentarian forces, as Lunenburg even in the 1780s was an area where a person's productive capital was more effectively measured by the size of his assembled labor force than by his accumulated acreage. The average holding of the entire group of supporters of the general assessment bill was nearly seven slaves, while the prominent members of that group averaged sixteen slaves each. The average holding in the county at large was not quite four slaves per household; only 20 percent of the county's households owned seven or more slaves and only 5 percent had slaveholdings of sixteen or more.[20]

The landholdings and slaveholdings of those who supported the general assessment proposal were generally similar to those of Episcopalians throughout the county at large. Among those 123 Lunenburg citizens who can definitely be identified as Episcopalians during the decade 1775–84, the average landholding was 481 acres, the average slaveholding nearly nine.[21] Thus, the Lunenburg Episcopalians generally, as well as those who went on record supporting the establishmentarian position, were notably more wealthy than most of their fellow residents.

Other indications of the background and attachments of the proponents of the establishmentarian position were their age and length of residence in the county. In a highly mobile society, where individuals disappeared from the tax rolls during the prerevolutionary years at rates varying from 10 to 25 percent of the total listings each year, a striking 79 percent of the signers of the 1783 general assessment petition had appeared on the last complete prerevolutionary tax list for the county compiled in 1769. Some 50 percent of the signers of the more widely circulated 1784 petition had also appeared on the 1769 tax list. Although this last figure is not as convincing an evidence of residential continuity, it is an indication of substantially greater persistence than characterized the population at large.[22] These facts are evidence of a greater tendency to establishmentarianism among long-standing residents, and they also draw attention to the high average age of the group supporting the general assessment proposal.

TABLE 3 WEALTH OF ADVOCATES AND OPPONENTS OF GENERAL ASSESSMENT PROPOSAL

Wealth of Advocates		
Acres	*No. of Holdings*	*% of Holdings*
0	14	10.0
1–100	14	10.0
101–150	8	5.7
151–250	21	15.0
251–350	24	17.1
351–450	20	14.3
451–700	24	17.1
701–1,000	12	8.6
1,000 and over	3	2.1
	140	99.9
Slaves	*No. of Holdings*	*% of Holdings*
0	36	25.7
1–3	26	18.6
4–6	23	16.4
7–10	16	11.4
11 and over	39	27.9
	140	100.0
Wealth of Opponents		
Acres	*No. of Holdings*	*% of Holdings*
0	12	16.2
1–100	8	10.8
101–150	8	10.8
151–250	12	16.2
251–350	11	14.9
351–450	10	13.5
451–700	9	12.2
701–1,000	2	2.7
1,000 and over	2	2.7
	74	100.0
Slaves	*No. of Holdings*	*% of Holdings*
0	29	39.2
1–3	24	32.4
4–6	9	12.2
7–10	6	8.1
11 and over	6	8.1
	74	100.0

SOURCE: Petitions of November 8, 1783, November 9, 1785, December 1, 1785, Lunenburg County, Virginia Religious Petitions; Real and Personal Property Tax Lists, Lunenburg County, 1782, Virginia State Library, Richmond, Va.

The picture that emerges from this analysis of the supporters of the establishmentarian position is of a group of Episcopalians with longer-standing attachments to those institutional arrangements and societal conceptions that characterized the traditional Virginia order. Indeed, for the very first time in the county's history, we can see a group of individuals whose roots were sunk deeply enough in the region to allow for development of some permanent attachment to a particular conception of their community. In the case of the leaders of the establishmentarian forces in Lunenburg, those attachments were buttressed by the fact that these same individuals had for so many years possessed a disproportionate share of the economic, political, and social power within that community.

The opponents of the general assessment proposal were undoubtedly a more diverse group than the supporters of the plan, but it is possible to make some tentative generalizations about the economic characteristics of these petitioners. Evangelical groups such as the Separate Baptists formed the core of Lunenburg's anti-establishmentarian forces, and their view of the proper relationship between religion and secular society was explicit.[23] They shared with their co-petitioners across the state a basic commitment to the divinely appointed separateness of religion from all other concerns in the world. Their insistence on the separation of religious and secular authority represented both an insistence on a deeply felt piety and an explicit rejection of traditional, organic conceptions of society. That rejection demonstrated a practical distrust of an alienation from the institutions that had oppressed them in the past.

It was probably this fundamental alienation from the manner in which traditional institutions of authority had operated that tied together the Baptist signers of the anti-establishmentarian petitions and many others who had no strong commitment to any denomination at all. Pious and secular-minded signers shared a sense of estrangement from the individuals who occupied prominent positions within the traditional structures of civil and religious authority. The importance of this estrangement can be most clearly deduced from the absence among those who signed anti-establishment petitions of persons who sat on the county bench or parish vestry. It appears also in the fact that only seven of the seventy-four signatories can be identified as members of the Episcopal church. Most of the anti-establishment petitioners were not politically powerful, and they were either dissenters or individuals whose ties to organized religion were uncertain or nonexistent.

The economic holdings of the anti-establishment group as a whole were roughly similar to those of the taxpaying population at large, and so were dramatically less impressive than those of either the Episcopalians or the groups of people identifying themselves with the establishment position. The average landholding among the seventy-four individuals whose wealth could be traced was 279 acres, and the average slaveholding was approximately three slaves per person, compared to the average of 267 acres and nearly four slaves for county taxpayers as a whole (see Table 3).[24]

If the anti-establishment group is broken down into groups of Episcopalians, Baptists, and individuals whose religious affiliation could not be determined, the results underscore the extent to which the Baptists, more than any other social group in the region, were drawn from the lower ranks in the economic order. Predictably, the few Episcopalians who signed the anti-establishment petition were among the wealthiest of the group, with average landholdings and slaveholdings of 287 acres and 6.3 slaves respectively. The thirty-six individuals whose religion could not be determined followed next, with average holdings of 312 acres and 3.2 slaves. And finally, the thirty-one identifiable Baptists who signed the petition held an average of 190 acres and 2.4 slaves only.[25]

The calculations bearing on both the political power and the wealth of the establishmentarian and anti-establishmentarian camps in Lunenburg show a part of the gap that separated the two opposing groups. Similarly, the calculations respecting the age and length of residence for Lunenburg's anti-assessment petitions serve to confirm the explanations of the different conceptions of authority in terms of transience and nonparticipation. The proportions of signers of the pro-establishment petitions of 1783 and 1784 who had appeared on the 1769 tax list were 79 percent and 50 percent respectively, but for the signers of the anti-establishment petition it was only 32 percent.[26] The commitment of establishmentarians to the traditional structure of authority in Virginia was demonstrably related to the length of their association with the local embodiment of that structure.

If the alignment of opinion—indeed, of active commitment in the struggle—followed predictable patterns, the voting of Lunenburg's delegates did not. The county's delegation to the legislature throughout the entire period 1776–86 was exclusively Episcopalian, wealthy, and prominent in the affairs of both the county court and the Episcopal parish. Twelve of the thirteen representatives serving during these years had sat on the bench of the county court, and nine of the thirteen had served on the Episcopal vestry. Their landholdings, averaging 505 acres for the group, and their slaveholdings, averaging nearly twelve slaves apiece, were well above the county average.[27] Moreover, virtually all of them had been prominent signers of most of the establishmentarian petitions, including the important petitions circulated by the pro-assessment forces in Lunenburg in 1783 and 1784. Yet on every recorded vote from 1776 to 1786, the Lunenburg representatives voted against the establishmentarian position, siding with those dissenting sects whose demands they had so energetically worked to counteract at the constituency level.[28]

Certainly the pressure of numbers had something to do with their change of heart on this momentous issue. Contemporary observers considered popular opinion to have been strongly against assessment in the state at large; it would not have been less so in a county where dissent was as general as was the case in Lunenburg.[29] The Lunenburg delegates, like many others in Virginia in the fall of 1785, must have had to choose between voting for separation or facing a popular revolt at the polls. Continued political mobilization of religious dissent would only have weakened further the elite controls the establishmentarian gentry were trying to reinforce.[30]

One should not be too cynical about the decision of the delegates, however. Majorities are persuasive, especially majorities armed with an intense sense of moral rectitude. Lunenburg's delegates, and the many other Episcopalian representatives who joined them in voting against their private preferences in favor of disestablishment, had an important stake in preserving the consensual base of politics in their state, in maintaining a government that was truly representative. An interesting indication of this is contained in two memorials laid before the House of Delegates on November 28 and December 10, 1785, emanating from Dinwiddie and Amherst, two southwestern counties in the same geographic region as Lunenburg. The signatories to these documents had been moved by the progress of the petition campaign to declare, in the words of the Dinwiddie memorialists, "that they are now as decidedly opposed to a General assessment, as they were formerly in favor of it." The petitioners from Amherst noted that when they had supported the general assessment it had been as "One step at least towards Opening a Way for Obtaining a Supply of ministers who might be Instrumental . . . in Stoping the Prevailing Torrent of Iniquity." They had supposed the assessment "might be acceptable to at least a Majority of [their] Fellow-Citizens," but they were now aware that "On the Contrary . . . the Bill . . . has Distressed . . . many of our . . . Fellow-Citizens in Different Parts of the State who have Advanced Reasons . . . against it of no Small Weight & Importance."[31]

The sentiments of the Amherst and Dinwiddie representatives, together with the actions of many of their fellow backcountry legislators, suggest a conception of political leadership at variance from those deference-based modes of the traditional society. Representing communities that were far more diverse in their constituent parts than those of the east, backcountry legislators simply could not fall back on a ready-made consensus based on shared cultural traditions. Rather, if a consensus were to be shaped at all, it would have to be shaped by a contractual view of government which sought to represent the real interests of at least a majority of the citizens of the community.

The pattern of voting on the establishment issue demonstrates just how widespread this change in traditional attitudes toward political representation had become. On November 11, 1784, there was a substantial majority, 47 to 32, in favor of the general assessment. On December 17, 1785, the diametrically opposed bill for religious freedom carried the House, 74 to 20, with the most significant number of changes of opinion coming from the backcountry delegates.[32] The continuing political dominance of the cultured gentry was indicated by the role of legislative pilot played by James Madison and the fact that it was Thomas Jefferson who supplied the lapidary philosophic phrases in which the outcome was proclaimed. Nevertheless, the victory belonged to the counterculture of the evangelicals. For more than a decade a leader of the forces for disestablishment and the chief target of those seeking to suppress the dissenters, John Williams rejoiced at what he believed to be the dawning of a new era. He wrote:

We live in an extraordinary day, under the benign influence of the gospel sun, that seems to be rising to his meridian height; no nation or people, since government was first introduced into the world, ever enjoyed equal privileges with us. We boast not merely the enjoyment of civil, but of religious liberty, without any check or control from the hand of oppression. How ought every one to praise the Lord for his goodness and wonderful works to the children of men![33]

• THE AFTERMATH

The "New Lights" had effectively imposed on the society certain major social-cultural redefinitions. They had established a radically new definition of the role of religion in society and with that new definition a change in the conception of society itself. The gentry Patriot leaders had envisaged a continuation of the rank-ordered, organic community that had been the ideal of the traditional regime; the religious settlement of 1786 confirmed a contrary tendency in popular republicanism. It marked a decisive triumph for the egalitarian, voluntary contractualism of the evangelicals, who had long since demanded freedom to eschew the world and to seek salvation in their own exclusive gathered churches.

In 1776 the religious dissenters had been granted relief. By 1786, after a bitter struggle, they had succeeded in securing a major reorganization of social authority. The effects of that reorganization would be particularly dramatic in Lunenburg. The institutions of courthouse and church, which had so long stood as the twin pillars of a comprehensive gentry control in eastern Virginia, had never achieved that kind of dominance on the Southside frontier, so when the legislative battle over disestablishment was over, the defenders of the traditional order in Lunenburg—denied the force of either long-established tradition or prestigious leaders capable of commanding the deference of large numbers of the county's citizens—were left with little to defend. And with the weakening of the traditional framework of authority in Lunenburg, it would become even more difficult to uphold those traditional notions of authority elsewhere, as the moving frontier created successive Lunenburgs across the old Southwest.

It should be noted that it was not simply that the Baptists, joined perhaps by a few Methodists and Presbyterians, had managed to break away from the traditional religious establishment. One of the effects of that traditional religious establishment had been to bind, at least in a technical sense, the apathetic and the nonbelieving to the Anglican church, occasionally compelling church attendance, but more important, encouraging an acquiescence to the Anglican-gentry way. It is entirely possible that Lunenburg's delegates, when they yielded to the dissenters' pressure and voted in favor of disestablishment, may have believed that they were granting concessions to those already in open revolt against the established church but not endangering in any fundamental way their hegemony over the society at large. If that was their expectation, then within just a few years they would receive shocking evidence indicating that the religious establishment, far from being a strong, supportive pillar of the traditional order, was merely a weak reed held in place only by the compulsion of the law. Although the Episcopal church in Lunenburg after 1786 continued to list among its nominal members most of the wealthy and prominent members of the county, it nearly withered away for lack of support. The full magnitude of the decline in Episcopal dominance within the county is perhaps best revealed by William Hill, an itinerant Methodist minister who preached in the county in April 1791. Hill noted ruefully, "My old acquaintance Parson Craig came across my track again," but this time, by the terms of the 1786 statute on religious freedom, Hill had the same legal right as Craig to use what had previously been the exclusive church of the Episcopalians for his services. There was evidently some confusion on this occasion as to who had made an appointment to use the church first, and Hill, arriving after Craig, was forced to sit by and watch his old antagonist hold the Episcopal services. He noted with obvious satisfaction that Craig's congregation consisted only of a "few bigotted Episcopalians" and with equal pleasure that his own congregation was a "large and attentive one," some of whom "seemed to be deeply affected under the sermon."[34]

This picture of aging, inadequately supported Episcopal clergymen preaching to ever-dwindling congregations in meeting-houses whose doors were now open to the still-suspect, ever-burgeoning dissenters was something that the establishmentarian petitioners had warned against, but few of them probably imagined that the decline in support for their church would be so dramatic or precipitous.

It is tempting to use this important symbolic issue of disestablishment as a pivotal point at which the political culture of this never-fully-assimilated frontier region began to move decisively away from traditional, deferential styles and unambiguously toward full-fledged democracy—the triumph of "the plain folk of the Old South."[35] The elimination of state support for the Episcopal church, a move resulting from the joining of the evangelical and revolutionary movements, clearly weakened *one* of the principal pillars of traditional elite rule. Moreover, the hold of the traditional elite itself over the political process seems to have been at least marginally weakened in the aftermath of the Revolution, even in those areas of Virginia where the elite had been the most impressively endowed.[36] And we might expect these developments to operate with particular force in Lunenburg, where the basis of support for the church was never so secure and where the claims to political power and personal authority by the elite were more uncertain at the very outset.

In fact, though, it appears that long-term trends of economic growth and concentration of wealth were working as powerfully as short-term political changes to shape the contours of life in the county. Once the wartime disruption had cleared, the economy of postrevolutionary Lunenburg would be given over in thoroughgoing fashion to the cultivation of tobacco and investment in black slaves, developments that would lead Lunenburg into still-closer conformity with the more well-established counties to the east. Although the events of the Revolution would forever prevent the men who dominated economic and political life in postrevolutionary Lunenburg from achieving the unrivaled position of the county oligarchs in eastern Virginia (indeed, eastern county oligarchs themselves would never again enjoy that unfettered power in both the secular and religious spheres), they would continue their ascent up the social hierarchy. The evangelicals, for their part, were neither fully assimilated by official acceptance nor, given the increasing economic and political power of the traditional ruling elite, were they able to establish a comprehensive alternative social-cultural hegemony to replace the one dominated by the old Anglican gentry.

In the aftermath of the Revolution, then, we find in Lunenburg a disjointed, fractured culture, with its constituent parts moving in contradictory directions. Indeed, we find those contradictory qualities that W. J. Cash discerned throughout much of the expansive, antebellum South, qualities common both to the maintenance and perpetuation of aristocratic, cavalier styles on the one hand and to an egalitarian and democratic social world on the other. Although many of the differences in style and values between Episcopal gentry and evangelical plain folk would never be wholly eradicated, inexorable patterns of demographic and economic development would, within three decades of the religious settlement, serve to bring about a lasting accommodation between the two cultural camps.

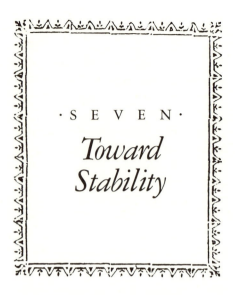

· S E V E N ·

Toward
Stability

As French historian Fernand Braudel notes, the disruption of wars and the upheavals of religious conflicts are often only "surface disturbances, crests of foam that the tides of history carry on their strong backs." According to Braudel, those slower but deeper currents of history are related at the most basic level to the relationship between human beings and their environment, and more generally to the long-term development of economic and social systems.[1] That wisdom appears to apply to Lunenburg in the eighteenth and early nineteenth centuries just as certainly as it does to the Mediterranean world in the sixteenth century. The only difference is that in the eighteenth- and early-nineteenth-century Virginia Southside those deeper currents of economic and demographic change were moving more rapidly than they had in almost any society in the early modern world.

The legal disestablishment of state-supported religion, though an important step in the acceptance of religious pluralism, did not eliminate all the cultural differences among Episcopalians, evangelicals, and unbelievers in a single stroke. Yet that event, together with postrevolutionary trends of economic and demographic development, would by the early nineteenth century produce a mode of community organization that was, though decidedly not a replica of the traditional, Anglican-gentry mode, nevertheless one with a more settled and uniform set of values and institutions. It is difficult to point to any one moment when the conjunction of these demographic and economic changes worked to mute the cultural conflict between Episcopal gentry and evangelicals or to create full-blown a single set of institutions that served to bring all the citizens of the county into a single, unified community, but in the last two decades of the eighteenth century and the first half of the nineteenth, the forces at work in Lunenburg were moving clearly toward continuity and conciliation rather than disruption and conflict.

• ECONOMIC INSURGENCE

The most important force behind this development was the decrease in the role of the eastern Chesapeake in the tobacco trade and the simultaneous increase in importance of Southside counties like Lunenburg in that same traffic. The Chesapeake tobacco economy had suffered from the dislocation of war. Many planters had been called away from their farms to wield a weapon rather than a plow or a hoe, but even had Virginians and Marylanders been able to keep tobacco production at prewar levels (which was not the case), they still were faced with the loss of a market that had absorbed nearly all their crop before the Revolution.

The decline in the Chesapeake tobacco economy, however, though it became dramatically apparent during the Revolution, had already been set in motion long before independence was declared, and it related less to the disruptions of war than to a shifting balance of economic power between an older, economically stagnating Tidewater and a steadily expanding Southside.[2] The stagnation of the tobacco economy of the eastern counties of Virginia was masked in the two decades immediately preceding the Revolution by an increase in continental demand for tobacco which raised prices and stimulated production, but in the east, unlike the Southside, production did not keep pace with the growth of the working population—which led to a definite squeeze in economic opportunity, particularly for whites who did not own land and whose labor was no longer highly valued.[3]

By the mid-1760s the spatial expansion of the part of eastern Virginia that had provided the bulk of the colony's tobacco exports and that had produced those families which set the opulent cultural styles for the colony as a whole had virtually ceased. There was simply very little new land on which to expand, and without the attraction of new land the economic incentive behind population growth (both for the immigration of free whites and for the purchase of additional slaves) in the Tidewater and Northern Neck disappeared. Moreover, by that time the gradual process of soil exhaustion was making it more difficult for the already intensely cultivated and populated Tidewater even to match previous levels of production. The Revolution, with its catastrophic disruption of the continental market for tobacco, only hastened the process of retreat from the tobacco economy in the Tidewater, and in the years from 1780 the trend within the Tidewater toward the raising of cattle, corn, wheat, and general farming accelerated.[4]

As world markets for tobacco returned to their prerevolutionary war conditions, it would be the Southside, not the Tidewater and Northern Neck, that was in the best position to satisfy those demands, and the combination of good land, a white landowning population that was expanding both numerically and spatially, and a dramatically increased commitment to slave labor would contribute to the expanded tobacco production that gave the Southside its extraordinary economic vitality.

In spite of the toll of the war, the white population of Lunenburg continued to grow at a rapid rate. The number of white heads of households in the population, which had stood at 434 in 1764, had risen to 881 eighteen years later, in 1782. Part of the reason for the increase was a slowing of migration out of the county. In the earliest years of Lunenburg's history, the rate of out-migration approached 20 percent of the existing population each year; by the 1760s that rate had decreased to slightly less than 10 percent, but that still represented a substantial flow of residents out of the county.[5] The disruption of war notwithstanding, the period between 1769 and 1782 witnessed a marked stabilization of the population, with the persistence rate during the thirteen-year period for heads of households standing at 48 percent, signifying a disappearance rate of only about 4 percent annually, with about half that caused by natural incidences of death. Still, in 1782 the overwhelming number of householders in Lunenburg had achieved that status only recently; of the 881 individuals paying taxes in 1782, some 690 (78 percent) had not appeared on the prerevolutionary list of 1769.[6]

Just as for those who migrated out, the lure for settlers who migrated into Lunenburg was land. In 1764, some 162,096 acres of land had been taken up within the county and made subject to tax; by 1782 that figure had jumped to 234,928 acres.[7] These increases both in households and in the occupation of land are persuasive indicators of the economic and demographic growth within the county, but they tell only part of the story, for the changing character of the labor force that worked those newly opened lands would also fundamentally alter the social fabric of the county.

In 1764 Lunenburg's population consisted of 434 white heads of households (36 percent of the tithable population of 1,185 and roughly 13 percent of the entire population), 175 white dependents over the age of sixteen (of whom about half were not the younger sons or relatives of the heads of household), and approximately 1,280 slaves. By 1782 the 881 heads of households in the county constituted nearly the same percentage of the tithable population (which numbered 2,372) as in previous years, but they now controlled fewer nonrelated white dependents and many more black slaves. The number of nonrelated white dependents in the population had fallen to below 50, and the number of slaves had risen to 3,378, a nearly threefold increase in less than twenty years.[8]

The trend is unmistakable. In 1750, with the county only thinly settled and only a fraction of the available land taken up, most of the agricultural labor in the county was performed by white planters and their families. Slaves constituted perhaps one-third of the county's total population at that time, but only one resident family in the entire population owned more than ten tithable slaves. By the mid-1760s, with more and more land being taken up, the number of slaves in the population had increased to 39 percent, the number of slaveowning families from 20 percent to 44 percent, and those residents who could afford to own ten or more tithable slaves now numbered five. By 1769 the number of slaves in the population had moved up to 44 percent, ten residents owned ten or more tithable slaves, and slaveowning families actually constituted a narrow majority among the county's households. During the period from 1769 to 1782, years in which the dislocation of political and military conflict might be expected to have slowed capital investments in slave labor, the commitment to slavery increased gradually but steadily. By 1782 the 3,378 slaves in Lunenburg constituted roughly 48 percent of the total population, with over 57 percent of the county's families owning at least one slave (see Table 4).[9]

Although already evident soon after the Revolution, these patterns of population change and economic investment became more marked in the last two decades of the eighteenth century, and then intensified dramatically in the first two decades of the nineteenth century. By 1795 the number of white heads of households had risen to 1,138, the amount of acreage being taxed to 248,000 acres, the proportion of slaves in the total population to 50 percent, while the proportion of slaveowning households to nonslaveowning households remained roughly equal to the 1782 level.[10] In the next twenty-five years, however, the reliance on slave labor took off dramatically. The amount of occupied land in the county remained virtually unchanged from 1795 to 1800, but the character of the population working that land changed markedly (see Table 5). By 1800 there were 4,372 whites and 5,876 slaves in the county, an increase of nearly 750 slaves over the previous five years and a decrease in the white population of over 700. The preponderance of blacks over whites continued to accelerate in the next twenty years. The white population rebounded from 4,372 in 1800 to 4,933 in 1810, but the slave population rose even more dramatically, from 5,876 to 7,155, creating a ratio of slaves to whites of 1.45 to 1. In the next decade both the white population and the slave population fell, but the decline among whites was so drastic that the ratio of slaves to whites jumped to 1.72 to 1 by 1820.[11]

When compared with the patterns of population change in Tidewater and Northern Neck counties, these demographic trends reveal a reversal in older patterns of slave ownership in Virginia. In most eastern counties the number of slaves in proportion to

TABLE 4 POPULATION AND SLAVEHOLDING, LUNENBURG COUNTY, 1750–1815

Year	Total Households	Slaveowning Households No.	Slaveowning Households %	Mean No. of Slaves per Household	Total Population	No. of Slaves	% of Total
1750	1,080	246	22.8	1.3	6,182	1,396	22.5
1764	434	193	44.5	3.0	3,278	1,280	39.0
1769	398	212	53.3	3.8	3,342	1,842	44.8
1782	881	505	57.3	3.8	6,984	3,378	48.4
1795	1,138	611	53.7	4.5	10,140	5,131	50.6
1815	978	686	70.1	7.0	10,973	6,884	62.7

SOURCE: Landon C. Bell, *Sunlight on the Southside: List of Tithes, Lunenburg County, Virginia, 1748–1783* (Philadelphia, 1931), pp. 58–86, 122–61, 228–46, 269–85. Real and Personal Property Tax Lists, Lunenburg County, 1782, 1795, 1815, Virginia State Library, Richmond, Va.

NOTE: See note 11 for Chapter 7.

TABLE 5 SLAVE/WHITE POPULATION OF SELECTED VIRGINIA COUNTIES, ACCORDING TO THE FIRST FOUR U.S. CENSUSES

County	1790				1800			
	White	Slave	Total Black	No. Slaves per White	White	Slave	Total Black	No. Slaves per White
Lunenburg	4,547	4,332	4,412	0.95	4,372	5,876	6,009	1.34
Lancaster	2,259	3,236	3,379	1.43	2,090	3,126	3,285	1.50
Richmond[a]	2,918	3,984	4,067	1.37	5,334	7,826	8,410	1.47
James City	1,519	2,405	2,551	1.58	1,374	2,389	2,557	1.74
Surry	2,762	3,097	3,465	1.12	2,777	3,258	3,758	1.17

County	1810				1820			
	White	Slave	Total Black	No. Slaves per White	White	Slave	Total Black	No. Slaves per White
Lunenburg	4,933	7,155	7,332	1.45	3,873	6,663	6,789	1.72
Lancaster	2,276	3,112	3,316	1.37	2,388	2,944	3,129	1.23
Richmond[a]	2,775	3,178	3,439	1.15	2,749	2,664	2,957	0.97
James City	1,354	2,320	2,740	1.71	1,017	1,677	2,144	1.65
Surry	2,751	3,440	4,104	1.25	2,642	3,340	3,952	1.26

SOURCE: U.S. Census, 1790, 1800, 1810, 1826.

[a]Combined with Westmoreland County in 1800.

whites was either remaining roughly constant or declining during the period 1790–1820, yet in Lunenburg that ratio had nearly doubled, from 0.95 to 1.72 (see Table 5), a figure which placed Lunenburg near the top of the state in both the percentage and the absolute number of slaves living within its borders.[12]

The consequences of these changes on the county economy and social structure were profound. At the most obvious level, the total wealth of the county increased significantly. In the prerevolutionary period the provincial government made no provision for inspection warehouses west of the Fall Line, so Southside planters had to bring their tobacco east for inspection. This fact both indicates the impediments to Southside tobacco production and makes it difficult to calculate the region's share of the overall market during those years. It is highly unlikely, however, that the Southside's share of prerevolutionary tobacco production was more than 25 percent of the Virginia total; it was probably closer to 20 percent.[13]

After the Revolution a number of factors combined to encourage increased production of tobacco in the Southside. Although planters in the region continued to be hampered by an inferior system of river transport, the combination of improved roads and a more efficient system of rolling hogsheads along those roads greatly reduced the time and expense involved in getting the crop to market. Most important, the postrevolutionary government in Richmond established additional inspection warehouses west of the Fall Line, greatly reducing the distances that Southside planters had to travel to get their crop to market. Before the Revolution, Lunenburg's planters had to bring their tobacco at least forty miles, to the eastern edge of Dinwiddie or Prince George County, for inspection, but by the early nineteenth century there were warehouses spread all over the Southside, including several in neighboring Prince Edward and Mecklenburg counties (see Map 4).[14]

By 1784–85, annual production of tobacco in the Southside had risen to 19,654 hogsheads, or 33 percent of the total production throughout the entire state. By 1790–91 that figure had increased to 29,143 hogsheads, 40 percent of Virginia's total. Tobacco production throughout the Old Dominion declined

1765

Fall Line

|||||| Lunenburg County

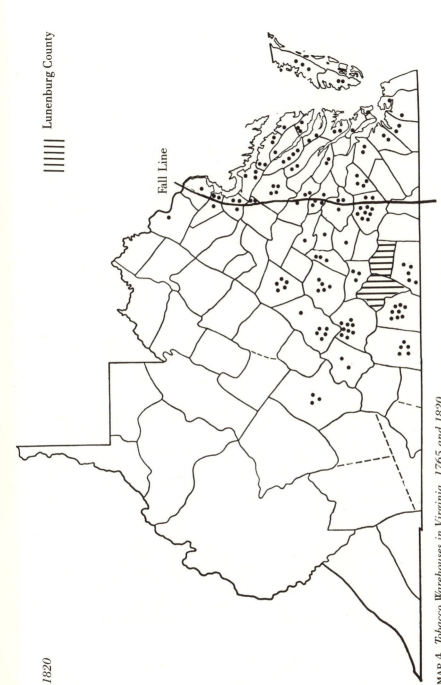

MAP 4. *Tobacco Warehouses in Virginia, 1765 and 1820*

SOURCE: These maps are based on information from George Melvin Herndon, "A History of Tobacco in Virginia, 1613–1860" (M.A. thesis, University of Virginia, 1956), pp. 100–105.

Lunenburg County

Fall Line

1820

substantially in the mid-1790s as a consequence of the collapse of the French market, but the Southside's share of the overall market in those depressed years increased to 53 percent. From that point on the region's production continued to rise; in 1840 it stood at 47,053 hogsheads and 62 percent of the market, and in 1860 at 69,209 hogsheads and 55 percent of the market.[15]

The effects of this increasing dependence on a single crop— tobacco—and a single system of labor—chattel slavery—were in many respects harmful to the long-term economic development of the Southside, but by the beginning of the nineteenth century residents of Lunenburg must have marveled at the economic transition that had taken place. Far from being a backwater, Lunenburg by 1800 stood at the very center of the market economy of the Old Dominion.

• A CHANGING SOCIAL STRUCTURE

The increase in the Southside's productivity was reflected in the property that individuals were able to accumulate, with the mean and median values of estate inventories, even after adjustments for inflation, more than doubling between the decade of the 1760s and that of the 1780s.[16] By far the most important factor in this increase in estate value was the greater number of slaves appearing in the inventories of the period, as slaves generally constituted between 70 and 80 percent of the total value of an estate in which slaves were listed.

The increase in black chattels signified more than an increased commitment to tobacco production. The entire racial and social balance of the county was changing, with the numbers of blacks in the population increasing fourfold between the Revolution and 1820, and the number of whites doubling between the Revolution and 1794 and then declining slightly thereafter. Much of the black population increase was due to reproduction rather than slave purchase. Although there is no evidence that Southside Virginians actively pursued slave-breeding, it is clear that young women of childbearing age were among the most highly valued slaves in most of the inventories recorded in the early nineteenth century.[17] In the case of the white population, there had always been a rapid turnover, with steady rates of out-migration every year. Up until the 1790s, that out-migration had always been matched by substantial in-migration, either from the eastern parts of Virginia or from out of state, but by at least 1795 the number of those leaving the county was beginning to exceed those who were coming in.[18]

This decrease in the number of white settlers, together with the dramatically increased proportion of slaves in the population, suggests that economic opportunity in the county, at least for some, was gradually becoming more straitened, while concentration of wealth, particularly in the form of slaveholdings, was becoming more pronounced. The decline in the white population, which dropped at the precipitous rate of 20 percent in the decade between 1810 and 1820, marked a dramatic reversal from the unimpeded growth of the county's population in the eighteenth century. The history of Lunenburg had always been marked by a significant out-migration of men and women, particularly those at the lower end of the economic scale, moving farther south and west in search of greater opportunity, but by the beginning of the nineteenth century, with the best land in the county already occupied and the price of available land in the county steadily rising, few new settlers were likely to regard Lunenburg as the ideal place to gain their independent freehold.

For white householders who stayed in the community, most of whom had already carved out their freehold, the slightly decreasing availability of inexpensive land did not create serious obstacles to prosperity. Indeed, when one looks at those who sunk their roots in Lunenburg—by the late eighteenth century the overwhelming majority of the population—it is apparent that while the affluent continued to build their estates, most ordinary planters were able to improve their position as well. While relatively few middling planters improved the size of their landholdings, large numbers of them did choose to invest substantial amounts of capital in an expanding slave labor force, and it was that expanding labor force, rather than larger landholdings, that provided the key to greater prosperity. As a consequence, the middling planters of Lunenburg were able to stay in the same relative position vis-à-vis the large planters they had been in over the course of the years between 1764 and 1815.

One reason for this relatively stable distribution of wealth within the county was that while the rich were gradually becoming richer, they were never able to exert the kind of dominance enjoyed by those gentry who controlled the tobacco economy of Virginia in the first half of the eighteenth century. While the productive capacity of the largest Southside planters increased markedly during the late eighteenth and early nineteenth centuries, those planters were never able to gain control over the operation of the tobacco economy itself. Although the Scots merchants had been temporarily purged from the Southside during the 1780s and had been replaced with French mercantile intermediaries, neither the French nor the local merchants had the capital or organizational expertise to make the system work. As a consequence, by the 1790s the large merchant firms of Glasgow once again regained dominance in the Southside tobacco trade. Therefore the only individuals who enjoyed a truly dramatic increase in wealth relative to the rest of the population were those outsiders, living in Scotland, overseeing the credit system that underpinned the Virginia tobacco economy.[19]

The percentage of people owning land in the county varied in a fashion consistent with the patterns of growth and decline in the white population. In 1764 and 1769, with the white population still expanding into vacant lands within the county, the proportion of landowning households varied between 76 percent and 80 percent. That pattern of expansion continued during the years of the Revolution, and in spite of a near doubling of the number of white households between 1764 and 1782, the number of households listed as owning land in 1782 remained at 75 percent. It seems clear that most of the good land in the county had been taken up by 1795, however, and with a still-expanding white population the number of households owning land fell to 65 percent. In the next twenty years, however, the movement of whites (predominantly though not exclusively landless whites) out of the county swelled the percentage of landowning households once again; in 1815 some 78 percent of the county's heads of households owned at least some land.[20]

As one might expect in an economy that was growing both spatially and in terms of productivity, the heightened competition for good land resulted in higher land prices and a corresponding reduction in the average size of individual holdings, a reduction from 373 acres per household in 1764 to 267 acres in 1782, to 218 acres in 1795, rebounding to 260 acres again in 1815. The principal effect of these trends was to reduce the ranks of Lunenburg's middling planters. Whereas before the Revolution approximately 40 percent of Lunenburg's heads of households had owned between 200 and 500 acres, by 1815 the number had dropped to 27 percent (see Table 6).

In spite of the apparent squeeze in the amount of acreage available to Lunenburg's middling planters, there is little evidence, at least among the white citizens, of any dramatic cleavage between rich and poor. Both the percentage of citizens in the county owning no land and that of citizens owning more than one thousand acres remained roughly the same in 1815 as they had been before the Revolution. Moreover, at no point in the county's history did any one or two individuals have an unusually disproportionate share of land (see Appendix 1). David Garland's holdings of 3,190 acres in 1769, William Barrott's of 3,069 acres in 1782, and William Buford's holdings of 3,186 acres in 1815 were all roughly similar. As was the case throughout the county's history, however, the index of landownership tells only a small part of the story. David Garland's 3,190 acres in 1769 were mostly uncultivated, while William Buford's 3,186 acres, divided among seven separate plantations and tended by a corps of forty-four slaves, had an appreciably higher productive capacity.[21]

Similarly, the decrease in the size of the landholdings of middling planters, which might at first be a sign of declining opportunity, takes on a different cast when viewed in the light of dramatically rising individual slaveholdings and significantly increased estate valuation. As we have already seen, the proportion of households able to afford an investment in slave labor rose steadily during the history of the county. If the slaveholdings of the county's twenty richest men in 1815 were three and a half times that of the economic elite in the 1760s, the average slaveholdings in the county at large had managed nearly to double, from 3.8 to 7.0 per household, during the same period (see Table 7 and Appendix 1).[22]

TABLE 6 DISTRIBUTION OF LANDHOLDINGS, LUNENBURG COUNTY, 1764–1815

Acres	1764		1769		1782	
	No. of Households	% of Households	No. of Households	% of Households	No. of Households	% of Households
0	102	23.5	78	19.6	223	25.3
1–99	9	2.1	10	2.5	40	4.5
100–199	58	13.3	74	18.6	187	21.2
200–299	71	16.4	74	18.6	136	15.4
300–399	49	11.3	44	11.0	77	8.7
400–499	52	12.0	42	10.6	90	10.2
500–999	60	13.8	52	13.1	97	11.0
1,000–1,999	27	6.2	22	5.5	26	3.1
2,000 or more	6	1.4	2	0.5	5	0.6
	434	100.0	398	100.0	881	100.0

Acres	1795		1815	
	No. of Households	% of Households	No. of Households	% of Households
0	395	34.7	205	21.1
1–99	98	8.6	142	14.5
100–199	211	18.6	221	22.6
200–299	160	14.0	130	13.3
300–399	74	6.5	79	8.1
400–499	63	5.5	54	5.5
500–999	98	8.6	103	10.5
1,000–1,999	34	3.1	35	3.6
2,000 or more	5	0.4	9	0.8
	1,138	100.0	978	100.0

SOURCE: Landon C. Bell, *Sunlight on the Southside: List of Tithes, Lunenburg County, Virginia, 1748–1783* (Philadelphia, 1931), pp. 228–46, 269–85; Real Property Tax Lists, Lunenburg County, 1782, 1795, 1815, Virginia State Library, Richmond, Va.

TABLE 7 DISTRIBUTION OF SLAVEHOLDINGS, LUNENBURG COUNTY, 1750–1815

Tithable Slaves	1750[a]		1764		1769[b]	
	No. of Households	% of Households	No. of Households	% of Households	No. of Households	% of Households
0	834	77.2	241	55.5	186	46.7
1–2	158	14.6	94	21.7	93	23.4
3–5	68	6.3	69	15.9	81	20.4
6–15	18	1.7	29	6.7	38	9.5
16–30	1	0.1	1	0.2	0	0.0
31 or more	1	0.1	0	0.0	0	0.0
	1,080	100.0	434	100.0	398	100.0

Tithable Slaves	1782[c]		1795		1815[b]	
	No. of Households	% of Households	No. of Households	% of Households	No. of Households	% of Households
0	376	42.7	527	46.3	292	29.9
1–2	157	17.8	248	21.8	221	22.6
3–5	127	14.4	187	16.4	169	17.3
6–15	175	19.9	161	14.2	234	24.0
16–30	42	4.8	14	1.2	49	5.0
31 or more	4	0.4	1	0.1	8	0.8
	881	100.0	1,138	100.0	978	100.0

SOURCE: Landon C. Bell, *Sunlight on the Southside: List of Tithes, Lunenburg County, Virginia, 1748–1783* (Philadelphia, 1931), pp. 122–61, 228–46, 269–85; Personal Property Tax Lists, Lunenburg County, 1782, 1795, 1815, Virginia State Library, Richmond, Va.

[a] The tithable population of Lunenburg in 1750 was more than twice that in 1764 and 1769 because the county's boundaries initially encompassed a much larger territory. By 1764, after successive divisions of the county, Lunenburg was only one-tenth the geographic size it had been in 1750.

[b] The number of independent householders on the 1769 tithable list is less than that for 1764 because the returns for two of the county's districts are missing for that year.

[c] The calculations for 1782 are skewed by the fact that *all* slaves, rather than tithable slaves sixteen years and over, were included in the tax lists for that year.

These patterns of investment resulted in the emergence of a middle-class, slave-based society. The total number of slaves whose productive capacity could be marshaled to generate wealth was significantly higher than it had ever been in the county's history; indeed, by 1815 there were two or three men in that society who could marshal the labor of forty or fifty slaves, but their holdings were dwarfed by those of the wealthiest planters in the eastern Chesapeake both before and after the Revolution. The distinctive phenomenon in Lunenburg and in most of the remainder of the Southside up to the Civil War was the evenness with which slaves were accumulated throughout the white population as a whole. Some 70 percent of the population owned at least one slave, 82 percent of those households owned between one and ten slaves, and only 2.5 percent of the households owned more than twenty slaves. Lunenburg had become a society in which the vast majority of householders worked side by side with a small slave labor force.[23] And conversely, that class of small landholders working their land without slaves had largely disappeared.

The increase in estate valuations at all economic levels in the county corresponded almost directly to the increased investment in slaves. As Table 8 shows, the median estate value in the period 1746 to 1752, a period when only 20 percent of the county's households owned slaves and when less than 1 percent owned more than ten slaves, was a mere £42 (the average was £72). By 1762–66 the median valuation had risen to £73. The striking thing about the median at that time is that it is the point at which the estates of that half of the population which now owned slaves began to appear; the dramatically increased values of the estates of slave-owners whose inventories placed them above the median helps account for the high average estate valuations during the 1762–66 period of £221. These increases in estate valuations during the prerevolutionary period do not appear to be skewed unduly by inflation. Slave prices did increase by perhaps 35 percent during the fifteen years separating the two samples, but there was virtually no increase in the other most common farm commodities such as horses, cattle, sheep, hogs, and basic farm implements. The dramatic jump in estate valuations would come in the next fifty years. By 1782–86, median estate valuations had risen to £333, average

1746–1752

Estate Value in Pounds	No. of Inventories	% of total
0–25	11	36.7
26–50	6	20.0
51–100	4	13.3
101–200	8	26.7
201–300	1	3.3
301–500	0	0.0
501–1,000	0	0.0
1,001–2,000	0	0.0
2,000–4,000	0	0.0
4,000 and over	0	0.0
	30	100.0

1762–1766

Estate Value in Pounds	No. of Inventories	% of total
0–25	11	18.6
26–50	10	16.9
51–100	11	18.6
101–200	7	11.9
201–300	8	13.6
301–500	4	6.8
501–1,000	6	10.2
1,001–2,000	1	1.7
2,000–4,000	1	1.7
4,000 and over	0	0.0
	59	100.0

1782–1786

Estate Value in Pounds	No. of Inventories	% of total
0–25	3	4.9
26–50	4	6.6
51–100	9	14.8
101–200	8	13.1
201–300	6	9.8
301–500	12	19.6
501–1,000	13	21.3
1,001–2,000	4	6.6
2,000–4,000	2	3.3
4,000 and over	0	0.0
	61	100.0

1802–1806

Estate Value in Pounds	No. of Inventories	% of total
0–25	4	6.6
26–50	3	4.9
51–100	5	8.2
101–200	7	11.5
201–300	6	9.8
301–500	8	13.1
501–1,000	16	26.2
1,001–2,000	7	11.5
2,000–4,000	5	8.2
4,000 and over	0	0.0
	61	100.0

1812–1816

Estate Value in Pounds	No. of Inventories	% of total
0–25	9	11.4
26–50	7	8.9
51–100	4	5.1
101–200	8	10.1
201–300	6	7.6
301–500	17	21.5
501–1,000	10	12.6
1,001–2,000	12	15.2
2,000–4,000	4	5.1
4,000 and over	2	2.5
	79	100.0

	1746–1752	1762–1766	1782–1786	1802–1806	1812–1816
Mean estate value (£)	72	221	461	649	724
Median estate value (£)	42	73	333	472	425

SOURCE: Lunenburg County Will Books, no. 1 (1746–60), no. 2 (1760–78), no. 3 (1778–91), no. 6 (1799–1808), no. 7 (1803–16), Virginia State Library, Richmond, Va.

valuations to £461; by 1812–16 the median value remained roughly constant and the average had risen to £724 (see Table 8). Inflation contributed to some of that increase, but even after allowing for inflation the median estate valuations in that last period stood at nearly three times the level fifty years earlier.[24]

For all but the county's wealthiest residents, these estate valuations (not including the value of current crops) reflected almost exclusively an investment in slaves, horses, and livestock. When we go beyond the values of increased slaveholdings, increased land values, and increased production of tobacco, we wonder what qualitative benefits ordinary planters were receiving from their larger slave forces and tobacco crops. At the bottom of the economic scale, among those planters whose estates were valued below £20 in 1762–66 and below £50 in 1812–16, the quality of material life seems to have changed hardly at all. In 1763 an individual such as Abraham Roberson, with his rock-bottom estate valued at £8 5s., might have a horse, a cow, a heifer, a young steer, and a bed. Or moving up the economic scale a bit, but still not to the point where the householder could afford an investment in slaves, a man like Richard Sunday had accumulated two horses, nine head of cattle, ten hogs, the usual complement of kitchen implements, some farm tools, saws and wedges for firewood, two spinning wheels, a bed and a bedstead, a chamber pot, and at least two sets of clothes by the time of his death in 1764. The only items in his inventory that probably would not have been in an inventory of someone of his social rank fifteen years earlier were his sets of knives and forks and a pepper box. By 1812 the quality of the possessions of people at the bottom of the economic hierarchy remained virtually unchanged. They may have owned a few more horses or a few more cattle, but in general these people lived much the same kind of hard, plain life as that of their forebears in the county forty or fifty years earlier.[25]

The members of the "middling ranks" were most affected by the economic and demographic changes of the postrevolutionary years. Their ownership of slaves allowed them to generate the profits that promoted investment in still more slaves and a few additional consumer goods. Still we look in vain for dramatic signs of an increase in luxury items in this middle sector of the population. It is true that such items as dutch ovens, spice mortars, knives and forks, feather beds, teakettles, and "smoothing irons" (all items virtually unheard of in the 1740s and only infrequently found in the 1760s) become more prevalent in inventories, but in general we are struck by the continuities of material life. Carpenters tools, cross-cut saws and splitting wedges, shears for cutting the wool of the sheep, spinning wheels, shoemaker tools, grinding stones—these are all signs that Lunenburg had emerged from its wilderness, pioneer stage. Yet they were still the tools of a middle class creating for themselves a life of self-sufficiency, not of a gentry enjoying affluence and luxury. Through their reinvestment in slaves and farm implements, they may have been working toward the goal of affluence, but for the most part the environment of Lunenburg offered them few opportunities for great wealth.[26]

The best sense of the plain style of life of the great mass of Lunenburg's citizens is conveyed through a detailed tax assessment levied in 1815. Virginia's legislators, who throughout their history were concerned mainly with taxing land, slaves, livestock, and an occasional luxury item deemed particularly frivolous (for example, the tax of £15 levied on billiard tables), decided in 1815 and in that year alone to tax all manner of domestic furniture, silver, and household ornaments. Although it yielded little extra revenue for the commonwealth from a county like Lunenburg, the result was a remarkable accounting of the domestic goods in the county.

The 1815 tax list, which consciously sought to identify luxury items in the households of all Virginia's citizens, confirms the impression given by the Lunenburg inventories for the period. It is notable for the paucity of such items. As in the inventories, the vast majority of capital was tied up in slaves—by valuation 72 percent of the total personal property taxes paid in the county. While items like earthenware pottery, knives and forks, spices, and other ornamental items began to appear more frequently in Lunenburg households, only a tiny minority of the county's households were willing or able to invest in luxury items that were common in other parts of the Chesapeake. While more and more citizens could afford an investment in simple country furniture (there were 260 pine chests of drawers spread among the population), only sixteen households possessed a mahogany chest of drawers, and only twenty-five owned mahogany tables. Even fewer residents owned items suggestive of real luxury rather than mere comfort. There were only three portraits in oil and seven in crayon in the entire county, and only twenty-four smaller pictures of any kind. One householder was able to boast of a carpet, four houses possessed pianos, one a silver teapot, and a few dozen had curtains, but the unmistakable impression continued to be of a spartan style of life.[27]

The most dramatic evidence of this modest life-style is in the dwellings themselves. Only 9 of Lunenburg's 978 households owned plantation houses valued over $1,000, and there were only twenty-five in excess of $500.[28] Even at the very upper end of the social order, those plantation houses remained modest structures. Nearly all were constructed with simple pine weatherboards rather than brick, and few seem to have had more than six rooms, a detached kitchen, and perhaps an office building. All traces of the slaves' quarters have disappeared, but given the modest character of the main house, it seems likely that they were modest in the extreme. The only exception to this humble style seems to have been Brickland, the home of Sterling Neblett. Valued at $700 in 1815, it was constructed entirely of brick and on completion in 1818 contained ten rooms, five chimneys, and a portico reminiscent of some Tidewater homes.[29]

The houses of Lunenburg's middling planters were even less imposing. Describing the state of Virginia's housing in the mid-1780s, Thomas Jefferson lamented, "It is impossible to devise things more ugly, uncomfortable, and happily more perishable." He went on to observe, "A country whose buildings are of wood can never increase in its improvements to any considerable degree. Their duration is highly estimated at fifty years. Every half century then our country becomes a *tabula rasa*, whereon we have to set out anew, as in the first moment of seating it." And when that rebuilding took place the new edifices were usually as primitive as their predecessors.[30]

The very impermanence of Lunenburg's housing stock makes any systematic tracing of architectural styles among ordinary settlers extremely difficult, but a survey of housing, compiled in neighboring Halifax County in 1785, gives us some indication of

FIGURE 5. *Magnolia Grove Plantation, Lunenburg County. Original construction circa 1800. Photo by the author.*

FIGURE 6. *Brickland Plantation, Lunenburg County. Original construction circa 1818. Photo by the author.*

the simplicity of domestic architecture in the Southside. Of the 239 households in Halifax, 27 owned no dwellings of any kind, 67 lived in buildings listed merely as "cabins," and 145 lived in dwellings listed as "farms" or "plantations." Of the 145 dwellings that merited further description, the smallest was an 8-by-8-feet structure listed as a "small house," and the largest was a 42-by-28-feet structure accompanied by several outbuildings. Nearly 80 percent of the homes contained less than 400 square feet, an area comparable to that of a large modern American living room. In Halifax, as in Lunenburg, brick or stone construction was virtually unheard of, and even among those houses constructed of wood the overwhelming number (76 of the 80 explicitly described in the survey) had log rather than frame walls.

Thomas Jefferson's other complaint about the character of most architecture in Virginia was its lack of variety, and here too the homes of most Southside residents would have merited his scorn. The dimensions of most houses in the Halifax survey show little variation; there are large clusters of dwellings of 20 by 16 feet, 16 by 12 feet, 16 feet square, and 24 by 16 feet; indeed, 80 percent of houses that merited descriptions had either a length or a width of 16 feet. And although Henry Glassie and others have pointed to a "great rebuilding" in Virginia in the nineteenth century, much of that rebuilding apparently proceeded along lines that connected the present with the past. In 1934, when the federal government surveyed the housing stock in Halifax, it discovered that 42 percent of the farmhouses in the county were still constructed of logs.[31]

The other impression emerging from this composite of the county's material wealth is that of an economy becoming more self-sufficient in some areas but less diversified in others. During the eighteenth century, cattle-raising had been an important part of almost every planter's agricultural operation, providing both a source of food for domestic consumption and a substantial surplus for sale elsewhere. By 1815, beef production had dropped by more than a third from previous decades and would continue to decline. Grazing land was now being planted in tobacco and to a lesser extent in grains, by means of an increased slave labor force. Moreover, the increase in the number of tobacco inspection warehouses within easy reach of Lunenburg (by 1800 there were at least twelve within that part of the Southside) and a gradual improvement in the road system, which made it easier to transport the tobacco to those warehouses, made it much less expensive to market the crop once it was out of the ground. The number of plantations in the county with mills on their property had also increased to thirty-one by 1815, and though it does not appear that the Southside had made a switch from tobacco to wheat of the same magnitude as that occurring in the eastern and northern Chesapeake, it does seem likely that by the early nineteenth century wheat was becoming a significant secondary crop in Lunenburg.[32]

Given the level of capital necessary to support an investment in slaves, one suspects that many Lunenburg families could have marshaled resources sufficient to purchase at least some of the linens, silver plate, fine porcelain, or walnut furniture more often found among the gentry of traditional Chesapeake society. But even among those at the very top of the hierarchy in Lunenburg—individuals like Henry Blagrave, who died in 1781 leaving an estate valued at £3,753 and containing thirty-three slaves—the character of domestic consumption was strikingly different from more prestigious gentry to the east.[33] Even by 1815, when the total wealth of Lunenburgers at the very top of the hierarchy was two or three times that of the leaders of the prerevolutionary generation, their consumption expectations were far different from those that guided the Byrds, Carters, or Tayloes, all of whom not only enjoyed affluence in the eighteenth century but also continued that tradition well into the nineteenth century. The estate of Henry Stokes, appraised in 1814 at $28,829 (the equivalent of £8,657), was an impressive one by the standards of any previous generation within the county, even after adjustment for inflation. Some $19,250 of that estate (68 percent) was tied up in slaves, but that left $9,000 for the more than three hundred other entries in Stokes' inventory. The nonslave entries, however, reveal a high percentage of capital invested directly in the business of production, in over five hundred barrels of corn from Stokes's six working plantations in the county, in hogs, sheep, bulls, and horses, and in an extraordinary expansion in the number and variety of farm animals and tools—horses, oxen, rakes, harrowers, grubbing hoes, tilling hoes, scythes, carts, and the like. Certainly that vastly increased production allowed Stokes to live in handsome style, and his inventory of household furniture (which included a walnut chest, twenty-four knives and forty-three forks, twenty-eight wine glasses, a silver watch, and a four-wheeled coach) is testimony to the comforts with which he was able to surround himself.[34]

Yet in spite of all the productive capacity and material comforts that Stokes was able to marshal, his style of life was altogether different from that of the traditional Chesapeake ruling elite. We search in vain for a description, even a remnant, of his plantation house, but it has disappeared without a trace, leaving no mark on either the landscape or the collective memory of the county's citizens. And when one searches the inventory for the other trappings of gentility—an extensive library, musical instruments, or any of the paraphernalia suggestive of a rich and extensive social life with other residents in the county—what one finds instead are the tools of a diligent farmer, not of a gentleman.

In this sense Henry Blagrave's or even Henry Stokes's estates are strikingly different from that of Lunenburg's single bona fide resident gentleman of an earlier generation, Clement Read, who died in 1764. Read's estate, valued at £3,804, was more than twice the value of the next highest estate probated in the county during the period 1762–66 and more than fifty times higher than the median estate value for that period. Most important, it contained goods that marked a gentleman: silver plate, a carpet (a unique possession in Lunenburg in the eighteenth century), fine china, twenty-five leather chairs, and a chariot.[35] Stokes's estate, though worth more than twice that of Read even after adjustments for inflation, simply did not reflect that same set of aspirations.

Clement Read had come of age at a time when the trappings of personal authority expected of a gentleman were all clearly defined and commonly accepted by people from all ranks of society. The state of social and economic development in Lunenburg made it exceptionally difficult for any locally based citizens (as opposed to an absentee grandee like William Byrd) to acquire those trappings, which accounts for the rough-and-tumble way the county's social and political system operated in the prerevolutionary years. But when someone like Read did come along, even Lunenburgers who had little previous connection with the eastern Chesapeake society that had produced a man of Read's tastes and aspirations were prepared to honor his claim to public office and social deference.

The values of nineteenth-century Southsiders were moving in a different direction. Those citizens clearly respected economic achievement, but the traditional system of power and authority, based on the tripodal foundation of church, court, and plantation house, was on the wane. Lunenburg County was moving toward a replication of traditional Virginia standards in terms of the accumulation of real and personal property, but the ethics underlying the wealth of its citizens were different from the members of the Byrd or Randolph families who initially charted the course of settlement for the county.

It is a mistake, however, to see in these differences a major source of conflict between backcountry Lunenburg and the eastern Chesapeake. In the first place, the traditional Chesapeake culture, deprived of many of the legal and economic advantages it had previously enjoyed, was itself undergoing considerable change. Even more important, Lunenburg's citizens could increasingly look to the south and west for cultural models that were wholly consonant with their own. Landon Carter III might attempt to continue the traditions established by his grandfather at Sabine Hall, Richard Bland Lee would actually enhance the grandeur of Stratford, and the Tayloe family plantation, Mount Airy, would persist in displaying the facade if not the substance of gentry dominance well into the nineteenth century, but those worlds were indisputably a part of the past. Nineteenth-century Southerners, fond of history and tradition as well as rising profits, would continue to pay homage—selectively—to some of the ideals of that old gentry culture, but there were far too many of them, spread out over the vast expanse of the old Southwest and displaying an ethnic and religious diversity that would have been unthinkable in the time of King Carter or even William Byrd, for any one family or group of families to claim undisputed cultural or economic hegemony. The pressures of economic competition and the friction produced by competing socioreligious systems would persist in causing tension in the social order of Lunenburg and of the antebellum South more generally, but in the long run the common commitment to expanded agricultural productivity, and to the slave system that made that productivity possible, led to an accommodation of differences and an unprecedented solidarity based on an allegiance to a "Southern" way of life.

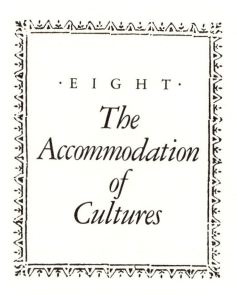

· E I G H T ·

The Accommodation of Cultures

The forces of economic and demographic growth that gave most Lunenburg households an increased level of agricultural output and a slightly enhanced standard of physical comfort appear to have cut across the religious and ethnic lines that had worked to divide the white citizens of the county during the prerevolutionary period. While growing similarities in economic circumstance did not eliminate the cultural differences that separated evangelicals, Episcopalians, and unbelievers, they did, in combination with a revised institutional structure that removed the privileges and powers of sanction from the Episcopal church, greatly reduce the conflicts those differences had previously generated.

• TOWARD RELIGIOUS PLURALISM

The unequal distribution of economic and political power which gave disproportionate advantage to the members of the Anglican gentry elite in the prerevolutionary period did not disappear completely after the war, but there was a marked trend toward an evening of those imbalances. The formal power of the Protestant

Episcopal Church had declined markedly; most obvious, it no longer possessed the legal power to command attendance at its weekly services, and it could not command the taxpayers to support either its doctrines or its ministers. And in a display not so much of militant repudiation as of unconcern and apathy, many of Lunenburg's citizens—both well-to-do and middling—simply ceased to take an interest in the affairs of the church once compulsory support had been eliminated.

The members of the church vestry, who in the decade before the Revolution constituted a group nearly synonymous with wealth and political power in the county, were by the end of the eighteenth century steadily losing their claim to preeminence. By 1795 fewer than half the members of the county court had also served the Episcopal church as vestrymen, and only five of the twenty wealthiest men in the county had held that post. By 1815 the separation of secular authority and the old church was even more marked. Only three of the eighteen justices and only five of the twenty wealthiest men in the county had served as vestrymen.[1] As might be expected, certain prominent family names closely associated with positions of leadership in the economic, political, and religious life of the county in earlier years (Chambers, Billups, Stokes, and Taylor) continued to appear on the lists of court justices and of the affluent, but in many cases those sons and relations of the pillars of the prerevolutionary Anglican church did not choose to follow the example of their elders and devote their time to serving the Episcopal church.[2] Disestablishment facilitated the movement of at least a few prominent Lunenburg citizens out of the ranks of the Episcopal church altogether and into the ranks of what previously had been defined as "dissenting" religions. The most prominent example of this trend was the Rev. Clement Read, the ·grandson of the great patriarch of Lunenburg and one of the pillars of the Anglican church during the formative years of the county. The younger Read, after completing a course of study at the newly established Presbyterian college of Hampden-Sydney in neighboring Prince Edward County, was received as a candidate in the Presbyterian ministry in 1788. Ultimately Read spurned Presbyterianism, becoming instead one of the leaders in the emergent Republican Methodist Church.[3] The growth of the Republican

Methodists, just one of the variants of Methodism that was making its influence felt in the Southside by the turn of the century, was itself another sign of the growing acceptance within the county of a pluralistic cultural-religious standard. The Republican Methodists, like the Presbyterians, constituted a thoroughly "respectable" group within Lunenburg, and while Episcopalians continued to enjoy a slight preponderance among the economic and political elite of the county, members of other denominations increasingly appeared in the ranks of the wealthy and powerful. Even the Separate Baptists, who in Lunenburg continued to represent the most radical and numerically significant alternative to the values of traditional religion, had by 1815 managed to place four of their members on the county court; one, Joseph Yarborough, could be counted among the fifteen wealthiest men in the county, and several other members could boast of landholdings and slaveholdings that placed them in the upper 10 percent of the county's population.[4]

Those members of the Baptist rank and file who continued to live in Lunenburg through both the pre- and postrevolutionary eras also showed a tendency to improve their fortunes in the years following their decision to join the church. They were men like Benjamin Evans, who owned neither land nor slaves when he first joined the Baptist church in 1769, but who by 1782 owned 660 acres and five slaves and by the time of his death in 1806 possessed eight slaves, five horses, and an estate worth over $3,000. Similarly, Benjamin Hawkins, who like Evans owned no land or slaves when he joined the Meherrin church in 1771, had become a solid member of Lunenburg's middling planter class at his death in 1802, leaving an estate of 100 acres and four slaves. Other Baptists converts also indicated the growing appeal of the Baptists to men and women endowed with more substantial material advantages. William Stone, who was listed as a tithable on his father's medium-sized plantation in 1769, deserted the Anglicans for the Meherrin church in 1776. By the time of his death in 1802, he had accumulated an estate of nearly 1,000 acres and six slaves worth over $2,000.[5]

The narrowing of the gap between Episcopalians and dissenters was perhaps best symbolized, though not typified, by the estates of the two leading religious figures in the county's eighteenth-century history, those of James Craig, Anglican minister of Cumberland Parish, and John Williams, minister of the Meherrin church and spiritual leader of perhaps a dozen other Baptist congregations within and outside the county. Antagonists for over a quarter of a century, Craig and Williams died within a few months of one another in 1795. Craig, who presided first over the move toward respectability and subsequently the spiritual and financial decline of the Episcopal church in Lunenburg, had over the course of his thirty-five-year tenure as minister acquired virtually all the trappings of a Virginia gentleman. His estate, valued at £2,744, contained forty-two slaves, eight feather beds, a variety of walnut furniture, an eight-day clock, a substantial quantity of silver plate, and all the equipment—stills, boilers, hydrometers—to run a distillery! The quantity of slaves, horses, cattle, hogs, and farm implements in Craig's estate indicates that his was a working plantation designed to produce an income substantially above that which he received as minister of his flock. His inventory listed over 10,000 pounds of tobacco in his possession at the time of his death, and his gristmill, probably the busiest in the county, served not only his own needs but also those of many of his parishioners and neighbors.[6] All in all, Craig's estate suggests the life not only of a genteel and learned parson but of a country gentleman as well.

Although far more modest than Craig's estate, the estate of John Williams was not that of a man shut off from worldly concerns. Williams had earlier attempted, apparently without success, to persuade the Meherrin church to provide him with an independent income that would allow him to pursue his ministerial duties free from the distractions of the tobacco fields or the marketplace, but when that support proved inadequate, he evidently devoted his own efforts to those concerns, with results that left him a comfortable if not opulent estate at his death.[7] Valued at £902, Williams's estate included sixteen slaves, a walnut chest, a library of nearly one hundred books, and the usual farm implements found on a plantation devoted to the raising of wheat and tobacco. Williams's accumulation of slaves, which had increased steadily, coincided both with the growing reliance of many of his Baptist congregants on unfree labor and with the noticeable quieting of Baptist opposition to the peculiar institution. Williams himself appears to have fallen into a mode of antislavery sentiment that stressed amelioration rather than abolition. In his will he provided that any of his legatees found guilty of mistreating the slaves in their possession be disinherited, and he stipulated "that if any of the Negroes are sold, it should be at a private sale, and to only those that are of indisputable Human characters, or Such if possible, that the Negroes should choose to serve."[8]

Lunenburg's Baptists had always been ambivalent about the institution of slavery, and even during the fervent years of evangelical awakening in the 1760s and early 1770s the church stopped short of outright condemnation of slavery. The evangelical Baptists were not premillennialists; their primary concern was the redemption of individual sinners and not the radical change of a whole social system. Slavery had always been a part of the social system in which they had lived, and while the Baptists of the prerevolutionary period showed far more concern for both the material and spiritual condition of individual slaves, they never meant their stewardship of black laborers to be transformed into a crusade against the institution itself.

Yet the tenor of the Baptists' attitudes toward their own black bondsmen and bondswomen and those of their neighbors had changed unmistakably between the time when they were a distinct, countercultural force in the prerevolutionary years and the early nineteenth century, when Lunenburg's Baptists began to approach the standard of the county's other citizens in economic circumstances and social station. For example, the Meherrin congregation remained much more active than any other religious group in encouraging slaves to become members, but the records show both a marked decrease in efforts to prevent cruelty at the hands of white Baptist masters and an increased tendency to use the doctrines of the church as a means of oppression. Whereas in 1772 the church went on record as opposing excessive cruelty in the whipping of slaves and in that same year moved against a member for mistreating his slaves, by the late 1790s the record is silent with respect to censures directed at white masters for cruel treatment and more abundant in its chronicle of punishments of black members such as "Robertson's George," who was disciplined for "several elopements from his master . . . and of sundry other evils which circumstances are well known," or Winn's Ben, who was excommunicated "for attempting to bead with a white woman."[9]

The wavering of moral concern about the institution of slavery was not confined to the Meherrin Baptists. By the early 1790s, John Leland, one of the Virginia Baptist leaders whose abhorrence of slavery was stern and consistent, found to his dismay that fellow Baptists in the state were growing decidedly touchy about his efforts to make antislavery ideology a central part of Baptist church policy. Leland was able to use his considerable influence to persuade the Virginia Baptist General Committee to pass a resolution denouncing slavery as a moral evil, but when that resolution was transmitted to individual congregations, he discovered that the combination of a growing defensiveness about their own ownership of slaves and a continuing determination to defend congregational autonomy produced a chilly reaction among his brethren. The Roanoke Association, a group of separate Baptist churches immediately to the west of Lunenburg in Pittsylvania County, responded that they were "not unanimously clear" about either the morality or immorality of slavery, but then asserted that "neither the General Committee nor any Religious Society whatever has the least right to concern therein." The message was much the same from the churches within the Strawberry Association, serving Bedford, Botetourt, and Franklin counties; they answered in 1792 with the injunction "We advise them not to interfere with it."[10]

We cannot discount those feelings of humanitarianism and limited egalitarianism which continued to evoke in the Baptists a greater concern for the spiritual life of their black bondsmen and bondswomen than that evinced by most other white citizens of the region. Yet the increased dependence of the rank and file of the church on slave labor may have contributed to a decline in antislavery zeal among the evangelicals. As a disillusioned Baptist leader, Richard Dozier, put it in 1783: "They have taken themselves out of the world, and at the same time [are] following the world."[11] To follow the world of the late-eighteenth-century Virginia Southside meant to avert one's eyes from the moral dilemma of slavery.

The twin developments of a general rise in prosperity and an evening of the distribution of wealth and power among the different cultural-religious groups in the county were not sufficient to quell conflict among those groups altogether. In those time-honored displays of hostility, nurtured both by an instinctive suspicion of the unknown and by heightened competition for souls in a marketplace that was now officially guaranteed to be an open one, Episcopalians, Presbyterians, Baptists, and Methodists continued to cast invective freely at one another. James Craig, in spite of losing his legal monopoly over the meetinghouses of the parish, continued to regard the use of those buildings by other sects as an insult both to the Divine Being and to standards of gentility and decency. For their part, the Presbyterians continued to practice their brand of Calvinism in a fairly "respectable" fashion, often feeling more comfortable with the styles of the formerly established church than with those of the other dissenting sects with whom they had much more in common doctrinally. In 1801 a group of six Presbyterians from the area around Lunenburg did meet with ten Baptists and ten Methodists to discuss the differences that had divided them in the past and to see if they could agree on a means for living "more friendly than we have done, and even to commune together," but in spite of an agreement reached by the representatives of each of those sects, the legacy of suspicion continued. The Presbyterians in particular resisted a union with the other, more enthusiastic and less genteel congregations, and their ministers continued to view with disdain the excesses of the Methodists and the Baptists.[12]

The Methodists, whose growth throughout the state of Virginia in the last decade of the eighteenth century and first decade of the nineteenth was probably more dramatic than that of any other sect, continued to concentrate their successes in conversion in Brunswick County, to the south of Lunenburg, but they counted among their converts such prominent Lunenburg citizens as John Glenn and Nicholas Hobson, both members of the county court and representatives to the House of Delegates. The diary of Bishop John Early, raised as a Baptist but by 1807 a Methodist itinerant who preached throughout the Southside, indicates clearly that whatever the Baptists and Methodists might have had in common in terms of rhetorical style, denominational jealousies kept the members of the two sects apart. Like all good evangelicals, Early viewed the impiety and sinfulness around him both as a reproach to the inadequacy of the prevailing religious leaders and as a rich and fertile field for his own efforts; appraising the "wavering minds of these people," he prayed to "Lord Jesus . . . [to] deprive the devil and the Baptists of their expectations (for John's people—the Baptists—are contented if they can divide the Methodist classes and then plunge them under the water. They put out the fire and cry out to heaven all their lives and depend on their conversion and Baptism to carry them to heaven without any more trouble)."[13] The theological differences separating the Baptists and Methodists— the Methodists' revulsion at the Baptists' continued commitment to the rite of adult baptism, and the strict "Calvinism" of the Baptists as opposed to the Arminian tendencies of the Methodists—were probably accentuated by the competition for converts between the two sects.

The precise dating of upswings and downturns in religious fervor in early America is a difficult business, as the variations in circumstance among localities even caused the impact of the First Great Awakening to be felt in Virginia some thirty years after the first stirrings of the movement were felt in Pennsylvania and New England. The Second Great Awakening, rather than being a single explosion of religious piety, appears to have consisted of many ripples of enthusiasm, emanating not from a central source of inspiration but rather from multitudinous local agencies of evangelicalism and stimulated by competition among the growing number of religious sects in America. It is reasonably clear that the competition in Lunenburg had reached one of its high points by the end of the first decade of the nineteenth century, for the Baptist and Methodist preachers of the period record with satisfaction the conversion of dozens, sometimes hundreds, of souls at a single meeting.

Early's successes on behalf of the Methodists during this period seem as emotional and dramatic as those of the Baptists forty years earlier. Preaching at Prospect, about ten miles from Lunenburg, he recorded

a powerful, awful, happy, solemn time indeed. Night and day the work went on. The preachers and people were united as one heart. Sinners trembled, saints rejoiced aloud, and great preaching indeed. My poor soul was truly fed and made fat and about fifty converted and nineteen joined the Society. Of what great things my God can do.[14]

The Baptist pioneer John Williams, dead for more than a decade when Early recorded his experiences, could not have wished for more. The only important difference between the revivals promoted by Williams and his followers in the 1760s and 1770s and those fostered by Methodists like Early in the early nineteenth century was the more self-conscious way in which the Methodists organized and orchestrated their revivals. As Early was led to exclaim in 1807: "A great institution, that of camp meeting. An awful sight to hear preachers preaching and prayers and singing, crying and shouting in every direction. The tents, erected and stretched out for shelter; candles and fire and the cries that were heard night and day."[15] Those camp meetings, lasting four and five days at a time and sometimes staffed by batteries of preachers and exhorters, were designed both to awaken the fervor of those neglected souls of the Virginia Southside and to provide that same feeling of close-knit community that was such an important part of the emotional experience of the Baptists in the prerevolutionary years. Unlike the Baptist revivals, which were highly individualized from congregation to congregation and from preacher to preacher, the Methodist revivals were, as Donald Mathews has noted, an "organizing process." After the camp meeting had ended and the tents had been folded, the leaders of the Methodist hierarchy would make certain that other representatives of the faith would follow up on that initial awakening of enthusiasm, attempting to enroll the recently converted more permanently in the ranks of the Society and ultimately supplying those newly formed congregations of the awakened with trained ministers capable of sustaining and nourishing their faith.[16] That organizing process, which worked so well in Kentucky and even in counties like Brunswick to the south of Lunenburg, never took hold quite so firmly in Lunenburg itself. The sinners were awakened and converted temporarily, but as often as not they either lapsed back into lives that did not include regular church attendance or, perhaps just as dangerous from the point of view of many, they fell under the influence of the equally fervent and more firmly entrenched Baptists.

The Baptists remained the one denomination that continued to evoke the greatest suspicion and distrust from all the others, for in spite of the growing wealth and respectability of many Baptists, and in spite of some signs of a cooling of their evangelical ardor, they continued too often in style and doctrine to offer the most dramatic repudiation of the norms of the traditional society. The ups and downs of the Baptists' fortunes during the years between the disestablishment of the Anglican church and the Second Great Awakening were probably typical of those of the sect elsewhere in the state. In 1808 the membership of the county's five Baptist churches stood at 315, and by most accounts that number was on the increase after a steady downturn in membership in the previous decade.[17] During his tour of Virginia and North Carolina in 1797, Isaac Backus received steady complaints from Southside ministers about the low state of religion in the area. "Iniquity abounds," he noted, "and the love of many waxes cold." The Meherrin church had fallen on particularly hard times. It struggled without success for more than a decade to find a replacement for John Williams after his death in 1795. By 1803 the membership at Meherrin had dwindled to only eighteen, a condition which evidently persisted for a few more years, as the minute books of the church for 1807 carry the desultory notation that "the year 1807 was in a very languid state indeed . . . and no supply to the Church as a Pastor, so that there was no business enter'd on record."[18]

The seeds for that decline were probably sown even before the disestablishment controversy had been resolved. In October 1776, John Williams had claimed that he felt it "an Intolerable burden upon his hands to support his family and live while things keep him so immersed in the world that he believes God is dishonored and the success of the Gospel in a great measure prevented." Williams desired "to live a more retired life, the things of the world taken off his hands," and to that end he proposed to turn over "the whole or at least the greater part of his Estate" if his parishioners would take over its management and provide him with the proceeds from it for his salary. The request probably could not have come at a worse time, with a substantial portion of the county's able-bodied male citizens away on militia duty and with complaints about economic hardship throughout the county in general at an all-time high. As a consequence, the Meherrin meeting, in spite of its obvious affection and loyalty to Williams, refused to accede.[19] Whether this dispute led in any direct way to Williams's decision to move out of the district is not clear, but in the spring of 1779 he and about a dozen members of the Meherrin church obtained leave from the meeting to settle on the Yadkin River in Surry County in northwestern North Carolina.

Williams's new church on the Yadkin was covenanted in June 1779, but the settlers soon "met with such distress from the Tories and other ill-advised persons and the British army that they were obliged to move back again to Virginia in the fall of the year 1780, and lived in a scattered and dispersed circumstance till the beginning of the year 1784."[20] This move, coming as it did when the War of Independence was taking its heaviest toll on church membership, shattered the stability of the Meherrin church. The records of the period indicate only sporadic meetings and, with the departure of Elijah Baker for the Virginia Eastern Shore just a few years before Williams's move, a desperate lack of leadership. Williams returned to the congregation in 1784 at the height of the disestablishment controversy and took charge almost immediately. By 1790 he had worked out an arrangement whereby some of the duties of his plantation were taken over by others, but with his death in 1795 the congregation once again suffered from the effects of his absence.[21]

One of Williams's principal strengths as both a religious and a political leader had been his ability to steer his flock down a relatively moderate course. Although he embraced a strictly Calvinist doctrine and chose to identify with the Separatist rather than the Regular Baptist tradition, Williams was sufficiently moderate in his own personal demeanor that he was generally able to keep his congregation from indulging in dangerous schisms. In December 1774 he had persuaded the Meherrin congregation to offer "free and open communion kept up with all orderly Baptists without distinction with regard to the Term Regular & Separate." In the following year, in the midst of a bitter divisive feud among Baptists throughout the colony between Arminians and Calvinists, Williams, though clearly identified with the Calvinist wing when the two groups broke up into separate bodies at the meeting of the district association, was the one who ultimately restored some semblance of harmony to the association.[22]

The tendency toward schism was something with which the Separate Baptists always had to contend, and after Williams's death those tendencies would be given freer rein, a development that would affect not only the Meherrin congregation but also the congregations in Reedy Creek and Flat Rock. Those congregations, now under the direction of James Shelburne, a mechanic by trade, were in the forefront of the "restoration movement," claiming that the Scriptures and the Scriptures alone "were a sufficient rule of faith and practice" and that all human addition in the form of creeds or confessions of faith were invalid. This position, which in the 1830s became the basis of the Campbellite and later the Disciples of Christ movement, only added confusion to a religious climate in which virtually every sect was seeking to prove that it was truer to the meaning of the Scriptures than all the rest.[23]

The Baptists then had to contend not only with the customary suspicion of traditionalists from the Episcopal church, the continuing scorn of those unbelievers who viewed their rites as superstitious delusions, and the heightened competition from the Methodists, but also with discord within their own ranks. In spite of these obstacles, and in the face of fluctuating waves of piety that would cause Baptist ministers alternatively to bemoan the spiritual lethargy of the citizenry and then to praise the power of the Lord in awakening those same citizens from their slumbers, the number of Baptist congregations in the Meherrin Association grew from six at the time of the Revolution to sixteen in 1810.[24]

The competition and conflict evident in the religious life of the county in the era following disestablishment must be seen in a context entirely different from that which shaped the conflicts of the prerevolutionary years. In that earlier period the notion of a single religious-cultural orthodoxy, established by law and charged with overseeing the virtue of all the citizens, made the notion of religious or cultural pluralism seem dangerous and threatening to most of the men charged with upholding order in their communities. That "order," always in a fragile condition in the inherently unstable environment of the frontier, was dramatically threatened by the evangelicals, who took advantage of the formlessness of the cultural and institutional life of the region by attempting to offer new alternatives not only in religious belief but in social behavior and organization as well. As we have seen, the evangelicals did not succeed entirely in overthrowing the old sociocultural value system and replacing it with their own, but by the time of the passage of Jefferson's Bill for Religious Freedom they had at least been guaranteed the right to compete for the minds and souls of the county's citizens on equal terms with the Episcopal gentry culture. With the legal backing of the state removed from their arsenal, the men who stood for the values of the traditional religious culture were less capable than ever before of retaining their monopoly. The competition for converts that ensued may have caused jealousy and even anger among contending religious groups, but no longer could the Episcopal gentry argue that the preservation of the social order itself hung in the balance. Even in those areas where traditional gentry values were least threatened, the state of Virginia had committed itself to a more open-ended definition of how salvation was to be achieved and how life on this earth was to be lived. Once that decision to secularize the state had been made, a sizable area of contention between the evangelical and gentry cultures disappeared.

At precisely the time when legal safeguards to the physical safety and institutional equality of the dissenting sects were being adopted, those sects themselves began to offer somewhat less of a threat to the established order than they had in previous times. For at least a quarter of a century after the Revolution the combination of wartime disruption, an increased attention to the worldly concern of a growing tobacco economy, and the absence of a formidable officially sanctioned opposition such as had existed before the Revolution all served to render most of the evangelical sects in Lunenburg less distinct on socioeconomic grounds and less self-consciously militant in their rejection of the values and life-styles of their opponents. As we have seen, there is clear evidence that the Baptists, Methodists, and Presbyterians were approaching at least approximate parity with the Episcopalians in terms of wealth and political power. But as the evangelicals became more comfortably placed in the social structure of their region, they began to organize and comport themselves in a fashion less indicative of an emotional attachment to an undifferentiated community of pure and true believers and more closely congruent with the less intense, more explicitly hierarchical ordering associated with a structural, status-defining mode of social organization. The 1770 journal of the Rev. John Williams bursts with references to the brethren "joining together," "all . . . warm with the love of God," "Christians all afire with the love of God; Assembly praising of God with a loud voice," and "the Christians . . . shouting, sinners trembling and falling down convulsed, the devil raging and blaspheming, which kindled the flame of the Christians." Williams described the mode of preaching which produced those reactions variously as "sweet exhortation," "feeling the gift," or preaching with liberty."[25] By the 1790s, however, that tone had begun to change, with Williams noting in the Meherrin church minute book in 1794 that he had "discoursed learnedly" to his congregation. To some extent this attitude was in keeping with the aspirations of a man who late in life was working toward the establishment of a Baptist seminary of higher learning and who at the time of his death was the one Baptist preacher in the state to be entrusted with writing the denomination's official history, but it also suggests an altered emphasis within the faith.[26] In effect the enthusiasm of a shared emotional and spiritual experience—the exemplification of what Victor Turner has called *communitas*—appears to have been giving way to the more decorous and well-ordered form of the "learned discourse," a form long familiar to the Episcopal-gentry world.[27]

The Methodist camp meetings of the early nineteenth century do suggest a return to that spirit of *communitas*, with hundreds of Southside citizens gathering for days at a time in huge voluntary associations in which "sinners trembled and cried aloud for mercy," "saints rejoiced," and the ordinary folk, many of them simply curious about the spectacle, could be heard "crying and shouting in every direction."[28] However important these meetings may have been as an emotional release and a means of achieving a sense of common identity and purpose among residents of a still highly individualistic and mobile society, the ties that bound the Methodist communicants together were not reinforced by the intense feelings of both legal and cultural alienation that the Baptists had felt when they set their faces against the established church in the prerevolutionary years. In the postrevolutionary period the

Methodists, and to some extent the Baptists too, may have rejected the decorous forms of traditional religion, but in their economic aspirations and daily social behavior they were moving toward at least a partial accommodation with those who had upheld the standard of traditional society.

• TOWARD A VARIEGATED COMMUNITY

The multiplication of religious denominations in Lunenburg was paralleled by the multiplication of a host of other public and private services and institutions that brought the county's citizens together on a more consistent and more varied basis. The individual church meetinghouse had always served as an institution that simultaneously bound individuals together and set them apart from others of differing religious belief, while the proliferation of secular avenues of community involvement tended to cut across denominational lines, reaching out ever more widely to all the population.

It is not surprising that most of these developments were tied to the continuing development of Lunenburg's economy. The county's road system, crucial to the marketing of tobacco, steadily expanded, reaching out in all directions beyond the county while at the same time adding new arteries of transportation and communication within the county. Long-distance travel was still not an easy matter even by the nineteenth century. Most of Lunenburg's residents only rarely traveled beyond the county's borders, but for those merchants and peddlers who did need to cover long distances, the condition of the roads was a constant trial. One itinerant peddler, traveling through Lunenburg in 1807, recorded a series of mishaps—rivers and streams that became impossible to ford after even a slight rainfall, bridges out of repair, ferries running on unpredictable schedules, and main roads so poorly maintained that the peddler would lose his way even within a few miles of the courthouse.[29] And the peddler was doing most of his traveling on those primary roads of the region connecting one courthouse to another. It is plain that the secondary roads connecting settlements within the county were little more than dirt paths, suitable perhaps for riders on horseback but not for wagons rolling hogsheads of tobacco to market. Still, the state of transportation in the county had improved markedly since 1750, when there was only one tolerable road running across the center of the county and, even since 1780, when fully half the citizens remained unconnected with any major roads leading out of the county.[30]

The settlements located along those roads continued to be both widely dispersed and relatively modest in size, but they had made some progress between the time of the Revolution and the 1830s. The Lunenburg courthouse, now located at a site that had achieved the status of a township and renamed Lewiston, was by 1827 constructed of brick with two large pillars adorning its entrance and surrounded by twenty dwellings, including two large general stores and two taverns (see Figure 7). By that time the town had a resident population of some seventy-five citizens, including wheelwrights, saddle and harness makers, blacksmiths, two lawyers, and a physician, and was served by a daily stagecoach running between Petersburg and Williamsburg, North Carolina. And if Lewiston had become the center of both government and transportation in the county, there were other sites (Byrdie's Store in the northern part of the county; Columbian Grove in the south, near the Mecklenburg County line; Haleysburg, in the west, on the border between Lunenburg and Charlotte) that provided regular postal service, at least one general store, and an ordinary for the convivial entertainment of the nearby residents.[31]

The development of these centers of activity, spread relatively evenly throughout the county, gives us our first glimpse of something resembling neighborhoods. There were other sites, perhaps not sufficiently well established to be designated post office centers, but nevertheless serving as important points of congregation for settlers in their vicinity. Moore's Ordinary in the northwest corner of the county, near the Prince Edward County line, served citizens in both Lunenburg and Prince Edward, providing a well-stocked general store and, attached to it, one of the county's most popular taverns. Taverns such as Moore's and Meriwether Hunt's provided one sort of convivial entertainment, complete with food,

FIGURE 7. *Lunenburg County Courthouse. Construction completed in 1827. Photo by the author.*

drink, and lodging, but there were probably a dozen other publicly recognized but not legally sanctioned houses of "private entertainment" which also served as points of coming together for male and female citizens of the county alike.[32]

The most obvious basis for these local neighborhood centers was the ever more densely populated network of kin relations within the county. Even in 1750, with a young, newly arrived, and highly mobile population, ties of kinship probably constituted the most meaningful basis of association within the fragile network of community relations within the county. Those who had kin ties in Lunenburg in those early years were likely to patent or purchase land adjacent to their relatives, creating at least one network of familiar—and familial—association in an otherwise socially frag-

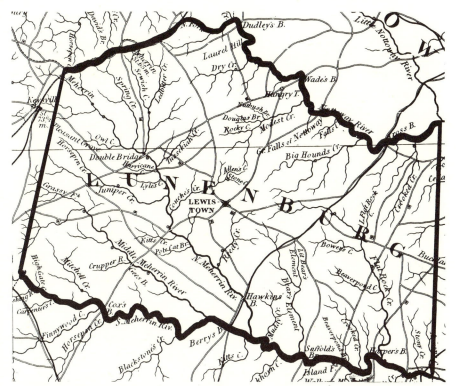

MAP 5. *Lunenburg County, 1859. This is a small section of a nine-piece map drafted by Ludwig von Bucholtz in 1859. Bucholtz's work was based in considerable measure on Herman Boye's 1825 map of Virginia. Courtesy of Virginia State Library, Richmond, Va.*

mented environment. By the 1780s, as the population of the county began to stabilize, the density of related households in the county had increased dramatically, with nearly 75 percent of the households sharing patrilineal kin ties with others, and over 10 percent of the households being part of an extended patrilineal network of ten or more families. By 1815 the patterns of patrilineal kinship had become still more extended, with nearly 20 percent of the households of the county sharing the same surname with ten or more other households. See Figure 8.[33]

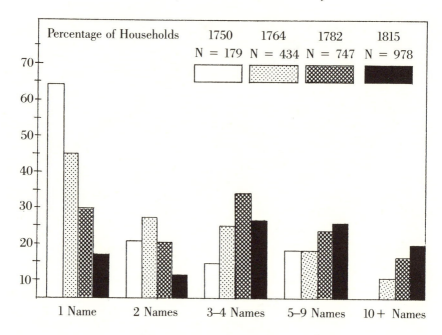

FIGURE 8. *Patrilineal Kinship in Lunenburg County, 1750–1815.*
SOURCE: Landon C. Bell, *Sunlight on the Southside: Lists of Tithes, Lunenburg County, Virginia, 1748–1783* (Philadelphia, 1931), pp. 122–61, 228–46; Real and Personal Property Tax Lists, Lunenburg County, 1782, 1815, Virginia State Library, Richmond, Va.

Occurring among residents whose roots in the county went back in time the longest, this growing concentration of kin ties was similarly reflected in the structure of power within the county. By 1815 a handful of families (the Blackwells, the Stokeses, the Ragsdales, the Gees) appeared far more numerously and consistently among the economic and political elite of the county. Most of these families had begun to achieve prominence just after the Revolution, but judging from the frequency with which their names appeared on the list of the county's economic and political leaders thereafter, they had also acquired an ability, not enjoyed by previous leaders of the county, to pass down their privileged positions from one generation to the next.[34]

The courthouse site was the place where the enhanced power of the political elite was displayed most openly, and it remained the spot at which the legal, mercantile, and convivial activities of all the individual neighborhoods of the county came together. By the first decade of the nineteenth century, itinerant peddlers in the Southside and western Piedmont had organized a series of mercantile fairs held at each of the courthouses of the region at least once a month on court day. The success of those fairs depended on a sufficient number of people coming together to allow the dozen or so peddlers who converged on the courthouse site to sell enough of their wares to make the miles and sometimes days of travel worth their while. It did not always work out as the peddlers hoped. The pair that traveled through Lunenburg in December 1807 nearly had their prospects wiped out by a rainstorm that caused "not more than 10 Dollars taken among the 5 which were there." Similarly, when they had arrived in Bedford County two weeks earlier, bad weather also plagued them, one of the peddlers noting: "A very Poor Court, no fighting or gouging, very few Drunken People." But there were good times as well. In nearby Pittsylvania County, business on court days for the two was brisk:

There we[re] a Number of People Collected there to see quarter Races which they had that day and the preceding one. Grog as usual had Great effect upon them and created much Noise (no fighting for a Wonder, neither was there any at Henry altho the Noisyed Crew ¾'s of them in the state of intoxication drinking out of the tin Cups there being not a Single Glass upon the premises).[35]

The decorum (or lack of it) that often prevailed on court day was indicative of a society whose manners and mores were still shaped in large measure by the openness, independent spirit, and occasional crudeness of the frontier, but the very fact that the travels of peddlers across the Southside had become sufficiently routinized that mercantile fairs, and often the horse races, cockfights, and drinking bouts that accompanied them, had become publicly scheduled events was another sign that the county and its constituent neighborhoods were developing an interconnectedness not apparent in previous eras.

In spite of the increased prosperity, the expanded transportation networks, and the multiplication of centers of community congregation, Lunenburg remained as closely attached to the backcountry culture of its early history as it did to the culture of the Old Dominion. In common with the rest of the commonwealth, Tidewater and backcountry alike, Lunenburg's citizens continued to display a nearly complete unconcern for public education. In spite of the high-sounding proposals of such luminaries as Thomas Jefferson, who firmly believed that an educated citizenry was essential for the continuation of America's experiment in republican liberty, Virginia's political leaders did almost nothing to provide an equal and easily accessible means of educating the youth of the state. Belatedly, in 1796, the General Assembly passed legislation that would have enabled each county to establish its own public school system, but it left the funding of that plan up to the counties themselves, a provision which doomed public education in virtually every county in the commonwealth. In Lunenburg, lack of concern for public education seems also to have extended to private institutions of learning, for there is no indication that the gentry of the county ever made a move to establish private academies of the type that were common in eastern Virginia. As in so many aspects of its cultural life, Lunenburg's successful adoption of the agricultural economy of eastern Virginia was not accompanied by a corresponding commitment to those values of learning and gentility which had originally been such an important part of the gentry ideal.[36]

This lack of concern for formal institutions of learning and for the high culture automatically associated with those institutions did not mean that the citizenry was content with the low levels of "practical" learning that marked the county's early history. In the mid-eighteenth century, when most householders were subsistence farmers in the most fundamental sense, the literacy rate among male heads of households stood at around 50 percent of the population. By the time of the Revolution that rate had risen to 60 percent, and by the early nineteenth century, a time in which the vast majority of households grew crops for a world market and consistently entered into a wide variety of mercantile agreements, the number of literate males had risen to over 80 percent of the population.[37] This improvement in the literacy rate, an advance that allowed ever greater numbers of citizens to share in a print culture that in earlier years was the exclusive preserve of a privileged few, was yet another force working toward more cohesive and inclusive forms of community life.

• THE AFRO-AMERICAN COMMUNITY

The black population of Lunenburg, so vitally important to the county's improved position in the tobacco economy of the Old Dominion, remains only barely visible in our survey of the expansion of economic opportunity and proliferation of religious and community institutions in the county. That population, which by 1820 accounted for 64 percent of the people living in the county, probably experienced as substantial a change in circumstance between the mid-eighteenth century and the early nineteenth century as any other part of the population, yet the very looseness of the bonds of social organization in places like Lunenburg makes the history of those changes extraordinarily difficult to reconstruct. In the earliest years of the county's history, when blacks were a distinct minority and when most of the slaveowning households possessed just one or two slaves, the material condition of most slaves was probably not drastically different from that of most whites. If blacks lived in crude housing and possessed only the scantest material comforts, then so too did most whites, freeholders and dependent laborers alike. And for better and for worse, those blacks living on small plantations could not have experienced too much separation from their white masters; the demands of an intensive agricultural system and the constraints imposed by the modest housing stock of the region made it necessary for most blacks and whites to live and work closely together.

Even as the slave population of Lunenburg increased (see Table 7), the pattern of concentration of those slaves remained essentially different from that prevailing in eastern Virginia. At no point in the county's history did anyone accumulate the amount of capital that enabled a Robert Carter or a William Byrd to assemble nearly complete villages of bondsmen and bondswomen, many with highly specialized skills, on their plantations. The smaller scale of plantation life in Lunenburg permitted a degree of personal interaction between white and black that was not possible on more elaborately structured plantations, but at the same time the dispersion of blacks among many relatively isolated farmsteads worked to inhibit the development of the slave family life and community institutions that came into being in areas of Virginia where the concentration of slaves was greater.[38]

The one community institution that seemed to reach out most aggressively to include blacks within its ranks was the Baptist church meeting. Much of the early suspicion and distrust that Anglican gentry felt toward the Baptists was provoked by those open-air meetings for exhortation and baptism in which large numbers of blacks and whites alike came together, confessed their sins, and accepted in common God's gift of the new birth. For a brief time in the late 1750s and early 1760s, a portion of the black community around Lunenburg was given an even stronger and more distinctive sense of its own religious identity through its affiliation with the Bluestone Baptist church. A substantial portion of the membership of that church was composed of blacks from one of William Byrd's plantations in the area, one of the few plantations to support more than just a handful of slaves. For a time the church had a black preacher and some fifty black members who could be counted "bright and shining Christians." When Byrd sold his holdings in the region and the slaves were dispersed, the Bluestone church itself faded from existence, weakening still further the bonds of community that those black slaves had once enjoyed.[39]

As we have already seen, by the postrevolutionary period the attitude of white Baptists toward their black brethren had begun to harden. More solidly connected to the county, with substantial holdings in slaves themselves, white Baptist leaders tended increasingly to use the religious doctrines of their church as a means of social control over the slave population rather than as a requirement of mutual submission. As slaves came to outnumber whites in the county, the need for control over blacks was perceived to be much greater. By the time of the Methodist insurgence in the first decade of the nineteenth century, evangelical religion was still an important spiritual and social gathering point for Lunenburg's black residents, but the Southside Methodists, even more than the Baptists, were committed to a society in which blacks were kept under close surveillance.[40]

In some senses, then, slave life in early-nineteenth-century Lunenburg may have combined all the worst features of chattel slavery across the antebellum South. The black men and women who lived under the slave regimen were part of an economic system dependent on the continued expansion of production of a single crop, tobacco, without much of the diversification of skills that marked the Tidewater economy even during the years of its most concerted commitment to that same crop. Few if any of the plantation owners who controlled those slaves had either the economic resources or the inclination to indulge the instincts toward patriarchy that motivated some of the Tidewater's principal planters; and, living on plantations lacking the scale of Westover, Nomini Hall, or Mount Airy, Lunenburg's slaves were generally denied the benefit of numbers that permitted creation of alternative modes of community life on larger plantations.

One institution that probably did afford black slaves in Lunenburg, as well as slaves nearly everywhere in North America, some degree of autonomy and protection was that of the family. In a study of the eastern Chesapeake, Allan Kulikoff has demonstrated the way increases in population density, together with increases in the size of slave labor forces working on individual plantations, worked by the time of the Revolution both to increase the opportunity for family formation and to provide some measure of protection for those slave families that had come into being. Few plantations in Lunenburg ever developed the concentrations of slaves typical of the eastern Chesapeake, but population trends in Lunenburg in the early nineteenth century, trends which brought ever larger numbers of slaves in closer proximity to one another both within individual plantations and throughout the county at large, made it much easier for slave families to form and to stay together.[41]

Although we lack direct testimony indicating that life for black slaves in Lunenburg was bleaker than it was for slaves elsewhere in Virginia, the extraordinarily small size of the free black population in the county suggests some of the difficulty of obtaining freedom in a region where the slave-based tobacco economy was still expanding. Even if freedom were attained, the prospects for free blacks in an economic order dominated by unfree labor were decidedly less promising. In well-settled but economically stagnating Virginia counties like Richmond or Westmoreland, free blacks accounted for over 10 percent of the total black population and more than 5 percent of the population as a whole. In well-settled and increasingly urbanized areas, such as James City County, the number of free blacks in the population was even greater; in 1820 free blacks constituted 22 percent of the black population of James City County and 15 percent of the total population (see Table 5). In Lunenburg, by contrast, free blacks comprised less than 2 percent of the black population and just 1.2 percent of the total.

The handful of free blacks living in Lunenburg appears to have been scattered fairly widely across the county. All but a few remained dependent on whites for their livelihood, residing on plantations owned by others and serving as agricultural laborers, spinners, weavers, or, most common, simply "hirelings." A few had acquired skills, such as Zechariah Valentine, who was a shoemaker and also managed to maintain a small farm at the head of Kettlestick Creek; a few others had learned more specialized trades, such as coopering, which gave them the ability to contract out their services to a larger number of people within the county. On the whole, however, the lives of the free blacks in Lunenburg, like those of the slave population, were marked by a condition of harsh dependence, with scant opportunity within the county to improve that position.[42] Given those facts, it is not surprising that most blacks in Lunenburg chose to move on to more promising parts when they acquired freedom.

The twin forces of economic development and a partial religious accommodation did little to improve the lot of black people in the county by the early nineteenth century, but they were working to mitigate those conditions that had served to divide Lunenburg's white population in the past and to create new avenues of association that would bring the county's free white citizens in closer contact with one another. Moreover, the growing dependence of Lunenburg's planters on racial slavery, a dependence that reverberated with increasing force throughout the social and economic life of the county, would serve ever more powerfully to diminish previous sources of division and conflict and to create among the white citizens of the county not only a common system of values, but also a link between the cavalier culture of old Virginia and the newer, more expansive culture of the antebellum South. Like their counterparts in the Tidewater and Northern Neck a century earlier, the tobacco planters of Lunenburg had increased their production and their profits through an ever-greater reliance on unfree labor, and perhaps even more self-consciously than their counterparts to the east, the group identity and system of values of Lunenburg's white citizens would come to be shaped by the changing dynamic of black-white relations in the antebellum American South.

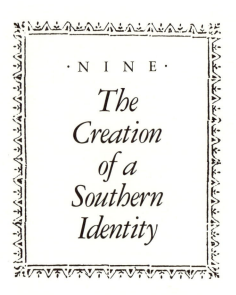

· N I N E ·

The Creation of a Southern Identity

From his vantage point in western North Carolina more than three decades ago, Wilbur J. Cash wrote about the transmission of the cavalier culture of traditional Virginia society to the frontier. He noted that there "was indeed a genuine, if small aristocracy in colonial Virginia . . . but this Virginia was not the great South. By paradox, it was not even all of Virginia. . . . All the rest, at the close of the Revolution, was still in the frontier or semi-frontier stage." With that combination of acuteness and overstatement that has made his work such an enduring one, Cash further argued that

to ignore the frontier and the [dimension of] time in setting up a conception of the social state of the Old South is to abandon reality. For the history of this South throughout a very great part of the period from the opening of the nineteenth century to the Civil War . . . is mainly the history of the roll of frontier upon frontier—and on to the frontier beyond.[1]

Cash went on to invent a parable to illustrate the process by which backcountry Southwestern frontiersmen and women were transformed into antebellum Southern aristocrats. That parable featured "a stout young Irishman [who] brought his bride into the

Carolina upcountry about 1800. He cleared a bit of land, built a log cabin of two rooms, and sat down to the pioneer life." The combination of cheap land, slave labor, and a newly profitable staple crop—cotton—would transform the lives of that Irishman and his family. Through the steady acquisition of more land, and most important, more slaves, he would produce ever more cotton, and from the returns of that crop his two-room log cabin would grow to six rooms and eventually be replaced altogether by a "big house."

It was not, to be truthful, a very grand house really. Built of lumber sawed on the place, it was a little crude and had not cost above a thousand dollars, even when the marble mantel was counted in. . . . But it was a house, it had great columns in front, and it was eventually painted white, and so, in this land of wide fields and pinewoods it seemed very imposing.

With the Irishman's growing wealth came enhanced personal authority. At the end of his life he served in the legislature, "grew extremely mellow in age and liked to pass his time in company arguing about Predestination and infant damnation, proving conclusively that cotton was king and that the damnyankee didn't dare do anything about it."[2]

There were significant differences between Cash's young Irishman and the hundreds of English and Irish men and women, Baptists, Presbyterians, and Methodists who settled in eighteenth- and early-nineteenth-century Lunenburg. Cash's archetype landed in the Carolina upcountry, thus sharing in the phenomenal prosperity brought by the cotton boom, a prosperity that was duplicated by others not only in South Carolina but also on other parts of the southwestern frontier as those settlers expanded westward in successive waves into Tennessee, Mississippi, Alabama, and Texas. In that sense the experience of Cash's agricultural entrepreneur was typical of many of those eighteenth- and early-nineteenth-century pioneers who *left* Lunenburg for parts farther south and westward. The most famous name connected with the history of Lunenburg is probably that of South Carolina's John C. Calhoun, grandson of John Caldwell, one of the first justices of the Lunenburg court and the leader of the group of Presbyterians who settled on Cub Creek in 1739. The Caldwells, along with many of the Presbyterians who formed the Cub Creek community, left the county for South Carolina in the late 1750s, where they appear to have settled once again as a group.[3]

Most of the men and women who chose to settle in Lunenburg were committing themselves to an agricultural economy that was not so specialized or expansive as the cotton monoculture of other parts of the South, yet whatever the differences between cotton and tobacco in terms of profitability or the precise rhythms of agricultural labor associated with each crop, it is plain that both Lunenburg tobacco growers and Carolina cotton planters came to share a common commitment to agrarianism and to the system of racial slavery that supported their agricultural economies. That commitment would be affirmed gradually and implicitly over the last two decades of the eighteenth century and the early decades of the nineteenth as Lunenburgers of all ethnic and religious affiliations expanded their investments in tobacco and slaves. During those years, however, their attachment to slave-based agriculture came also to have explicit expression in the political posture of the county in both state and national affairs. And while an identification as a "Virginian" was often insufficient to provide a unifying cultural standard for every citizen of Lunenburg in the prerevolutionary era, the constellation of values denoting a "Southerner" came increasingly to give Lunenburgers a sense of common identity among both themselves and their fellow agrarians below the Mason-Dixon Line.

• POLITICAL SOLIDARITY

The process by which this common identity came into being unfolded haltingly in the decade after the Revolution and then gained momentum. As Jackson T. Main has argued, planters from Southside counties like Lunenburg were still sufficiently handicapped by imperfect systems of transport for their agricultural products during the immediate postrevolutionary era that they tended to perceive at least some of their economic interests as being different from those of their fellow Virginians in the Tidewater and Northern Neck.[4] It is likely, though, that Main overstated the importance of these economic and geographic conflicts between the Southside and the eastern Chesapeake, for those differences were rapidly narrowing. The more important cause of the occasional political disagreements between the Southside and the eastern Chesapeake during the early 1780s was the perception—a product both of history and of still-imperfect communications—among Southsiders that they were somehow out of the political and cultural mainstream of Virginia. These differences, both real and perceived, may have been the cause of the Southside's advocacy of debtor relief legislation, its continued evasion of the provision in the Treaty of Paris requiring repayment of debts to British and particularly Scottish merchants, and its support of legislation postponing the collection of state taxes. Most decisive, the cultural influence of dissenting religious groups in the Southside, mobilized into political action for the first time in the decade following independence, produced a distinct split between that region and the eastern Chesapeake on the issue of disestablishment.

As the dust from the religious controversy settled and as the commitment of Lunenburgers to tobacco and slaves increased, factors of geographic distance and an imperfect system of river transport which may initially have differentiated the Southside from the Tidewater and Northern Neck came to seem less important. Part of the mechanism for this joining of interests was political. Lunenburg, which had voted with an Anti-Federalist minority in the Virginia Ratifying Convention of 1788, became part of an overwhelming Republican states' rights majority in the 1790s. Jefferson's margin of victory over John Adams in the election of 1800 in Virginia was slightly over three to one; in Lunenburg that margin was ten to one.[5] Thereafter Lunenburg would remain steadfast in its partnership with the Jeffersonian Republican and later the Democratic party consensus within Virginia on most national political issues up to the Civil War. It should be noted that the Democratic consensus within Virginia became increasingly a *Southern* Democratic consensus. Its guiding principles—states' rights, strict constructionism, a firm opposition to protective tariffs and federally financed internal improvements—were generally embraced by most Virginians, but the dedication to them among Southside Virginians was particularly steadfast and fervent.[6]

This increasing commitment to what most Lunenburgers would

have called "fundamental principles" or "traditional values" was exhibited even more clearly in local politics. Whereas Lunenburg's perception of itself in the prerevolutionary days had been as a "western" or even a "frontier" county, by 1829 (at the time of Virginia's first constitutional convention since the Revolution) its representative was making a clear and close identification of the residents of the Southside with those of other slaveowning counties to the east. Indeed, by that time Southsiders were explicitly antagonistic toward "those persons of the West most prominent in moving reform and trying to stir up dissatisfaction in the minds of our peaceful and happy citizens." The great majority of Lunenburg's citizens did not even wish to call a constitutional convention, for fear that the "fundamental principles" of 1776 might be disturbed. But when a majority of Virginians voted for a convention, Lunenburg's representative, William H. Brodnax, did everything possible to see that the reforms proposed by the "West" went unaccomplished.[7]

The county court system, staffed by a cadre of appointed, self-perpetuating, and, most frequently, ill-trained justices, had long been under attack in some quarters of Virginia, but Brodnax conceived that system to be "the first link in the chain" of good government and "the most valuable part of our present judicial system."[8] Brodnax's assessment may have been accurate had he been surveying the system of Virginia justice in 1750 (although even then the actual legal expertise of the gentlemen justices sitting on the county benches was negligible), but by 1829, at a time when individuals with legal complaints were attempting to circumvent the county courts by going over the heads of local justices to the better-trained district court judges, that claim could be made only by a man like Brodnax, who continued to sit on the county bench after seventeen years of service.[9]

Similarly, whereas in the 1780s the Southside counties may have exhibited a slightly more democratic temper than their wealthier and more well-established counterparts to the east, by the time of the Virginia Convention the citizens of that region, although there were few aristocrats within their own ranks, were deeply suspicious of "foreigners, artisans of various kinds, and itinerants" who were without freeholds and who could not give "sufficient evidence of permanent interest with and allegiance to the community." In Brodnax's view, "all are for drawing some line of limitation to many, and none are for letting the women and children and negroes and convicts and paupers vote," so one could never claim to have a truly "open suffrage."[10] It was simply a question of where to draw the line, and for Brodnax and most of the Southside delegates that line was to be drawn at a *status quo* that denied the franchise to those who were without property. That suspicion of the propertyless was no doubt a reflection of a society that was itself becoming increasingly less flexible in its economic structure, but even more important it was the consequence of the Southside's long-standing commitment to the ideal of an "independent" citizenry. Throughout their history, Southsiders had sought to avoid the condition of "dependence," but by the early nineteenth century, when that condition was even more closely associated with enslavement and debasement, the virtue of an independent freehold and the disabilities associated with not owning property were more strikingly manifest.

Many of the issues raised at the constitutional convention—the construction of the court system, the extent of the suffrage, the power of the executive—were fought along lines that the participants themselves described as "east" versus "west," with Lunenburg's representative consistently identifying himself with the "east." In fact, though, the lines of division were determined not by simple lines of geography running from east to west but rather by the extent of a region's commitment to slavery. This identification both with the "east" and with a militant proslavery position was expressed most vehemently and explicitly in the debate over the apportionment of representation in the legislature. Lunenburg's citizens insisted that "representation and taxation should go hand in hand" and that "according to our eastern exposition of that maxim . . . our slave population should not be totally disregarded in the adjustment of the ratio of representation."[11] It is not surprising that Lunenburg's freeholders should come around to this position. In 1750, with a small, widely scattered white population and a negligible black population, Lunenburg's claims to power in the legislature were frail. By 1829, Lunenburg's free white population stood at approximately 3,500 (slightly higher than that of the average county in Virginia), but its black population, which numbered some 6,500, placed the county among the top 10 percent of Virginia's counties in terms of overall population. Thus, when Lunenburg's representatives spoke of defending the interests of the "east" or of the importance of preserving the "fundamental principles" of the Revolution, those interests and principles were increasingly not determined by geography or by the fundamental testaments of revolutionary republicanism, but rather by the need to protect the social and economic institution that had come to provide the central point of definition for the Southside's white citizens. That institution was racial slavery.

• RACIAL SOLIDARITY

As early as the mid-1780s, it was beginning to become apparent that black slavery served as the basis for the joining of interests between the well-established, eastern regions of Virginia and the Southside. Reacting to the efforts of a few Quakers and Methodist ministers (Thomas Coke and Francis Asbury in particular) to arouse sentiment within Virginia in favor of a legislative bill for the general emancipation of slaves, the Southside counties of Amelia, Mecklenburg, Pittsylvania, Brunswick, Halifax, and Lunenburg each sent petitions to the legislature defending their right to own slaves and, what is more striking, defending the benevolence of the institution itself. The Virginia House of Delegates rejected the arguments of the antislavery activists out of hand. Indeed, it was so hostile to any talk of emancipation that it nearly went so far as to repeal an existing act allowing for private manumission of slaves. Judging from the hysterical tone of the Southside proslavery petitions, however, one would think that the abolitionist threat within Virginia had reached dangerous proportions.[12] The rhetoric of the 1785 petitions suggests that the traditional assumption that the South aggressively advocated slavery only in reaction to Northern abolitionist agitation in the 1830s requires some revision. Most of those Methodists who preached in the Southside in the 1780s had long been associated with the region, yet such was the uneasiness of Southsiders about their growing dependence on slavery that they were quick to lash out at anyone who seemed to threaten either their physical security or their economic security.

Like their counterparts from the other Southside counties, the Lunenburg petitioners attempted to bend revolutionary principles to defend their right to own human property, reminding the members of the legislature that "in order . . . to Fix a Tenure on our property on a Basis of Security not to be shaken in the future, we dissolved our union with our parent County." They viewed the agitation for general emancipation as "flagrant Contempt of the constitutional powers of the Commonwealth" and predicted that it would result in

Want, Poverty, Distress & Ruin to the free Citizens; the Horrors of all the Rapes, Robberies, Murderers, and Outrages, which an innumerable Host of unprincipled, unpropertied, vindictive, and remorseless Banditti are capable of perpetrating; Neglect, Famine and Death to the abandoned black infant and superannuated Parent; inevitable Bankruptcy to the Revenue; Desperation and revolt to the disappointed, oppressed Citizen; and sure and final ruin to this happy, free and flourishing Country.

All in all, it was seen as quite a despicable scheme, and one that in the petitioners' view was consistent "with the principles and Designs of a Bute or a North" but that was in this case perpetrated by a cabal of those evil tyrants working in unison "with a proscribed Coke, and imperious Asb[ur]y, and other contemptible Emissaries and Hirelings of Britain."[13]

The 161 Lunenburg freeholders who signed the petition not only went on record opposing the principle of general emancipation, they also enjoined the delegates to repeal the act allowing for voluntary manumission and "to provide effectively for the good Government and due restraint of those already set free, whose disorderly conduct and thefts and outrages are so generally the just subject of Complaint." The Lunenburg citizens concluded their petition with what to them was the most powerful example of those "just subjects of complaint" provoked by the free black community, namely, the "Insolences and Violences so frequently of late committed to and on our respectable Maids and Matrons."[14] This concern about the dangers posed by free blacks, a concern that is strikingly apparent in all the 1785 proslavery petitions, is difficult to penetrate. By 1790, free blacks in Lunenburg numbered eighty, less than 1 percent of the population, and the court records indicate only minor incidences of crime by either slaves or free blacks. But the mere possibility of such crime, even before the black rebellion in Santo Domingo became part of the public consciousness in 1792–94, was plainly enough to cause the white population of Lunenburg to raise the alarm.

All the proslavery petitions from the Southside were nearly identical, indicating perhaps that only a few people had taken a hand in drafting and then circulating them more widely throughout the region. The only item missing from the Lunenburg petition that was a standard part of the arguments of virtually all the others was a lengthy religious and moral justification of the institution itself. That justification was generally based on biblical texts, the most common from chapter 9 of Genesis, reciting the story of God's curse on Canaan, and that from chapter 25 of Leviticus, in which the right to hold "Bond-men and Bond-maids" was asserted. Those biblical references, designed (in the words of the Brunswick County petitioners) to prove "that it was ordained by the Great and Wise Disposer of all things, that some Nations should serve others; and that all Nations have not been equally free," seem to carry the Southside defenders of slavery well beyond the confused and apologetic defenses that most historians have seen as typical of the late-eighteenth-century Virginia attitude toward slavery.[15] Rather, as early as the mid-1780s we can perceive a notable combativeness and aggressiveness in the Southside Virginia defense. It was not that white Virginians were assuming a burden laid on them by the prerevolutionary British policies respecting the slave trade, nor was it merely that the right to own chattel slaves was an important ingredient in the Southside economy, although that fact was readily observable and readily acknowledged. Rather, in the eyes of the Southside petitioners,

It hath been the practice and custom for above 3500 Years, down to the present time, for one Nation to buy and keep Slaves of another Nation: That God so particularly (as above recited) Licensed or Commanded his People, to buy of other Nations and to keep them for Slaves: And that Christ and his Apostles hath in the mean time come into the World, and past out of it again, leaving behind them the New Testament, full of all instructions necessary to our Salvation; and hath not forbid it: But left that matter as they found it, giving exhortations to Masters and Servants how to conduct themselves to each other.[16]

It is not surprising that the 161 signers of the Lunenburg petition were predominantly those whose own economic and social position would incline them toward a defense of slavery. Men like Christopher Billups, Edward Brodnax, virtually all the members of the prominent Ragsdale and Garland families, and James Craig were featured prominently at the head of the list of signatories. Indeed, every resident of the county owning thirty or more slaves signed the petition, as did about two-thirds of the county court and Episcopal vestry. Members of dissenting religious groups were not as enthusiastic in their support of the peculiar institution. It is difficult to trace the names of individual Methodists who lived within the county in 1785, but given the involvement of prominent Southside Methodists in the antislavery movement, it seems probable that the few Methodists in Lunenburg refrained from signing the petition. The Baptists, far more numerous than the Methodists in Lunenburg, were conspicuous by their absence among the signatories of the petition.[17] Most of the Baptists were still not slave owners and were engaged in a bitter political struggle with an Anglican slave-owning class over the issue of separation of church and state at precisely the time that the proslavery petition was circulated. In subsequent decades, however, as the mild, antislavery ideology of the Baptist church waned still further and as Baptist congregants themselves joined the ranks of the slave owners, the consensus within the Southside on a militant defense of slavery would become nearly complete.

In ensuing years, as Southsiders heard reports of the slave revolution in Santo Domingo, and then of Gabriel's rebellion in Richmond, closer to home, they would become more fearful of the dangers posed by free blacks and more defensive about demonstrating the benevolence of their slave system.[18] The intensity of feeling in the Southside on those subjects was given its greatest impulse in January 1832 in the aftermath of Nat Turner's rebellion in nearby Southampton County, when the Virginia General Assembly debated the status of slavery within the commonwealth. No substantive legislation would result from the more than two weeks of discussion on the subject, but the Virginia slavery debates, coming as they did at the time the South began to assume a more militant proslavery stance in the face of Northern attacks on the institution, are remarkable for both the candor and the range of opinion expressed by Virginia's postrevolutionary ruling class.[19]

William O. Goode of Mecklenburg County, Lunenburg's immediate neighbor to the south, stood at one extreme of the spectrum of opinion, introducing a resolution on January 10 instructing the Virginia Assembly to cease consideration "of all petitions, memorials, and resolutions which have for their object the manumission of persons held in servitude under the existing laws of this commonwealth."[20] Thomas Jefferson Randolph, Jefferson's grandson, countered with a motion calling for a statewide referendum on the propriety of a law stipulating that the children of slaves born after July 4, 1840, should become wards of the state until they could be emancipated and removed beyond the limits of the United States.[21] Randolph's resolution was hardly a hallmark in American egalitarianism, as the provision requiring that slaves leave the country after manumission was indicative of a racist ideology that the Albemarle County planter shared with his recently deceased grandfather and virtually everyone else in Virginia. Yet the resolution's rejection of slavery on grounds of both morality and practicality, coming as it did from a man of Randolph's stature, marked the most serious assault on the peculiar institution in the history of the Old Dominion.

The two-week debate that followed the introduction of the opposing resolutions was perhaps the last to occur in the South before the Civil War in which both egalitarian and aggressively proslavery sentiments were expressed with equal liberty. Samuel McDowell Moore, representing the predominantly white nonslaveholding county of Rockbridge, chose to follow the logic of the Declaration of Independence to its conclusion, asserting that "the right to the enjoyment of liberty is one of those perfect, inherent, and inalienable rights, which pertain to the whole human race, and of which they [the slaves] can never be divested except by an act of gross injustice."[22] At the other extreme, and ultimately expressing the majority view, were the delegates from the Virginia Southside.

Alexander Knox of Mecklenburg, who together with William Goode and John Street of Lunenburg was among the most uncompromising of the proslavery advocates, proclaimed:

I cannot force my mind, even by calling to its aid humanity, religion or philanthropy, to the conclusion that slavery, as it exists in Virginia, is an evil. But, Sir, on the contrary, I consider it susceptible of demonstration that it is to this very cause, that we may trace the high and elevated character which she has heretofore sustained; and moreover, that its existence is indispensably requisite in order to preserve the forms of a Republican Government.[23]

The Southside proslavery argument encompassed all the sentiments that had been expressed in the legislative petitions of the mid-1780s and added a few new considerations produced by the simultaneous occurrence of Northern abolitionist agitation and servile insurrection (which many Virginians believed were causally linked). Once again the legal basis on which the proslavery argument rested was that the right to own property in slaves was a fundamental natural and constitutional right not subject to legislative encroachment. Although disturbed by the "dangerous and incendiary productions" of Northern antislavery advocates, the Southside delegates argued that the general contentment of the slave population would win out over abolitionist agitation. James Gholson of Brunswick County argued:

The Slaves of Virginia are as happy a laboring class as exists upon the habitable earth. They are as well fed, well clothed and as well treated. In health, but reasonable labour is required of them—in sickness, they are nursed and attended to. In times of plenty, they live in waste—in times of scarcity, they do not want—they are content to-day, and have no care or anxiety for to-morrow. Cruel treatment of them is discountenanced by society, and until of late, their privileges were daily extending. Among what labouring class will you find more happiness and less misery? Not among the serfs and labouring poor of Europe! No, Sir.— Nor among the servants to the North of us.[24]

The happy condition of the slaves, though certainly facilitated by the natural benevolence of Virginia masters, was not simply the result of the white man shouldering the "burden" of slavery, for unlike their more apologetic proslavery colleagues from the eastern

Chesapeake, the Southside delegates were also prepared to argue that the slave system in Virginia was still the basis for a prosperous and expanding economy. The Southsiders contended that all the recent improvements in agriculture—better methods of plowing and fertilizing and a greater attention to the rotation of crops—had occurred on those "estates on which slave labor most abounds."[25]

Taken in its entirety, the Southside argument contained all the ingredients of the militant Southern defense of slavery. An uncivilized but essentially docile slave population, a benevolent, paternalistic labor system far preferable to the wage slavery of the North, and a healthful physical environment all combined to bring into being an agricultural system that was expansive and innovative and that allowed those white planters who were a part of it an independence which had for so long been their primary goal in life.

When the debates were over and the votes on a wide array of proposals were recorded, the status of the Negro—slave and free—remained virtually unchanged. Yet the fact that the subject had been explored in an open political forum in thoroughgoing fashion was in itself unprecedented in the history of the state. According to some observers, those debates, while they did not result in a legislative breakthrough, at least yielded something approaching a consensus on slavery within the state. In the interpretation of the editor of the Richmond *Constitutional Whig*, the discussion in the House of Delegates seemed to prove:

1. That it is not expedient, at this session, to legislate on abolition. (2) That the coloured population of Virginia is a great evil. (3) That humanity and policy in the *first place*, demand the removal of the free, and those who will become free (looking to an extensive voluntary manumission). (4) That this will absorb our present means. (5) (Undeniable Implication) That when public opinion is more developed; when the people have spoken more explicitly, and the *means* are better devised, that it is expedient to commence a system of abolition. The House of Delegates have gone this far, and in our opinion it had no right to go farther.[26]

The views expressed by the *Constitutional Whig* did not represent a uniform consensus. While that interpretation probably served as an acceptable compromise between delegates from nonslaveholding regions in the northwest and those from the moderate, proslavery portions of the Tidewater, it is plain that Southside delegates like Lunenburg's John Street were inclined toward a more pugnacious view of their peculiar institution, a view that would in future years align them more readily with Fire-eaters from South Carolina than with compromisers from the Old Dominion. Though Street joined enthusiastically with the eastern delegates in voting for a resolution stating that it was not "expedient, at this session, to legislate on abolition," he denied that the slave population of Virginia was an "evil." And though he would have joined his fellow Virginians in encouraging the removal of free blacks from the state, he was even more fervently opposed to any measure that might, even by the voluntary act of individual slave owners, allow granting slaves their freedom in the first place. It is clear that neither Street nor any other Southside delegate would ever assent to the proposition that the House of Delegates should *ever* work toward a program of abolition.

So it had come to pass that Lunenburg County, which had its origins as a spacious, open-ended, frontier society peopled overwhelmingly by individuals with few claims to hereditary privilege and scant association with slavery, became a defender of a political system that was increasingly oligarchic and archaic and a militant champion of an economic and social system that condemned nearly two-thirds of the county's population to a condition of enforced and perpetual dependence. It is paradoxical that these increasingly inegalitarian institutional arrangements should arise in a region that had initially offered equality of opportunity on a nearly unprecedented scale to almost all its citizens. In that sense though, the history of Lunenburg County in the one hundred years between the mid-eighteenth and the mid-nineteenth centuries followed the same pattern as the history of eastern Virginia over the first century of settlement. No single individual in Lunenburg was ever able to acquire a labor force sufficient to exploit the abundant land of the region in quite the fashion achieved by the great planters of the eastern Chesapeake, and therefore no one in Lunenburg ever could assert claims to economic and social dominance in quite the same way those claims were lodged in the traditional Virginia culture. Yet for the great mass of the white settlers in Lunenburg, as in the eastern Chesapeake a century earlier, freedom—or more pre-cisely, *independence*—came to depend on an economic system based heavily on slavery. But there was a fundamental difference. Though that paradoxical combination of slavery and freedom pro-vided unprecedented levels of economic opportunity for Lunen-burg's white citizens, it also served to wed them to a social and political system that, however well suited to the eastern Chesa-peake a century before, was nearly wholly out of step with the pace of American development in the nineteenth century.

Ultimately it was the dimension of time, even more than differ-ences in settlement patterns or in economic development, that divided the history of Lunenburg from that of the eastern Chesa-peake world which had given the Southside its original political identity. As we have seen, the world in which Lunenburg's tobacco planters lived was simply too big and too complexly ordered to allow anyone in Lunenburg (or anywhere else in Virginia) to enjoy a monopoly of economic, social, and political power. Perhaps even more important, it would prove impossible for anyone in Lunen-burg, no matter how wealthy or powerful, to operate in the wider world outside that region with the sense of self-confidence and mastery enjoyed by previous generations of Virginians. By the end of the revolutionary era, and continuing into the nineteenth cen-tury, the very basis of the system that supported Lunenburg's way of life was under attack. While the county's citizens may have inherited the basic ingredients of their economic system from east-ern Virginia, their formulation of an increasingly unyielding de-fense of that system drew on sources of inspiration that reached far beyond the borders of the Old Dominion. In the mid-eighteenth century the factors that gave Lunenburg its identity—political in-stitutions imported westward from Williamsburg, a spacious phys-ical environment, extraordinary geographic mobility among both inward- and outward-bound settlers, and remarkable economic op-portunity for those free white settlers who chose to stay in the county—were the consequence of influences that can be associ-ated both with the culture of Virginia and the culture of the Amer-ican frontier. In the aftermath of Nat Turner's rebellion, however, the imperatives of racial slavery caused Lunenburg's identity to be forged in a fashion that was distinctly, and militantly, Southern.

Epilogue

In the process of defending themselves from Northern attacks on the slave system and justifying the way of life that system encouraged, white Lunenburgers came to acquire a sense of group solidarity unprecedented in the previous history of their county. That solidarity would be given its most dramatic expression on the afternoon of March 11, 1861, at a meeting of the county's citizens at the courthouse "for the purpose of taking into consideration the great crisis" created by those twin villains, Abraham Lincoln and abolitionism. The assembled freeholders unanimously passed a set of resolutions that left no doubt about Lunenburg's loyalties:

Resolved, That Secession, *direct, straight out, eternal*, is the salvation of Virginia.

Resolved, That as far as we are concerned, Abraham Lincoln should never have waved his sceptre over the state that boasts of a Washington's grave.

Resolved, That we are irreconcilably opposed to *any* border State Convention, and do hereby request our delegate in the State Convention now in session, to oppose every effort tending to that end, and to press with all his might and ability the *immediate* and *everlasting* separation of Virginia from *all* the non-slaveholding states, and to a union of the cotton states.

Resolved, That in the Peace Congress report, we recognize a willful and deliberate encroachment upon the rights of the South, consequently we repudiate it, we scorn and regard it as "the *scum* that rises when a nation boils."

Resolved, That we have ever been and are now opposed to compromise of any character with Lincoln's party or sympathizers.

Resolved, That we are *for the South, the whole South, and nothing but the South*, so help us God.[1]

David Stokes, a member of a Lunenburg family dating back to the founding of the county in 1746, presided over that gathering. In the covering letter that conveyed the resolutions to the state convention, he attempted to describe the feelings of his constituents on the question of slavery and secession:

Upon the brow of every man was written in unmistakable and indelible characters "my home is in the South, my grave shall be there too." If ever determination characterized the action of any people, it is stamped upon the actions of the people of Lunenburg. . . . They have witnessed the downfall of the nation's citadel of honor, and now desire to leave its dishonored ruins to the care of those who wantonly undermined its once grand and lofty pillars. They are eager to detach "the old mother of states and statesmen" from the accursed North, ere its fierce and desolating tide of furious fanaticism shall sweep her hallowed soil. Their ardent affections are closely entwined around the destiny of the Old Dominion. May oblivion never shroud her splendor is their only prayer. But if their mother state should ever conclude to cling to the North, in all its hideousness and heinousness, we dare say every citizen of Lunenburg will leave her to the *owls* and *bats* of abolition and seek some spot of earth where the sceptre of Lincoln can never desecrate their graves.[2]

It is clear that the citizens of the "Old Free State" continued to feel some sense of community with "Mother Virginia," a nostalgic fondness for the traditions and institutions that had produced a Washington or even a William Byrd. Yet by 1861, as the county girded itself for a political and social crisis that was to them more urgent than the American Revolution itself, the one force that unified Lunenburgers most closely was that collection of beliefs which they defined as "Southern." The cultural and political imperatives of being "Southern," and in particular of the slave system that formed the social basis of the South, ultimately provided the mechanism by which the white citizens of Lunenburg, plain folk and gentry, cavaliers and frontiermen, Episcopalians and Baptists, were bound together.

Appendix 1

The Economic Elite
of Lunenburg County
1750–1815

1750[a]

Name	Tithable Slaves
Armistead Burrell*	11
Lewis Burrell*	8
Hutchison Burton*	5
William Byrd*	62
James Cocke*	11
John Cole*	10
George Corray*	5
John Davis	8
John Edloe	13
Philip Edloe	5
William Fuqua	13
William Hill	7
William Howard	7
Field Jefferson	9
William Jones	7
Abraham Martin	5
Julia Nichols*	15
Colonel Ruffin*	16
Luke Smith	6
Richard Witton	8

SOURCE: Landon C. Bell, *Sunlight on the Southside: Lists of Tithes, Lunenburg County, Virginia, 1748–1783* (Philadelphia, 1931), pp. 122–61, 269–85; Real and Personal Property Tax Lists, Lunenburg County, 1782, 1795, 1815, Virginia State Library, Richmond, Va.

*Denotes nonresidents of the county.

[a]The 1750 tithable lists, unlike those for subsequent years, do not include landholdings, and thus the basis for calculating wealth in the county for that year is less secure than it is for subsequent years.

[b]The 1782 tax lists included *all* slaves rather than just tithable slaves sixteen years and over. Therefore the slaveholdings of the members of the elite for that year are distorted compared with other years.

1769

Name	Landholdings in Acres	Tithable Slaves
Lydall Bacon	1,060	8
John Bannister*	895	12
Joseph Billups	1,100	5
Henry Blagrave	2,170	12
Curtis Cates*	1,941	3
Thomas Chambers	940	10
Richard Claiborne	505	11
John Cross	400	7
Tscharner DeGraffenreid	1,500	14
William Embry	1,200	16
Lodowick Farmer	1,325	15
David Garland	3,190	12
Mary Glen	1,408	11
Charles Hamlin	1,176	11
Thomas Hardy	1,530	2
Peter Jones	3,525	4
Joseph Minor	1,105	9
Jonathon Patteson	1,069	5
Francis Smithson	1,246	4
Thomas Tabb	1,600	11

1782

Name	Landholdings in Acres	Slaves[b]
Roger Atkinson	4,531	61
John Ballard	1,398	25
John Barnes	652	21
William Barrott	3,069	22
Edward Brodnax	Unknown	40
Lewis Burrell	3,091	23
Thomas Chambers	1,614	42
James Craig	1,604	42
John Cross	400	24
Tscharner DeGraffenreid	435	28
Francis DeGraffenreid	1,043	24
William Dowsing	511	22
Mary Garland	—	27
Samuel Garland	500	28
Peter Jones	2,730	20
Frederick Nance	1,076	24
James Scott	783	25
Henry Stokes	1,172	20
William Taylor	900	26
Thomas Williams	404	21

1795

Name	Landholdings in Acres	Tithable Slaves
Roger Atkinson*	1,660	32
Edward Brodnax	350	20
Jeremy Burnett	1,355	14
Lewis Burrell*	2,481	15
Thomas Chambers	1,710	28
William Chambers	403	23
James Craig	2,584	30
John Cross	1,057	15
Francis DeGraffenreid	1,112	17
Agnis Hamlin	710	20
William Hatchett	1,794	20
Peter Jones	4,573	20
Edward Jordan	1,154	17
John Mason	108	15
James Scott	1,084	22
James Shelton	1,040	15
Henry Stokes	2,045	27
Anthony Street	673	23
William Taylor	1,611	26
Thomas Williams	1,408	21

1815

Name	Landholdings in Acres	Tithable Slaves
William Buford	3,186	44
Edward Chambers	1,098	59
George Craghead	760	28
George Craig	2,098	25
Peter Epps	2,692	36
William Fisher	1,119	28
John Hamlin	599	26
William Hatchett	2,435	45
Peter Jones	2,172	40
Thomas Jordan	1,943	39
James Macfarland	1,442	29
James Neal	2,180	20
Sterling Neblitt	991	25
John Ravinscroft	2,236	27
Robert Scott	1,660	27
James Smith	1,843	36
William Stokes	2,063	31
William Taylor	1,449	45
David Williams	1,201	26
Joseph Yarbrough	608	28

Appendix 2
Lunenburg County Court
1770–1815

	Lunenburg County Court, 1770			
Name	Total Years of Service	Land in Acres	No. of Slaves Owned[a]	Religious Service
Lydall Bacon	23	1,060	8	Anglican vestry (30 years)
Elisha Betts	10	815	5	Anglican vestry (3 years)
Christopher Billups	26	412	6	Anglican vestry (10 years)
Henry Blagrave	13	2,170	12	Anglican vestry[b] (11 years)
Thomas Chambers	17	949	10	Anglican vestry (11 years)
Richard Claiborne	9	505	11	Anglican vestry (5 years)
Everand Dowsing	11	462	8	Anglican
Lodowick Farmer	9	1,325	13	Anglican vestry (4 years)
David Garland	10	3,190	12	Anglican vestry (15 years)
Charles Hamlin	20	1,116	11	Anglican
Abraham Maury	10	535	6	Anglican
Jonathan Pattison	18	1,069	5	Anglican vestry
Thomas Pettus	6	330	5	Anglican vestry (20 years)
John Ragscale	21	625	2	Anglican vestry (47 years)[c]
Thomas Tabb	23	1,600	11	Anglican vestry (21 years)
Joseph Williams	16	535	5	Unknown
Thomas Winn	16	501	8	Anglican vestry (14 years)

SOURCE: Landon C. Bell, *The Old Free State: A Contribution to the History of Lunenburg County and Southside Virginia*, 2 vols. (Richmond, Va., 1927), 1:326–34; Landon C. Bell, *Sunlight on the Southside: Lists of Tithes, Lunenburg County, Virginia, 1748–1783* (Philadelphia, 1931), pp. 212–85; Landon C. Bell, *Cumberland Parish, Lunenburg County, Virginia, 1746–1816: Vestry Book* (Richmond, Va., 1930), pp. 26–31 and passim; Real and Personal Property Tax Lists, Lunenburg County, 1782, 1795, 1815, Virginia State Library, Richmond, Va.

[a]Includes only "tithable slaves" sixteen years and older.
[b]Blagrave left the Anglican church in 1768.
[c]This may represent the combined service of two men of the same name.
[d]This category includes *all* slaves.
[e]Includes slaves twelve years and older.
[f]Includes slaves nine years and older.

Lunenburg County Court, 1782

Name	Total Years of Service	Land in Acres	No. of Slaves Owned[d]	Religious Service
John Ballard	5	1,398	25	Episcopal vestry (4 years)
Christopher Billups	26	810	18	Episcopal vestry (10 years)
Robert Blackwell	11	327	13	Episcopal
Edward Brodnax	8	Unknown	40	Episcopal vestry (1 year)
Thomas Chambers	17	1,614	43	Episcopal vestry (11 years)
Francis DeGraffenreid	17	1,043	24	Unknown
Tscharner DeGraffenreid	5	435	28	Episcopal
Robert Dixon	2	636	9	Episcopal vestry (3 years)
John Glenn	9	600	10	Episcopal
Charles Hamlin	20	1,560	19	Episcopal
Nicholas Hobson	2	Unknown	16	Episcopal vestry (2 years)
James Johnson	3	140	7	Unknown
John Powell	3	350	6	Unknown
John Ragsdale	21	625	13	Episcopal vestry (47 years)[c]
Christopher Robertson	18	680	11	Episcopal vestry (18 years)
Henry Stokes	17	1,172	20	Episcopal vestry (21 years)
Anthony Street	12	300	14	Episcopal vestry (6 years)

Lunenburg County Court, 1795

Name	Total Years of Service	Land in Acres	No. of Slaves Owned[e]	Religious Service
Edmund Bacon	21	Unknown	Unknown	Episcopal vestry (26 years)
John Billups	16	887	11	Episcopal vestry (8 years)
Field Clarke	21	703	5	Baptist
William Craghead	19	563	13	Unknown
Francis DeGraffenreid	17	1,122	17	Presbyterian
William Fisher	11	1,061	13	Unknown
Edward Jordan	18	1,154	17	Episcopal vestry (7 years)
Peter Lampkin	17	829	12	Episcopal vestry (4 years)
Frederick Nance, Jr.	4	349	13	Episcopal
John Pettus, Jr.	5	1,025	9	Episcopal vestry (1 year)
Edward Ragsdale	12	360	10	Episcopal vestry (4 years)
Christopher Robertson	17	600	9	Episcopal vestry (19 years)
James Scott	16	1,084	22	Baptist
Abner Wells	16	220	2	Episcopal
Joseph Yarbrough	20	240	7	Baptist

Lunenburg County Court, 1815

Name	Total Years of Service	Land in Acres	No. of Slaves Owned	Religious Affiliation
Thomas Adams	14	415	11	Episcopalian
Charles Betts	8	284	17	Episcopalian
Joel Blackwell	14	671	13	Unknown
John Blackwell	6	613	14	Unknown
Thomas Blackwell	21	1,616	28	Unknown
Field Clarke	21	537	10	Baptist
William Ellis	15	382	19	Baptist
Jesse Hamlett	17	396	9	Unknown
Meriwether Hurt	10	554	12	Unknown
James Jeffress	18	1,167	17	Baptist
Lewis Jones	21	1,399	18	Unknown
Peter Jones	4	2,172	40	Unknown
John Knight	7	554	8	Unknown
James Smith	19	1,843	36	Episcopalian
William Stokes	10	2,063	31	Episcopalian
David Street	21	1,831	19	Episcopalian
Edmund Winn	26	1,100	20	Unknown
Joseph Yarbrough	20	608	28	Baptist

Notes

1. The law of Virginia stipulated only that the monthly courts be held in the most "convenient places" in the county, but the decision to locate the courthouse as close to the geographic center of the county as possible followed long-standing Virginia practice and was designed to ensure equal access to the services of the court. Phillip A. Bruce, *Institutional History of Virginia in the Seventeenth Century*, 2 vols. (New York, 1910), 1:485–86; Albert Ogden Porter, *County Government in Virginia: A Legislative History, 1607–1914* (New York, 1947), pp. 12–13.

2. Evelyn F. Arvin's *Antebellum Homes of Lunenburg* (Richmond, 1964) is an attempt to catalog and memorialize Lunenburg's grandest historical estates, but the overriding impression is one of plainness and simplicity, at least compared with the architecture in other parts of Virginia.

3. Kenneth Lockridge, *A New England Town: The First Hundred Years* (New York, 1970); Philip Greven, *Four Generations: Population, Land, and Family in Colonial Andover, Massachusetts* (Ithaca, N.Y., 1970). The earlier study by Charles Grant, *Democracy in the Connecticut Frontier Town of Kent* (New York, 1961), is an even more appropriate model for my own endeavor, although I was not sufficiently aware of it at the time.

4. See especially Robert Redfield, *The Little Community* (Chicago, 1956). These issues are explored more fully in Richard R. Beeman, "The New Social History and the Search for 'Community' in Colonial America," *American Quarterly* 29 (1977): 422–43. For a slightly different though by no means contradictory view, see Darrett B. Rutman, "The Social Web: A Prospectus for the Study of Early American Community," in William L. O'Neill, ed., *Insights and Parallels: Problems and Issues of American Social History* (Minneapolis, 1973), pp. 57–89; and idem, "Community Study" (Paper delivered at the Newberry Library Conference on Quantitative and Social Science Approaches in Early American History, Chicago, Ill., October 6–8, 1977).

5. Byrd patented land in the area as early as 1728 and by the 1740s had acquired over 100,000 acres. Richard Randolph, whose holdings exceeded 30,000 acres, began his patenting activity sometime in the 1730s. Landon C. Bell, *The Old Free State: A Contribution to the History of Lunenburg County and Southside Virginia*, 2 vols. (Richmond, 1927), 1:80–108; Abstracts of Patents and Grants, Virginia State Land Office, vol. 9, Brunswick County, books 17–25, Virginia State Library, Richmond, Va. (hereafter "Va. Abstracts," followed

by volume number of volume referred to); Va. Abstracts, vol. 20: Lunenburg County, books 27–31.

CHAPTER ONE
Settling the Wilderness

1. William Byrd, "A Journey to the Land of Eden, Anno 1733," in Louis B. Wright, ed., *The Prose Works of William Byrd of Westover: Narratives of a Colonial Virginian* (Cambridge, Mass., 1966), pp. 381–412.

2. William Byrd, "A Secret History of the Line," in ibid., pp. 143–45; Byrd, "Journey to the Land of Eden," p. 385.

3. The "traditional" character of eastern Chesapeake society was a hybrid version of those cultural styles transmitted from England and modified by the peculiar character of the seventeenth- and early-eighteenth-century Virginia landscape. The most insightful discussion of the essential character of that early modern English society which in turn shaped the American experience is Harold Perkin's *The Origins of Modern English Society, 1780–1880* (London, 1969), pp. 17–62.

In posing a single model of a traditional, eastern Chesapeake culture, I am setting up an ideal type, with all the attendant dangers of oversimplification. The leaders of Chesapeake society displayed considerable diversity among themselves, and the institutions they dominated (the plantation, the county courts, the church) did not function in a uniform fashion from one place to another. However, the societal ideal of the eastern gentry world was articulated in all the principal spheres of public activity in the Old Dominion, and if every member of the gentry was not a Robert Carter or a William Byrd, they nevertheless served as visible models of what a proper gentryman was supposed to be.

The literature on the eighteenth-century Virginia gentry is substantial, but the works that most influenced my own thinking are Rhys Isaac's *The Transformation of Virginia, 1740–1790* (Chapel Hill, N.C., 1982) and Charles Sydnor's *Gentlemen Freeholders: Political Practices in Washington's Virginia* (Chapel Hill, N.C., 1952).

4. Byrd, "Journey to the Land of Eden," p. 393. For the early Indian inhabitants of the region and for other details pertaining to the local history of Lunenburg, see also Bell's *Old Free State*, 1:39–42. Though linguistically part of the Iroquois, the Indians around Lunenburg tended to be identified by outsiders with the places in which they were encountered, e.g., the "Nottoways" or the "Meherrins."

5. Colonial Papers, folder 31, no. 19, Virginia State Library, Richmond, Va.

6. The best study of the early economic and social development of the Southside, one on which I have drawn heavily, is Michael L. Nicholls's "Origins of the Virginia Southside, 1703–1753: A Social and Economic Study" (Ph.D. diss., College of William and Mary, 1972), pp. 28–55.

7. Cary Carson, Norman Barka, William Kelso, Garry Wheeler Stone, and

Dell Upton ("Impermanent Architecture in the Southern Colonies," *Winterthur Portfolio* 16 [1981]: 135–96) have discovered that this impermanent style of architecture was typical even of the Tidewater well into the eighteenth century. Although evidence from the Southside is fragmentary, all indications point to an even more primitive style of building in that region. See, e.g., Byrd, "Journey to the Land of Eden," pp. 383, 384, 406, 409.

8. Nicholls, "Origins of the Virginia Southside," p. 139.

9. Ibid., pp. 44, 139–71.

10. Ibid., pp. 23–24; William Stevens Perry, ed., *Historical Collections Relating to the American Colonial Church*, vol. 1: *Virginia* (Hartford, Conn., 1870), pp. 261–322.

11. Bell, *Old Free State*, 1:76–108. Herbert C. Bradshaw, *History of Prince Edward County, Virginia, from Its Earliest Settlements Through Its Establishment in 1754 to Its Bicentennial Year* (Richmond, Va., 1955), pp. 1–21.

12. Richmond Croom Beatty and William J. Mulloy, eds., *William Byrd's Natural History of Virginia, or the Newly Discovered Eden* (Richmond, Va., 1940), p. xxii. We still lack a satisfactory history of the Scots-Irish immigration to America, but some of the background of that migration can be pieced together from J. C. Beckett, *The Making of Modern Ireland, 1603–1923* (New York, 1966); J. C. Beckett, *Protestant Dissent in Ireland, 1685–1785* (London, 1948); R. J. Dickson, *The Ulster Immigration to Colonial America, 1718–1775* (London, 1966); and Henry James Frost, *The Scotch-Irish in America* (Princeton, N.J., 1945).

13. Nicholls, "Origins of the Virginia Southside," p. 39; Robert D. Mitchell, *Commercialism and Frontier: Perspectives on the Early Shenandoah Valley* (Charlottesville, Va., 1977), pp. 16–19.

14. Richard J. Hooker, ed., *The Carolina Backcountry on the Eve of the Revolution: The Journal and Other Writings of Charles Woodmason, Anglican Itinerant* (Chapel Hill, N.C., 1953), pp. 52, 60–61.

15. Bell, *Old Free State*, 1:90–99. The surviving tithable lists for the county, which give some indication of the ethnic origins of Lunenburg's settlers, are printed in full in Landon C. Bell's *Sunlight on the Southside: Lists of Tithes, Lunenburg County, Virginia, 1748–1783* (Philadelphia, 1931).

16. Nicholls, "Origins of the Virginia Southside," pp. 28–31. See also Thomas Perkins Abernathy, *Three Virginia Frontiers* (Baton Rouge, La., 1940), p. 48, for an argument that overstates the extent to which the river system retarded the development of the Southside.

17. Melvin Herndon, *Tobacco in Colonial Virginia* (Williamsburg, Va., 1957), pp. 19–22.

18. Byrd, "Journey to the Land of Eden," pp. 384–412.

19. Nicholls, "Origins of the Virginia Southside," pp. 34–37.

20. William Waller Hening, ed., *The Statutes at Large: Being a Collection of All the Laws of Virginia from the First Session of the Legislature in the Year 1619*, 13 vols. (Richmond, Va., 1819–23), 5:57–58. Hereafter referred to as Hening, *Statutes at Large*.

21. Nicholls, "Origins of the Virginia Southside," pp. 41, 44.

22. For the different cultural and political systems in Virginia and the Carolinas, see Richard R. Beeman, "The Political Response to Social Conflict in the Southern Backcountry: A Comparative View of Virginia and the Carolinas During the Revolution," in Ronald Hoffman, Peter Albert, and Thad Tate, eds., *The Southern Backcountry in the American Revolution* (Charlottesville, Va., forthcoming).

23. Bell, *Old Free State*, 1:135–38; Hening, *Statutes at Large*, 5:310.

24. John P. Kennedy and H. R. McIlwaine, eds., *Journals of the House of Burgesses of Virginia*, 13 vols. (Richmond, Va., 1905–15), *1742–47*, pp. 92, 161, 179, 184. Hereafter cited as *JHB*.

25. The calculations of the proportions of heads of households, tithable slaves, and white dependents are based on the 1748 and 1750 tithe lists in Bell, *Sunlight*, pp. 58–86, 122–61. The formula for determining tithables varied, but for most of the prerevolutionary period, all white males sixteen years and older and all slaves (both male and female) sixteen and above were included among the tithable population. The rate by which one converts the tithable population to the total population depends on such variables as birthrate, male-female ratios, and number of slaves, but as a general rule the total population for areas like Lunenburg can be estimated by multiplying the number of white tithes by four and the number of black tithes by two.

26. Deloney immigrated to Lunenburg from Williamsburg, Cook from neighboring Amelia County, and John Edloe from William Byrd's Charles City County. Bell, *Old Free State*, 1:101–7; Landon C. Bell, *Cumberland Parish, Lunenburg County, Virginia, 1746–1816: Vestry Book* (Richmond, Va., 1930).

27. Bell, *Sunlight*, pp. 58–86, 122–61.

28. Ibid. For a provocative discussion of the importance of "independence" to eighteenth-century Americans, see Richard Bushman's " 'This New Man': Dependence and Independence, 1776," in Richard L. Bushman et al., *Uprooted Americans: Essays to Honor Oscar Handlin* (Boston, 1979), pp. 77–96.

29. Bell, *Sunlight*, pp. 58–86, 122–61.

30. Ibid., pp. 122–61; Va. Abstracts, vol. 20, books 27–31; Lunenburg County Deed Books, no. 1 (1746–51) and no. 2 (1750–52), Virginia State Library, Richmond, Va.

31. Nicholls, "Origins of the Virginia Southside," pp. 83–85.

32. Ibid., pp. 73–89, 244–25, has an excellent discussion of the method and the cost of the land-patenting process. He calculates the average cost of securing a patent to be just under £3 and, perhaps more important, the time involved to make the transaction from one to four years.

33. See Table 1; Lunenburg County Deed Books, no. 1 (1746–51) and no. 2 (1750–52). Nicholls, "Origins of the Virginia Southside," pp. 67–68, finds that fewer than 50 percent of Lunenburg's white tithable citizens had established legal title to land by 1750, but this figure, which excludes the significant number of those who were still going through the process of establishing legal title to their land, probably understates the case by as much as 20 or 25 percent.

34. Bell, *Sunlight*, pp. 122–61.

35. Ibid.

36. Lunenburg County Will Books, no. 1 (1746–60), Virginia State Library, Richmond, Va.

37. The best summary of the mechanics of tobacco cultivation is David O. Percy's "The Production of Tobacco Along the Colonial Potomac," *National Colonial Farm Research Report No. 1* (Accokeek Foundation, Accokeek, Md., 1979), esp. pp. 11–24.

38. William Tatham, *An Historical and Practical Essay on the Culture and Commerce of Tobacco* (London, 1800), pp. 56–57.

39. George M. Herndon, "A History of Tobacco in Virginia, 1613–1860," (M.A. thesis, University of Virginia, 1956), pp. 70–72.

40. Ibid.

41. Bell, *Sunlight*, pp. 122–61; Va. Abstracts, vol. 20, books 27–31; Lunenburg County Deed Books, no. 1 (1746–51) and no. 2 (1750–52); *JHB, 1752–55*, p. viii.

42. Byrd's activities as a land speculator had an impact on the economic life of the county, and during the late 1740s and early 1750s, when he still owned a working plantation utilizing the labor of scores of slaves, he undoubtedly influenced the networks of credit and transportation within the region. Yet the most striking fact is that he was rarely physically present in the county to impress on Lunenburg's citizens the values and styles of life he embodied. Rather, he chose to do his business in the region through intermediaries, such as Robert Munford and David Caldwell, who were certainly respectable but hardly of Byrd's social and economic standing. Rodney M. Baine, *Robert Munford, America's First Comic Dramatist* (Athens, Ga., 1967), pp. 3–5; Lunenburg County Deed Books, no. 2 (1750–52), pp. 39, 114ff.; Va. Abstracts, vol. 9, books 17–25, and vol. 20, books 27–31; Lunenburg County Deed Books, no. 1 (1746–51) and no. 2 (1750–52); Brunswick County Deeds, Wills, etc., book 1 (1732–40), and Deed Books 2 (1740–45) and 3 (1744–49); Bell, *Sunlight*, pp. 122–61.

43. Powhatan Bouldin, *The Old Trunk; or, Sketches of Colonial Days* (Richmond, Va., 1896), pp. 3–4, 14–32, 47–59. Alice Read Rouse, *The Reads and Their Relatives* (Richmond, Va., 1930), pp. 47–59; "Biographical Sketch of Clement Read," *William and Mary Quarterly*, 2d ser., 6:242–43.

44. Lunenburg County Will Books, no. 1 (1746–62), p. 57.

45. Ibid., pp. 76–77.

46. For all our study of the economic development of the colonial Chesapeake, we still have only a hazy idea of the actual rhythms of work which occupied Virginians, whether in the Tidewater or in the backcountry. David O. Percy and his staff at the National Colonial Farm in Accokeek, Maryland, have, in the course of actually cultivating the staple crops of the colonial Chesapeake, come closer than anyone else in arriving at reliable calculations on the number of hours spent on the multitude of chores that were a part of agricultural life in the eighteenth century. Their findings are summarized in David O. Percy, "Production of Tobacco Along the Colonial Potomac," "Corn: The Production of a Subsistence Crop on the Colonial Potomac," "English Grains Along the Colonial Potomac," and "Of Fast Horses, Black Cattle, Woods Hogs, and Rat-tailed

Sheep: Animal Husbandry Along the Colonial Potomac," Research Reports nos. 1, 2, 3, and 4, respectively, published by the Accokeek Foundation, Accokeek, Md.

CHAPTER TWO
Building Communities in the Wilderness

1. Hening, *Statutes at Large*, 5:489. The most recent treatment of the structure and function of the county court in Virginia is A. G. Roeber's, *Faithful Magistrates and Republican Lawyers: Creators of Virginia's Legal Culture, 1680–1810* (Chapel Hill, N.C., 1981). For an older but still useful description of the institutional structure of the court, see Albert O. Porter, *County Government in Virginia: A Legislative History, 1607–1904* (New York, 1947). A briefer but more illuminating discussion of the symbolic importance of the court is in Isaac, *Transformation of Virginia*, pp. 88–94, 124–31.

2. Lunenburg County Order Book, no. 1 (1746–48), no. 2 (1748–52), no. 12 (1766–69), no. 13 (1769–77), Virginia State Library, Richmond, Va.

3. The conduct of the Lunenburg justices was also slightly different from that of the justices of adjacent Amelia and Brunswick counties. By the standards of the eastern counties, the volume of court activity in all three Southside counties was slight, but the Lunenburg court was by far the least active of the three; this is most likely another reflection of the county's unsettled state. For a discussion of the courts in the Southside before 1750, see Nicholls, "Origins of the Virginia Southside," pp. 141–44, 151–52.

4. Richmond County Order Books, nos. 10–13, passim; no. 11, June 5, 1739, June 5, 1729, Virginia State Library.

5. Baine, *Munford*, p. 60; Byrd, "The Secret History of the Line," p. 144.

6. Lunenburg County Order Book, no. 1 (1746–48), pp. 70, 226, 327.

7. Ibid., passim.

8. Ibid., May 5, 1746, July 7, 1746.

9. Ibid., August 4, 1746.

10. Ibid., September 1747.

11. Ibid., passim.

12. The twelve original justices of the court were spread out among six of the county's eight tithable districts, and the concentration of justices from the northeast portion of the county was primarily a reflection of that region's denser population.

13. Lois Green Carr, "County Government in Maryland, 1689–1709" (Ph.D. diss., Harvard University, 1968), shows that individual justices working informally in the vicinity of their places of residence were able to enforce discipline by dint of their personal authority. See also Lorena S. Walsh, "Charles County, Maryland, 1658–1705: A Study of Chesapeake Social and Political Structure" (Ph.D. diss., Michigan State University, 1977), pp. 310, 339–51.

14. Bell, *Old Free State*, 1:290; H. R. McIlwaine, ed., *Executive Journals of the Council of Colonial Virginia* (Richmond, Va., 1930), 4:266, 301, 315, 333.

15. The original justices of the Lunenburg court were John Caldwell, William Caldwell, Cornelius Cargill, Abraham Cook, Lewis Deloney, William Hill, John Hall, Matthew Howard, Hugh Lawson, Thomas Lanier, John Phelps, and Matthew Talbot. Other than Deloney, only Hill, Hall, and Phelps appear to have patented or purchased more than four hundred acres in the area during the decade before the founding of the county; the remainder either did not record land patents or purchases, or received grants of relatively small tracts. Information on land acquisitions is derived from Nicholls, "Origins of the Virginia Southside," p. 84; Va. Abstracts, vol. 9, books 17–25, and vol. 20, books 27–31; Lunenburg County Deed Books, no. 1 (1746–51) and no. 2 (1750–52); Brunswick County Deeds, Wills, etc., book 1 (1732–40), and Deed Books 2 (1740–45) and 3 (1744–49).

16. See sources cited above in note 15. The justices' holdings were modest by the standards of the more settled Virginia counties, which is striking in view of the intense activity in selling and granting land in Lunenburg during that period. The average grant in Lunenburg for 1746–51 was 582 acres, and the average purchase was 330 acres. Thus we find that even those justices who did engage in land activity tended to do so on much the same scale as their neighbors. Va. Abstracts, vol. 20, books 27–31.

17. Bell, *Sunlight*, pp. 122–61.

18. Bell, *Old Free State*, 1:326–34. The high rate of turnover reflected not only the court's instability but also a process, just beginning, whereby the court would eventually strengthen itself. Over the course of the next two decades, the newer appointees to the court would have longer records of service than their predecessors and would gradually build higher levels of personal wealth as well.

19. *JHB, 1742–49*, p. 238; Bell, *Old Free State*, 2:68.

20. "Biographical Sketch of Clement Read," *William and Mary Quarterly*, 2d ser., 6:242–43.

21. Ibid.

22. *JHB, 1742–49*, p. ix. For a glimpse of Read's activities as a surveyor and an account of the importance of surveyors in Virginia generally, see Sarah S. Hughes, *Surveyors and Statesmen: Land Measuring in Colonial Virginia* (Richmond, Va., 1979), pp. 83, 151, 164, and passim.

23. *JHB, 1752–55*, p. viii.

24. Ibid., passim.

25. For the best account of the symbolic importance of the Anglican church in Virginia, see Isaac, *Transformation of Virginia*, esp. pp. 58–68, 120–24. For the English background of that tradition, see George W. O. Addleshaw and Frederick Etchells, *The Architectural Setting of Anglican Worship* (London, 1948).

26. The original vestry consisted of Lewis Deloney, Clement Read, Matthew Talbot, Abraham Martin, Lydall Bacon, Daniel Stokes, Daniel Ferth, Thomas Bouldin, and John Twitty. Of these men, Deloney, Read, and Twitty had pa-

tented or purchased more than a thousand acres of land either before the creation of the county or within five years of that date, and two others, Talbot and Martin, owned as many as five tithable slaves before 1750. Clement Read seems to have been the only man of high social standing as well as wealth. Va. Abstracts, vol. 9, books 17–25, and vol. 20, books 27–31; Brunswick County Deeds, Wills, etc., book 1 (1732–40), and Deed Books 2 (1740–45) and 3 (1744–49); Lunenburg County Deed Books, no. 1 (1746–51) and no. 2 (1750–52); Bell, *Old Free State*, 1:326–34; Bell, *Cumberland Parish*, p. 26.

27. William Meade, *Old Churches, Ministers, and Families of Virginia*, 2 vols. (Philadelphia, 1857), 1:482–84; 2:178–79, 217–18; Bell, *Cumberland Parish*, pp. 61–63.

28. Meade, *Old Churches*, 2:178–79; Bell, *Cumberland Parish*, pp. 64–65.

29. Bell, *Cumberland Parish*, pp. 68–70.

30. James Craig to Thomas Dawson, September 8, 1759, William Dawson Papers, 1728–75, vol. 2, p. 218, Library of Congress.

31. Bell, *Cumberland Parish*, pp. 32–33; Harold Wickliffe Rose, *The Colonial Houses of Worship in America, Built in the English Colonies Before the Republic, 1607–1789, and Still Standing* (New York, 1963); p. 465.

32. Bradshaw, *History of Prince Edward County*, pp. 10, 15, 16; William Henry Foote, *Sketches of Virginia, Historical and Biographical* (Philadelphia, 1850), pp. 103–4; Elizabeth Gaines, *The Cub Creek Church and Congregation* (Richmond, Va., 1931), pp. 9–10.

33. Gaines, *Cub Creek Church*, pp. 15–21.

34. We still lack a satisfactory history of Presbyterianism in Virginia, but for a survey of the contrasting styles within that denomination in Virginia, see D. C. Beard's "Origin and Early History of Presbyterianism in Virginia" (Ph.D. diss., University of Edinburgh, 1932). The most useful, though still unsystematic, published work remains Foote's *Sketches of Virginia*.

35. Gaines, *Cub Creek Church*, pp. 32–36; Bell, *Sunlight*, pp. 122–61.

36. Another member of the family, David Caldwell, also managed to achieve a position of some prominence in the county by dint of his position with William Byrd, for whom he served as principal agent in most of the latter's land transactions in Lunenburg during the late 1740s and early 1750s. Lunenburg County Deed Books, no. 1 (1746–51), pp. 114ff.

37. Bell, *Old Free State*, 1:290.

38. Nicholls, "Origins of the Virginia Southside," pp. 51–55.

CHAPTER THREE
A Southside Community in Transition

1. Bell, *Old Free State*, 1:132–55; Bell, *Cumberland Parish*, pp. 331–416.

2. Every move to divide the county brought forth petitions both favoring and strongly opposing the action. See, e.g., *JHB, 1742–49*, pp. 282, 306; ibid.,

1750–52, pp. 69, 85, 86, 115; ibid., *1752–57*, pp. 240–41, 425, 432, 445; ibid., *1758–60*, pp. 85, 191, 231; ibid., *1761–65*, p. 104

3. Bell, *Sunlight*, pp. 122–61. The one major exception to the slightly greater concentration of wealth in northeastern Lunenburg was the estate of William Byrd; with its more than 100,000 acres and sixty-two slaves, it tended to skew considerably the calculations for the "average" wealth in each of Lunenburg's tithable districts.

4. Although historians of early America have tended to use landholding as the principal index of wealth, it seems apparent that at least in prerevolutionary Lunenburg it was the control of a labor force, in addition to the accumulation of acreage, which separated affluent households from men and women of middling means. The two most commonly cited studies of Virginia social structure, Jackson T. Main's *The Social Structure of Revolutionary America* (Princeton, N.J., 1965) and Robert E. Brown and B. Katherine Brown's *Virginia, 1705–1786: Democracy or Aristocracy?* (East Lansing, Mich., 1964) both suffer from this tendency to equate land with wealth and status.

5. Bell, *Sunlight*, pp. 122–61, 228–46, 269–85.

6. The trend of land purchases was as follows:

Year	Mean Size (Acres)	Median Size (Acres)	Mean Price (Shillings per Acre)
1746	330	300	2.0
1751	336	253	2.5
1761	260	200	4.5
1766	270	220	8.0
1771	202	145	9.0

(Source: Lunenburg County Deed Books, nos. 1–11.)

7. Although "average" landholdings tended to decrease slightly during the period, the percentage of taxpayers in the population with legal title to land actually increased from 1750 to 1782.

8. Bell, *Sunlight*, pp. 269–85. My calculations, based on the 1769 rather than the 1764 tithable lists, are slightly lower than those of Main, *Social Structure*, pp. 168–85, but we agree on the higher level of opportunity to own land existing in frontier areas like Lunenburg.

9. Bell, *Sunlight*, pp. 269–85.

10. Lunenburg County Deed Books, no. 1 (1746–51) and no. 7 (1761–62).

11. Lunenburg County Will Books, no. 1 (1746–60) and No. 2 (1760–78). See also Table 8, p. 177.

12. This is the argument advanced so persuasively by Edmund S. Morgan in *American Slavery, American Freedom: The Ordeal of Colonial Virginia* (New York, 1975). The slave calculations for Lunenburg are based on the tithable lists in Bell, *Sunlight*, pp. 122–61, 228–46, 269–85. For comparable calculations for the east, see Main, *Social Structure*, pp. 45–46, and Allan Kulikoff, *Tobacco and Slaves* (Chapel Hill, N.C., forthcoming).

13. Bell, *Sunlight*, pp. 122–61, 228–46, 269–85.

14. Ibid.; Lunenburg County Deed Books, no. 1 (1746–51), p. 141; Bell, *Sunlight*, p. 279.

15. Lunenburg County Deed Books, no. 1 (1746–51); pp. 231, 236; Lunenburg County Will Books, no. 3 (1778–91), p. 244.

16. Va. Abstracts, vol. 20, book 29, p. 481; Bell, *Sunlight*, pp. 122–61, 269–85.

17. Lunenburg County Deed Books, no. 3 (1752–54), pp. 3, 34, 94, 356; no. 10 (1764–67), pp. 101, 159, 187, 189, 192, 321; no. 11 (1767–71), pp. 146, 291, 320; no. 12 (1771–77), pp. 67–69, 185, 202, 208, 282, 354, 356, 357, 360, 376; no. 4 (1754–57), p. 357; no. 6 (1760–61), p. 178; no. 7 (1761–62), p. 377; no. 8 (1762–63), pp. 90–93.

18. Bell, *Sunlight*, pp. 58–86, 122–61, 228–46, 269–85. The 265 white dependents do not include those 111 who appeared for the first time on the 1769 lists and therefore were not linked to any other previous tithe lists.

19. Ibid.

20. Ibid., pp. 212–85. The designation "economic elite" is an historian's construct. From the scanty information available in Lunenburg County's early tax lists, it is not possible to identify all the components of an individual's wealth. The capital of Lunenburg's residents was increasingly tied up in slaves, however, and for that reason I used slave ownership as the primary criterion for ranking the twenty wealthiest men in each year. In a few cases, where an individual's landholdings were exceptionally large, I used landownership as a secondary criterion.

21. Ibid., pp. 58–86, 212–85. See Appendix 1.

22. Lunenburg County Will Books, no. 3 (1778–91), pp. 252, 291; no. 7 (1803–16), pp. 278, 281.

23. Lunenburg County Deed Books, no. 7 (1761–62), pp. 195, 351.

24. Bell, *Cumberland Parish*, pp. 205–6, 287; *William and Mary Quarterly*, 1st ser., 13:123; Lunenburg County Deed Books, no. 1 (1746–51), p. 378; Bell, *Sunlight*, pp. 122–61, 228–46, 269–85.

25. Lunenburg County Deed Books, no. 1 (1746–51), p. 141, Bell, *Sunlight*, pp. 122–61, 212–85. Bacon was not recorded as having patented land in Brunswick County before Lunenburg was established, but he must have had some standing in the county or he would not have been appointed one of the original justices of the county.

26. Lunenburg County Deed Books, no. 2 (1750–52), pp. 20, 156; Lunenburg County Will Books, no. 3 (1778–91), p. 99.

27. Thomas P. DeGraffenreid, *History of the DeGraffenreid Family* (New York, 1925), pp. 58–69, 100–113.

28. The most prominent of DeGraffenreid's wives, Elizabeth Embry, was the daughter of Henry Embry, one of the original settlers of the county. Bell, *Old Free State*, 1:97; Bell, *Sunlight*, pp. 179, 212–85; Real and Personal Property Tax Lists, Lunenburg County, 1782, Virginia State Library, Richmond, Va. For a genealogy of the DeGraffenreid family, see Bell, *Old Free State*, 2:203–10.

29. Arvin, *Antebellum Homes of Lunenburg*, pp. 143–46, 159–60.

30. Lunenburg County Will Books, no. 3 (1778–91), p. 99.

31. Rhys Isaac, *Transformation of Virginia*, esp. pp. 18–42, delineates in compelling if overdrawn fashion the "gentry ideal." The two most important works by Eugene Genovese on this subject are *The World the Slaveholders Made: Two Essays in Interpretation* (New York, 1969) and, even more crucial, *Roll Jordan Roll: The World the Slaves Made* (New York, 1974).

32. The quote is from William Byrd II to Charles, Earl of Orrery, July 5, 1726, in "Virginia Council Journals, 1726–1753," *Virginia Magazine of History and Biography* 32 (1924): 27; but see Isaac, *Transformation of Virginia*, pp. 39–42, for a full analysis of the significance of Byrd's statement.

33. Genovese, *Roll Jordan Roll*, pp. 54, 85, 100–102, 188, 322, 393.

34. The two best general treatments of the role of the Scots merchants in the Virginia tobacco economy are Jacob M. Price, "The Rise of Glasgow in the Chesapeake Tobacco Trade, 1707–1775," *William and Mary Quarterly*, 3d ser., 11 (1954): 179–99, and James Soltow, "Scottish Traders in Virginia, 1750–1775," *Economic History Review*, 2d ser., 12 (1959–60): 83–98.

35. See sources cited above in note 34. For a glimpse of the overriding importance of the Scots merchants in the Southside, see Robert P. Thomson, "The Tobacco Exports of the Upper James Naval District, 1773–75," *William and Mary Quarterly*, 3d ser., 18 (1961): 393–407.

36. The exact effect of credit conditions in Great Britain on the Southside economy is not clear, but two useful accounts are Joseph A. Ernst's *Money and Politics in America, 1755–1775* (Chapel Hill, N.C., 1973), esp. pp. 45–46, 65–67, 231–33, 331–32; and Richard B. Sheridan's "The British Credit Crisis of 1772 and the American Colonies," *Journal of Economic History* 20 (1960): 161–86.

37. Bell, *Sunlight*, pp. 269–85; Bell, *Old Free State*, 1:326–34.

38. Bell, *Cumberland Parish*, pp. 26–31.

39. See Appendix 2.

40. Wilbur J. Cash, *The Mind of the South* (New York, 1941), esp. pp. 3–29. The Caldwells ended up in South Carolina; the Billups family moved to Georgia, and the Talbots moved to Tennessee and then to Georgia. Bell, *Cumberland Parish*, pp. 178–82, 291.

41. Lunenburg County Order Book, no. 12 (1766–69), June 12, 1776–June 11, 1767; no. 13 (1769–77), May 9, 1771–May 14, 1772, April 15, 1774–December 14, 1775.

42. Ibid., no. 1 (1746–48), June 1746–May 1747; no. 12 (1766–69), July 1766–June 1767.

43. For a discussion of the disposition of criminal cases in colonial Virginia, see Hugh F. Rankin, *Criminal Trial Proceedings in the General Court of Colonial Virginia* (Williamsburg, Va., 1965).

44. Lunenburg County Order Book, no. 12 (1766–69), September 11, 12, 1766; April 11 and June 11, 1767; no. 13 (1769–77), June 14, 1771.

45. *Virginia Gazette and General Advertiser* (Purdie and Dixon), August 15, 1771; Rhys Isaac, "Evangelical Revolt: The Nature of the Baptists' Challenge

to the Traditional Order in Virginia, 1765–1775," *William and Mary Quarterly*, 3d ser., 31 (1974): 345–68.

46. *Virginia Gazette* (Hunter), November 7, 1754, November 30, 1759; ibid. (Purdie and Dixon), September 26, 1766, September 30, 1773; ibid. (Purdie), December 10, 1772, April 5, 1776; ibid. (Rind), April 28, 1768.

47. Bell, *Cumberland Parish*, pp. 26–31, 68–70, 98.

48. Ibid., 26–31; Bell, *Old Free State*, 1:326–34; Bell, *Sunlight*, pp. 269–85.

49. Bell, *Cumberland Parish*, pp. 41–43.

50. For a more detailed discussion of the differences in political style between the Southside and more established, hierarchically ordered counties to the east, see Richard R. Beeman, "Robert Munford and the Political Culture of Frontier Virginia," *Journal of American Studies* 12 (1978): 169–83.

51. Jay Hubbell and Douglass Adair, eds., "Robert Munford's 'The Candidates,' " *William and Mary Quarterly*, 3d ser., 5 (1948): 217–57. *The Candidates* was first printed in 1798 by Munford's son William and was not reprinted until Hubbell and Adair undertook the task. All citations that follow refer to Hubbell and Adair's edition.

52. Baine, *Munford*, pp. 5–18.

53. *JHB, 1758–61*, March 8, 1758, pp. 83–84.

54. Munford, *The Candidates*, p. 232.

55. Hening, *Statutes at Large*, 3:243.

56. *JHB, 1758–61*, March 8, 1758, pp. 83–84.

57. Ibid.

58. Ibid.

59. Munford, *The Candidates*, pp. 243–44.

60. Ibid., p. 238.

61. *JHB, 1770–72*, February 11, 1772, pp. 251–54, 288–89.

62. Meherrin Baptist Church Minute Book, February and August 1774, Virginia Baptist Historical Society, Richmond, Va.

63. *JHB, 1756–58*, March 26, 1756, p. 339; May 7, 1757, pp. 456–58.

64. Ibid., 1758–61, March 8, 1758, pp. 83–84.

CHAPTER FOUR
The Evangelical Revolt in the Backcountry

1. James Craig to Thomas Dawson, September 8, 1759, William Dawson Papers, 1728–75, vol. 2, pp. 217–18. For the evangelical perspective in Lunenburg, the best source is the Journal of John Williams, 1771, Virginia Baptist Historical Society, Richmond, Va.

2. See esp. Isaac, *Transformation of Virginia*, pp. 163–64, 322; and Isaac, "Evangelical Revolt," pp. 345–68.

3. Beatty and Mulloy, eds., *William Byrd's Natural History*, p. xxii. Changes in population can be traced through the tithable lists printed in Bell, *Sunlight*, pp. 212–67.

4. Craig to Dawson, September 8, 1759, Dawson Papers.

5. Hooker, ed., *Carolina Backcountry*, p. 47.

6. Petition to the Legislature, Lunenburg County, March 8, 1782, Legislative Petitions, Virginia State Library, Richmond, Va.

7. Hooker, ed., *Carolina Backcountry*, pp. 88–89.

8. Even within those Anglican churches in the most well settled and traditionally ordered of Virginia's counties, there was a distinct tension between convivial and contestful styles of life, on the one hand, and genteel, decorous, and learned values on the other hand. Rhys Isaac, especially in "Evangelical Revolt," tends to emphasize the fondness of the Anglican culture for tippling, dancing, fiddling, cockfighting, horse-racing, and the like, a style of life which found its embodiment in men like William Byrd. Planter gentry like Robert Carter, who probably would have felt uncomfortable at a cockfight and who spent his evenings reading classical literature rather than tippling and gambling, represented the genteel, decorous ideal. James Craig, on his arrival in Virginia, probably carried within him images of a congregation led by men like Robert Carter, but he would be sorely disappointed.

9. Bell, *Old Free State*, 1:372–73; Gaines, *Cub Creek Church*, pp. 21–22; Bradshaw, *History of Prince Edward County*, pp. 75–76.

10. Bradshaw, *History of Prince Edward County*, pp. 75–76. All those families were represented on the Lunenburg Court at one time or another, and Christopher Billups and Thomas Pettus, whose families were closely associated with the founding of the Briery Presbyterian Church, both enjoyed long terms of service as vestrymen of Cumberland Parish.

11. Ibid.

12. William Robinson, the first Presbyterian to preach in Lunenburg, was an Englishman from a wealthy and prominent family. Robert Henry, the first permanent minister of the Cub Creek and Briery congregations, had been educated at Princeton. Foote, *Sketches of Virginia*, 1st ser., p. 125.

13. The other principal evangelical groups, the Methodists, came to the area later, shortly after the Revolution, and even then concentrated their efforts in the Southside in Brunswick County, to the southeast of Lunenburg (see Chapter 8).

14. Robert B. Semple, *History of the Rise and Progress of the Baptists in Virginia* (Richmond, Va., 1810), pp. 15–28. For an unusually lucid account of these events (and a novel appraisal of the key elements of American culture), see John Uno, "History of the Baptists in Virginia," a copy of which is available in the Virginia Baptist Historical Society, Richmond, Va.

15. Craig to Dawson, September 8, 1759, Dawson Papers.

16. For a biographical treatment of Harriss, see W. B. Hackley, "Sidelights on Samuel Harriss," *Virginia Baptist Historical Register* 10 (1971): 456–66.

17. Craig to Dawson, September 8, 1759, Dawson Papers.

18. Semple, *History*, pp. 291–92.

19. Ibid.

20. Lunenburg County Order Book, no. 13 (1769–77), December 13, 1770;

Virginia Redd, "The Meherrin Baptist Church, Lunenburg County, Virginia, 1771–1842," *Virginia Baptist Historical Register* 15 (1976): 706–18.

21. The calculations on Meherrin church membership are from the Meherrin Church Minute Book, 1771–81.

22. See, e.g., Meherrin Church Minute Book, December 8, 1771; January 5, 11, 12, February 8, March 22, April 2, May 20, and September 1, 1772; February, June, and August, 1774; and May 14, 1775.

23. Ibid., January 12, 26, May 20, July 5, and August 8 and 9, 1772; August 1773.

24. Ibid., February 22, 23, May 30, 31, June 1772; March 2, 1773.

25. Ibid., January 4, 26, May 30, 31, June 1772; March 2, 1773.

26. Ibid., February 22, 23, May 30, 31, June, July 5, October 1, 1772.

27. The most useful accounts of the importance of evangelical religion to slave life are Albert J. Raboteau's *Slave Religion: The "Invisible Institution" in the Antebellum South* (New York, 1978); Mechal Sobel's *Trabelin' On: The Slave Journey to an Afro-Baptist Faith* (Westport, Conn., 1979); Anne C. Loveland's *Southern Evangelicals and the Social Order, 1800–1860* (Baton Rouge, La., 1980); and Donald G. Mathews's *Religion in the Old South* (Chicago, 1977).

28. Meherrin Church Minute Book, January 12, May 20, 1772; July 1775; July 1776.

29. W. Harrison Daniel, "Virginia Baptists and the Negro in the Early Republic," *Virginia Magazine of History and Biography* 80 (1972): 64–65.

30. Raboteau, *Slave Religion*, p. 318.

31. Steven Kroll-Smith, "In Search of Status Power: Baptist Revival in Colonial Virginia" (Ph.D. diss., University of Pennsylvania, 1982).

32. Journal of John Williams, 1771.

33. Ibid.

34. The phrase "Christian, utopian, closed, corporate community" is from Kenneth Lockridge's *A New England Town: The First Hundred Years* (New York, 1970), esp. pp. 16–22, 57–58. Although Lockridge overemphasizes the insularity of early-seventeenth-century Dedham, Massachusetts, and exaggerates the similarity between Dedham and peasant communities of Central America and Indonesia, his comparative perspective is helpful in widening the focus on the historical and cultural roots of that form of community.

35. The most notable exception was Henry Blagrave, a wealthy landowner, gentleman justice, and former member of the Anglican vestry. Blagrave seems to have joined the Meherrin church in December 1771, becoming the Lunenburg Baptists' first genuinely wealthy and powerful convert. Meherrin Church Minute Books, December 8, 1771. The other exception was Francis DeGraffenreid, who seemed to float oddly through the ranks of the Baptists, Presbyterians, and Anglicans alike during the period and whose particular religious commitment defies precise categorization.

36. The tithable lists for 1769 and 1772 are in Bell, *Sunlight*, pp. 269–85, 287–309. Real and Personal Property Tax Lists, Lunenburg County, 1782.

37. Bell, *Sunlight*, pp. 269–85; Real and Personal Property Tax Lists,

Lunenburg County, 1782. Though Williams is not listed as owning any slaves, his journal makes note that "I had all my family given up to the Lord by prayer, the children black and white." Journal of John Williams, 1771.

38. Bell, *Sunlight*, pp. 269–85.

39. Meherrin Church Minute Books, 1772–82, passim. Bell, *Cumberland Parish*, pp. 424–48. Real and Personal Property Tax Lists, Lunenburg County, 1782. It is difficult to pinpoint the exact number of slaves of all ages belonging to any given household because the basis for calculating taxes on slaves kept changing periodically. Before the Revolution, tithable slaves (males and females above sixteen years of age) were included in the tax lists, and in 1782 the lists included slaves of all ages.

40. Bell, *Old Free State*, 1:76–131; 2:149–54.

41. Semple, *History*, pp. 11–13, 295–96; John S. Moore, "Writers of Early Virginia Baptist History: John Williams," *Virginia Baptist Historical Register* 14 (1975): 633–47.

42. Moore, "Writers of Early Virginia Baptist History," pp. 633–47.

43. Bell, *Sunlight*, pp. 121–61, 228–46, 269–85.

44. It is impossible to locate precisely where the members of the Anglican or Baptist churches lived, but by correlating the names of those church members with the names in the county's thirty-one processioning districts (printed in Bell, *Cumberland Parish*, pp. 421–24), it is possible to make some rough approximation of their area of residence. However, the correlation between residence and religious affiliation seems to be weak.

45. Hooker, ed., *Carolina Backcountry*, p. 101.

46. Ibid., pp. 16–17; Craig to Dawson, September 8, 1759, Dawson Papers.

47. Craig to Dawson, September 8, 1759, Dawson Papers.

48. *JHB*, 1770–72, pp. 160–61.

49. Ibid., p. 249; ibid., *1773–76*, pp. 92, 102; *Virginia Gazette* (Rind), June 10, 1773. For a general account of the prerevolutionary controversy over religious toleration, see Hamilton J. Eckenrode's *Separation of Church and State in Virginia: A Study in the Development of the Revolution* (Richmond, Va., 1910) and Thomas E. Buckley's *Church and State in Revolutionary Virginia, 1776–1787* (Charlottesville, Va., 1977).

CHAPTER FIVE
The Constitutional Revolt in the Backcountry

1. In general, the behavior of Virginians everywhere during the years 1763–74 conformed to the description given by Pauline Maier, *From Resistance to Revolution: Colonial Radicals and the Development of American Opposition to Britain, 1765–1776* (New York, 1972).

2. Robert Gross, *The Minutemen and Their World* (New York, 1976), pp. 42–67.

3. There is no wholly adequate account of the Revolution in Virginia. The

best remains Hamilton J. Eckenrode's *The Revolution in Virginia* (Boston, 1916). For Virginia's reaction to the Stamp Act Resolves, see Richard R. Beeman, *Patrick Henry: A Biography* (New York, 1975), pp. 33–44; and Edmund S. Morgan and Helen M. Morgan, *The Stamp Act Crisis: Prologue to Revolution* (Chapel Hill, N.C., 1953), pp. 120–32. For the responses of specific counties to the Stamp Act, see William J. Van Schreeven, Robert L. Scribner, and Brent Tarter, eds., *Revolutionary Virginia: The Road to Independence*, 6 vols. to date (Charlottesville, Va., 1977–   ), 1:19–49.

4. *Virginia Gazette* (Rind), June 4, 1769.

5. Maier, *From Resistance to Revolution*, esp. pp. 113–97.

6. *Virginia Gazette* (Rind), June 4, 1769.

7. Blagrave's conversion to the Baptist faith occurred about the time of the founding of the Meherrin church, for though he is listed as an original member of the congregation of that church, he had up until November 1768 been a vestryman of the Anglican church. Meherrin Church Minute Book, November 27, 1771; Bell, *Cumberland Parish*, p. 408.

8. Van Schreeven et al., *Revolutionary Virginia*, 1:204–5.

9. Ibid.

10. Ibid., 1:120–22; but see also pp. 145–47, 150–52. The wording of the resolutions from most of the Southside counties was essentially similar, suggesting some degree of coordination of the resistance movement by 1774.

11. Ibid., 1:120–22.

12. *JHB, 1770–72* and *1773–76*, passim; *Journal of the House of Delegates of the Commonwealth of Virginia*, 1776–80 (Richmond, 1827–28).

13. Van Schreeven et al., *Revolutionary Virginia*, 5:157.

14. Lunenburg County Order Book, no. 13 (1769–77), January 9 and 16, 1777.

15. Courtlandt Canby, ed., "Robert Munford's *The Patriots*," *William and Mary Quarterly*, 3d ser., 6 (1949): 437–503.

16. Ibid., p. 461.

17. Emory Evans, "Planter Indebtedness and the Coming of the Revolution in Virginia," *William and Mary Quarterly*, 3d ser., 19 (1962): 511–33, argues persuasively that the desire to escape paying back debts was not a primary cause of the Revolution in Virginia, but he underestimates the extent to which the Scots' domination of the system of trade and credit created an emotional climate that was bitterly hostile to the Scots.

18. The Journal of the Virginia Convention is printed in Peter Force, ed., *American Archives* (Washington, D.C., 1837), ser. 4, vol. 6, p. 1522.

19. The following discussion is informed by a reading of two of the most suggestive analyses of the social and intellectual meaning of the revolutionary war: John Shy's *A People Numerous and Armed: Reflections on the Military Struggle for American Independence* (New York, 1976), esp. pp. 193–224; and Charles Royster's *A Revolutionary People at War: The Continental Army and the American Character, 1775–1783* (New York, 1979).

20. Bell, *Old Free State*, 1:218.

21. Ibid., pp. 220–24.

22. Ibid., p. 213; W. P. Palmer and S. McRae, eds., *Calendar of Virginia State Papers*, 11 vols. (Richmond, Va., 1875–93), 2:245.

23. The story of Tarleton's raid and its aftermath in Lunenburg can be pieced together from a petition to Governor Thomas Nelson, August 12, 1781, in *Calendar of Va. State Papers*, 2:323–24; Meade, *Old Churches, Ministers, and Families of Virginia*, 1:484–85; and Bell, *Old Free State*, 1:252–56.

24. David Garland to Thomas Nelson, 1781, *Calendar of Va. State Papers*, 2:240–41.

25. Nicholas Hobson to William Davies, July 24, 1781, *Calendar of Va. State Papers*, 2:245.

26. Ibid.

27. General Nathanael Greene to General Robert Howe, December 29, 1780, and Greene to Robert Morris, March 7, 1782, Nathanael Greene Papers, Library of Congress. For a fuller comparison of the revolutionary situation in Lunenburg and the rest of the Southern backcountry, see Beeman, "Political Response to Social Conflict in the Southern Backcountry."

28. Bell, *Old Free State*, 1:262–63.

29. David Stokes to Thomas Nelson, October 1, 1781, *Calendar of Va. State Papers*, 2:515–16.

30. Ibid.

31. *JHB, 1756–58*, p. 360.

32. Louis B. Wright and Marion Tinling, eds., *The Secret Diary of William Byrd of Westover, 1709–1712* (Richmond, Va., 1947), pp. 414–15.

33. For an informative discussion of the role of alcohol in the fighting of the war, see Royster, *A Revolutionary People at War*, esp. pp. 144–46, 249–50.

34. These calculations are based on the Real and Personal Property Tax Lists, Lunenburg County, 1782; the information on court and vestry service provided by Bell, *Old Free State*, 1:326–34; and Bell, *Cumberland Parish*, pp. 26–31.

35. See the sources cited above in note 34. The muster roles (or at least those that have survived) are printed in Bell, *Old Free State*, 1:215–35.

36. See the sources cited above in note 34.

37. There is currently a vigorous argument among historians about the precise character of the social composition of the American revolutionary army. At one pole, Royster argues that in their ideological attachments if not always in their material circumstances, the militiamen embodied the ideals of a "republican" army (*A Revolutionary People at War*, esp. pp. 373–78). At the other extreme, Mark E. Lender, "The Mind of the Rank and File: Patriotism and Motivation in the Continental Line," in William C. Wright, ed., *New Jersey in the American Revolution, III, Papers Presented at the Seventh Annual New Jersey History Symposium* (Trenton, N.J., 1976), pp. 21–39; John R. Sellers, "The Common Soldier in the American Revolution," in Stanley J. Underdal, ed., *Military History of the American Revolution: Proceedings of the Sixth Military History Symposium, USAF Academy, 1974* (Washington, D.C., 1976), pp. 151–

66; and Edward C. Papenfuse and Gregory A. Stiverson, "General Smallwood's Recruits: The Peacetime Career of the Revolutionary War Private," *William and Mary Quarterly*, 3d ser., 30 (1973): 117–32, argue that the material condition and by implication the ideological orientation of the common soldier in America was more similar to that of the rank and file of the standing armies of Europe than it was of the idealized archetype of an "American republican."

38. Bell, *Old Free State*, 1:326–34; Real and Personal Property Tax Lists, Lunenburg County, 1782.

39. See the sources cited above in note 38.

40. Lunenburg County Order Book, no. 13 (1769–77), May 18, 1777.

41. Lunenburg County Order Book, no. 14 (1777–84), June 12, July 10, September 11, December 11, 1777; January 8, February 12, March 12, 1778.

42. Bell, *Old Free State*, 1:216; Real and Personal Property Tax Lists, Lunenburg County, 1795; Lunenburg County Will Books, no. 7 (1799–1810), 1810, p. 10.

43. For the constant cries of Lunenburg's residents for relief from debts, a situation they generally described as stemming from "a shortage of cash," see "Petition of John Ragsdale, Sheriff, to the Legislature, Nov. 19, 1783," "Petition of Jonathan Pattison, Sheriff, to the Legislature, Nov. 3, 1786," "Petition of the Debtors of Lunenburg to the Legislature, March 10, 1789," Legislative Petitions, Virginia State Library; *Calendar of Va. State Papers*, 4:10; 5:154; "List of Insolvents and Delinquents, Lunenburg Courts, 1788, 1789," Auditors Accounts, no. 148, Virginia State Library, Richmond, Va.

CHAPTER SIX
The Clash of Cultural Styles

1. *JHB, 1770–72*, pp. 160–61, 188, 249; ibid., *1773–76*, pp. 92–102. For a general account of the prerevolutionary controversy over religious toleration, see Eckenrode, *Separation of Church and State*, esp. pp. 31–40. See also Buckley, *Church and State*, pp. 8–14.

2. Meherrin Church Minute Book, September 2, 1774; Gordon Wood, *The Creation of the American Republic, 1776–1787* (Chapel Hill, N.C., 1969), pp. 91–124, makes a convincing case for the tendency among Americans to link their Revolution with the "moral reformation" of their society.

3. Bell, *Old Free State*, 1:213, 215–27, 233–35, 266–69, 326–34; Bell, *Cumberland Parish*, pp. 26–31; Meherrin Church Minute Books, 1774–84. One Baptist church member, Jeffrey Russel, Jr., was listed as a deserter from the Fourteenth Virginia Regiment in March 1777, but in general the county's citizens displayed a steadfast commitment to the war effort.

4. The continuity of the county court's leadership can be seen in the list of court members before and after the Revolution printed in Bell, *Old Free State*, 1:326–34. The continuity among Anglican vestrymen can be seen in Bell, *Cumberland Parish*, pp. 26–31.

5. Semple, *History*, p. 86.

6. A competent treatment of the legislative wranglings on church-state issues during this period is Buckley, *Church and State*, esp. pp. 29–37.

7. "Ten Thousand Name (Baptist) Petition," October 16, 1776, Virginia Religious Petitions, Virginia State Library, Richmond, Va.

8. Eckenrode, *Separation of Church and State*, pp. 46–54.

9. Ibid., p. 53.

10. *Journal of the House of Delegates of the Commonwealth of Virginia* (October 1777–January 1778), December 11, 1777, p. 75. The *Journals of the House of Delegates* cited hereafter are a four-volume reprinted compilation by Thomas W. White, covering the sessions from 1776 to 1790, which were published in Richmond in 1827 and 1828. The journal of each session is paginated separately. Subsequent references to these journals will be to *JHD*, with the session dates indicated in parentheses and the place and date of publication omitted.

11. Semple, *History*, p. 85.

12. The five pro-establishment petitions from Lunenburg are variously addressed, some to the House of Delegates and some to the General Assembly. Those dated November 3, 1780, November 8, 1783, and November 9, 1785, are found in the collection of Virginia Religious Petitions in the Virginia State Library; the other two petitions are found in *JHD* (October 1777–January 1778), December 11, 1777, p. 75; ibid. (October 1784–January 1785), November 20, 1784, p. 32. The anti-establishment petition addressed to the House of Delegates dated December 1, 1785, is also found in the collection of Virginia Religious Petitions.

13. For a more detailed survey of these events, see Buckley, *Church and State*, pp. 38–143.

14. The first quotation is found in *JHD* (October 1784–January 1785), November 20, 1784, p. 32. The second is from "A Bill Establishing a Provision for Teachers of the Christian Religion," a copy of which is attached to a petition in favor of the bill from Richmond County, dated November 3, 1779, also in the Virginia Religious Petitions.

15. "A Bill for Teachers of the Christian Religion," November 3, 1779.

16. Ibid.

17. Petition of December 1, 1785, Lunenburg County, Virginia Religious Petitions.

18. Ibid.; Petition to the House of Delegates from a Committee of Several Baptist Associations in Virginia, November 3, 1785, Virginia Religious Petitions.

19. I analyzed the establishmentarian petitions of November 8, 1783, and November 9, 1785, most intensely, because they had the largest number of signers and seem to have had the greatest impact on the course of decision-making in the House of Delegates. Information on the signers was gleaned from Bell, *Old Free State*, 1:326–34; Bell, *Cumberland Parish*, pp. 26–29; Real Property Tax Lists, 1782, Lunenburg County, Virginia State Library.

20. Personal Property Tax Lists, 1782, Lunenburg County, Virginia State Library.

21. A list of names of 123 Episcopalians gleaned from the Cumberland Parish Vestry Books covering 1775 84, in Bell, *Cumberland Parish*, was compared against the Real and Personal Property Tax Lists for 1782. It is difficult to say how typical those 123 men were of the membership of the Lunenburg County Episcopal church as a whole. That they were prominent enough to be mentioned in the vestry book could indicate that the sample is weighted toward those of wealth and social prominence; on the other hand, most entries in the vestry book relate to simple tasks and duties that an individual performed for the church, tasks dependent less on wealth or social prestige than on simple willingness to perform them.

22. Petitions, Lunenburg County, November 8, 1783, November 9, 1785; Lunenburg County Tithable Lists, 1748, 1750, 1764, and 1769, in Bell, *Sunlight*, pp. 58–86, 121–60, 212–85; Real and Personal Property Tax Lists, Lunenburg County, 1782.

23. Thirty-one of the seventy-four signers of the December 1, 1785, Lunenburg anti-assessment petition could be positively identified as Baptists, a fairly high proportion when one considers that the records for only two of the county's five Baptist churches exist from which to make such an identification.

24. Petition, Lunenburg County, December 1, 1785; Real and Personal Property Tax Lists, Lunenburg County, 1782.

25. See sources cited above in note 24.

26. Meherrin Church Minute Books, 1771–85; Tussekiah Baptist Church Minute Books, 1786, Virginia Baptist Historical Society, Richmond, Va.; Petition of December 1, 1785, Lunenburg County, Virginia Religious Petitions; tithable lists for 1769 in Bell, *Sunlight*, pp. 269–85; Real and Personal Property Tax Lists, Lunenburg County, 1782.

27. Earl G. Swen and John W. Williams, *A Register of the General Assembly of Virginia, 1776–1918, and of the Constitutional Conventions* (Richmond, 1918), pp. 3–25; Bell, *Old Free State*, 1:326–41; Bell, *Cumberland Parish*, pp. 26–31; Real and Personal Property Tax Lists, Lunenburg County, 1782.

28. The vote on the initial reform was not recorded. For the other votes, see *JHD* (May–June 1783), June 19, 1783, pp. 67, 78; ibid. (May–June 1784), June 28, 1784, p. 81; ibid. (October 1784–January 1785), November 12 and 19, December 22, 24, 1784, pp. 19, 27, 79, 82; ibid. (October 1785–January 1786), December 17, 1785, p. 96.

29. James Madison to James Monroe, April 13, 1785, in William T. Hutchinson et al., eds., *The Papers of James Madison*, 13 vols. to date (Chicago, London, and Charlottesville, 1962–), 8:261.

30. George Nicholas to Madison, April 22, 1785, in ibid., 8:264.

31. Virginia Religious Petitions, Dinwiddie County, November 28, 1785; Amherst County, December 10, 1785.

32. *JHD* (October 1784–January 1785), November 12, 1784, p. 19; ibid. (October 1785–January 1786), December 17, 1785, p. 96.

33. Quoted in Moore, "John Williams," pp. 633–47.

34. Journal of William Hill, Virginia Historical Society, Richmond, Va.

35. Frank Owsley, *Plain Folk of the Old South* (Baton Rouge, La., 1949), states the case most starkly.

36. Jackson T. Main, "Government by the People: The American Revolution and the Democratization of the Legislatures," *William and Mary Quarterly*, 3d ser., 23 (1966): 391–407, seeks to tie these changes directly to the Revolution. While this may be true in some very generalized sense, it is plain that the process was under way everywhere, and with particular force in frontier areas like Lunenburg, well before the Revolution.

CHAPTER SEVEN
Toward Stability

1. Fernand Braudel, *The Mediterranean and the Mediterranean World in the Age of Philip II*, 2 vols. (New York, 1972), 1:20–211.

2. The best treatment of these developments is in Allan Kulikoff, *Tobacco and Slaves: The Development of Southern Cultures in the Chesapeake Colonies, 1680–1800* (forthcoming); the best summary of these developments is Kulikoff's "The Colonial Chesapeake: Seedbed of Antebellum Southern Culture?" *Journal of Southern History* 45 (1979): 513–39. See also Avery O. Craven, *Soil Exhaustion as a Factor in the Agricultural History of Virginia and Maryland, 1606–1860* (Urbana, Ill., 1926); W. W. Low, "The Farmer in Post-revolutionary Virginia, 1783–1789," *Agricultural History* 25 (1951): 122–27; and George M. Herndon, "A History of Tobacco in Virginia, 1613–1860" (M.A. thesis, University of Virginia, 1956).

3. The decline in tobacco production in the east was both a cause and a reflection of the shift among many planters to the cultivation of wheat. That shift was in some respects a healthy sign of diversification and maximum utilization of land, but it does appear in general that the eastern economy was in a state of decline after the Revolution. See Kulikoff, *Tobacco and Slaves*, chap. 2. For the switch from tobacco to wheat in the eastern Chesapeake, see Paul G. E. Clemens, *The Atlantic Economy and Colonial Maryland's Eastern Shore: From Tobacco to Grain* (Ithaca, N.Y., 1980).

4. Kulikoff, "The Colonial Chesapeake," p. 537.

5. Bell, *Sunlight*, pp. 228–46, 269–85; Real and Personal Property Tax Lists, Lunenburg County, 1782.

6. See the sources cited above in note 5.

7. Ibid.

8. Ibid.

9. Ibid.

10. Real and Personal Property Tax Lists, Lunenburg County, 1795.

11. *U.S. Census, 1800* (Washington, D.C., 1801), p. 211; *U.S. Census, 1810* (Washington, D.C., 1811), p. 54a; *U.S. Census, 1820* (Washington, D.C., 1821), p. 24.

Comparing statistics on slave ownership over the period 1750–1820 is complicated by a number of factors. First, the population figures for 1750 are based on the tithable lists for the whole as-yet-undivided county. Therefore, the reduction in population from the year 1750 to 1764 indicates merely that by 1764 the county contained only one-tenth the land area of the original. Second, the tax bases for slaves varied over the period. From 1750 to 1776, male and female slaves sixteen years and over were counted as tithables; in 1782 apparently all slaves were taxed; in 1795, slaves twelve and older were taxed; and in 1815, slaves nine years and older were taxed. For the prerevolutionary period, I have used the traditional formula and merely doubled the number of tithable slaves in order to arrive at an estimate of the total slave population. The slave-owning figures on the tax lists of 1795 and 1815 have been adjusted by comparing them with the censuses of 1790, 1800, 1810, and 1820, which include slaves of all ages.

12. U.S. Censuses, 1790, 1800, 1810, 1820. Richard S. Dunn, "Black Society in the Chesapeake, 1776–1810," in Ira Berlin and Ronald Hoffman, eds., *Slavery and Freedom in the Age of the American Revolution* (Charlottesville, Va., 1983), pp. 49–82, has surveyed the changes in the black population in all Virginia counties during the period between the Revolution and the first decade of the nineteenth century and has concluded that "in most of the Chesapeake, especially in central Virginia where half of the blacks in the region lived, slaveholding became more widespread and more deeply entrenched than before 1776." Dunn's calculations, which are wholly congruent with mine, indicate that by far the largest portion of that increase was occurring in the Southside and central Piedmont.

13. These figures were furnished by Allan Kulikoff and are a part of his forthcoming book, *Tobacco and Slaves*.

14. W. A. Low, "The Farmer in Post-revolutionary Virginia, 1783–1789," *Agricultural History* 25 (1951): 126; Harold B. Gill, Jr., "Tobacco Culture in Colonial Virginia," Colonial Williamsburg Report, April 1972; Kulikoff, *Tobacco and Slaves*.

15. Kulikoff, *Tobacco and Slaves*.

16. Lunenburg County Will Books, no. 1 (1746–60), no. 2 (1760–78), no. 3 (1778–91), no. 6 (1799–1808), no. 7 (1803–16).

17. An analysis of Lunenburg County Will Books, no. 7 (1803–16), pp. 52–281, indicates that for the years 1812–16 the average adult male slave was valued at £127 and the average female slave at £100. Though a few exceptional males were valued as high as £150, there were also a few females, usually noted as being "young" or "able-bodied," who were valued at £120 or £130.

18. Real and Personal Property Tax Lists, Lunenburg County, 1795; U.S. Census, 1790, 1800, 1810, 1820.

19. George M. Herndon, "A History of Tobacco in Virginia, 1613–1860" (M.A. thesis, University of Virginia, 1956), pp. 110–16.

20. The total number of acres taxed in the county rose from 162,000 in 1764 to 234,928 in 1782, and then leveled off at 248,002 in 1795 and 254,882 in 1815. Bell, *Sunlight*, pp. 228–46, 269–85. Real and Personal Property Tax Lists, Lunenburg County, 1782, 1795, 1815.

21. The percentage of people owning between two hundred and five hundred acres declined from 39.7 percent in 1764 to 34.6 percent in 1782, to 24.7 percent in 1795, and then rose to 31.0 percent in 1815. Bell, *Sunlight*, pp. 228–46, 269–85; Real and Personal Property Tax Lists, Lunenburg County, 1782, 1795, 1815.

22. See the sources cited above in note 21.

23. Ibid.

24. Lunenburg County Will Books, no. 11 (1746–60), no. 2 (1760–78), no. 3 (1778–91), no. 6 (1799–1808), no. 7 (1803–16). The increasing price of adult male slaves is the best guide to inflation in the estate inventories, because those slaves made up the major component of the value of those inventories. The average price for an adult male slave was £75 in 1762–66, £100 in 1782–86, and £125 in 1812–16. Cattle prices provide another index; in 1762–66 the price was £1 per head, in 1782–86 it was £1 10s., and in 1812–16 it was roughly £2.

25. Lunenburg County Will Books, no. 2 (1760–78), May 14, 1763, July 11, 1764, p. 172.

26. A more decisive turn toward consumer goods of a luxury nature in the eastern regions of the Chesapeake has been documented by Lois Green Carr and Lorena Walsh, "Changing Life Styles in Colonial St. Mary's County," *Working Papers from the Regional Economic History Center*, Eleutherian-Mills Foundation, vol. 1, no. 6 (1978), pp. 73–118.

27. Real and Personal Property Tax Lists, Lunenburg County, 1815.

28. Ibid.

29. Ibid.; Arvin, *Antebellum Homes of Lunenburg*, pp. 41–50.

30. Thomas Jefferson, *Notes on the State of Virginia* (New York, 1964), pp. 145, 146, 148. The following discussion of Southside Virginia architecture is drawn from Michael L. Nichols's "Building the Virginia Southside: A Note on Architecture and Society in the Eighteenth Century" (unpublished paper). I am grateful to Professor Nichols of Utah State University for allowing me to use the material in the paper.

31. The most influential study of housing in nineteenth-century Virginia is Henry Glassie's *Folk Housing in Middle Virginia* (Knoxville, Tenn., 1975), but from the detailed evidence in Nichols, "Building the Virginia Southside," and from the patterns of consumption revealed in the estate inventories, cited earlier, it seems likely that the Virginia Southside was much slower in experiencing either a "great rebuilding" or a significant shift in consumer tastes.

32. Real and Personal Property Tax Lists, Lunenburg County, 1782, 1795, 1815.

33. Lunenburg County Will Books, no. 3 (1778–91), October 11, 1781, p. 99.

34. Ibid., no. 7 (1803–16), October 21, 1814, p. 125.

35. Ibid., no. 2 (1760–78), January 4, 1767, p. 278.

CHAPTER EIGHT
The Accommodation of Cultures

1. Bell, *Old Free State*, 1:326–34; Bell, *Cumberland Parish*, pp. 26–31; Real and Personal Property Tax Lists, Lunenburg County, 1795, 1815. See Appendix 2.

2. See the sources cited above in note 1.

3. Bell, *Old Free State*, 1:374–77.

4. Ibid.; Real and Personal Property Tax Lists, Lunenburg County, 1815. See Appendixes 1 and 2.

5. Bell, *Sunlight*, pp. 269–85; Real and Personal Property Tax Lists, 1782; Lunenburg County Will Books, no. 6 (1799–1810), October 1802, p. 9; ibid., January 1, 1806, p. 135a. For a more detailed view of the Baptists' mobility, see Kroll-Smith, "In Search of Status Power," chap. 4, esp. pp. 91–100.

6. Craig died sometime in the summer of 1795 and Williams died on April 30, 1795, although their wills were recorded on the same day, September 10, 1795. The inventory of Craig's estate is in Lunenburg County Will Books, no. 4 (1789–99), p. 110.

7. Moore, "John Williams," pp. 633–47.

8. Lunenburg County Will Books, no. 4 (1789–99), pp. 100, 104.

9. Meherrin Church Minute Book, May 30 and 31, 1772; March 2, 1773; December 14, 1794; Tussekiah Baptist Church Minute Book, May 28, 1791, Virginia Baptist Historical Society.

10. James David Essig, "A Very Wintry Season: Virginia Baptists and Slavery, 1785–1797," *Virginia Magazine of History and Biography* 88 (1980): 182. For a more sanguine view of the Baptists' attitudes toward slavery in this period, see Daniel, "Virginia Baptists and the Negro," pp. 60–69.

11. Essig, "A Very Wintry Season," p. 178.

12. Foote, *Sketches of Virginia*, 2d series, p. 578.

13. "Diary of Bishop John Early," *Virginia Magazine of History and Biography* 34 (1926): 303.

14. Ibid., p. 136.

15. Ibid., p. 134.

16. See Donald G. Mathews, "The Second Great Awakening as an Organizing Process, 1780–1830: An Hypothesis," *American Quarterly* 21 (1969): 23–43.

17. Semple, *History*, pp. 287–303.

18. Ibid.; "The State of the Virginia Baptists in 1797: Excerpts from the Letters of Isaac Backus," *Virginia Baptist Historical Register* 8 (1969): 381–84; Meherrin Church Minute Books, 1807.

19. Meherrin Church Minute Book, October 1, 1776.

20. Ibid., June 13, 1779, April 17, 1784.

21. Moore, "John Williams," pp. 633–47; Redd, "The Meherrin Church," pp. 7–18.

22. See the sources cited above in note 21; see also Semple, *History*, pp. 83–85; Meherrin Church Minute Book, October 1774.

23. Bell, *Old Free State*, 2:414–31.

24. Semple, *History*, p. 287.

25. Journal of John Williams, 1771.

26. Meherrin Church Minute Book, November 1794; Moore, "John Williams," pp. 633–47.

27. Turner's notions about these competing modes of social organization are presented succinctly in Victor W. Turner, *The Ritual Process: Structure and Anti-structure* (Chicago, 1969), esp. pp. 94–166, and in idem, *Dramas, Fields, and Metaphors: Symbolic Action in Human Society* (Ithaca, N.Y., 1974), esp. pp. 23–57, 272–98.

28. "Diary of Bishop John Early," pp. 134, 136.

29. Richard R. Beeman, ed., "Trade and Travel in Post-revolutionary Virginia: A Diary of an Itinerant Peddler, 1807–1808," *Virginia Magazine of History and Biography* 84 (1976): 174–88.

30. Edward Graham Roberts, "The Roads of Virginia, 1607–1840" (Ph.D. diss., University of Virginia, 1950).

31. Joseph Martin, *A New and Comprehensive Gazeteer of Virginia and the District of Columbia* (Charlottesville, Va., 1835), pp. 222–23.

32. Personal Property Tax Lists, Lunenburg County, 1815.

33. The measurement of patrilineal kin ties (admittedly a crude one) was taken by comparing the frequency with which last names occurred on the 1750, 1764, 1782, and 1815 Lunenburg tax lists. Bell, *Sunlight*, pp. 122–61; Real and Personal Property Tax Lists, Lunenburg County, 1782, 1815. I am grateful to Allan Kulikoff, who has incorporated some of this evidence in his forthcoming *Tobacco and Slaves*, for sharing his calculations on patrilineal kin ties with me.

34. Although Lunenburg's leading families enhanced their power within the county, they remained only moderately prominent in the affairs of the state as a whole. As we have seen, no one in the county ever ranked among the wealthiest individuals in the state, and in the area of politics Lunenburg's representatives in the legislature remained backbenchers, serving on only a few of the committees of the House of Delegates and participating only marginally in the initiation of legislation.

35. Beeman, "Diary of an Itinerant Peddler," pp. 181, 183, 184.

36. It is possible that many counties, including Lunenburg, had informal institutions of learning that have thus far escaped the historian's eye. It must also be said that the history of education in Virginia remains to be written. For a general discussion of the subject, see Richard Beale Davis, *Intellectual Life in Jeffersonian Virginia, 1790–1830* (Chapel Hill, N.C. 1964), pp. 27–70; and Lawrence Cremin's *American Education: The National Experience* (New York, 1980), pp. 107–14. Neighboring Prince Edward County was considerably more favored in the realm of education than was Lunenburg, for the Presbyterians had made that county the site of Hampden-Sydney College, founded in 1776 as an academy and elevated to a college in 1783. Only one Lunenburg resident,

William Cowan, seems to have been active in the affairs of the college, serving as a trustee, and only a few residents are recorded as having attended as students.

37. The literacy rates have been determined by examining signatures and marks on wills in Lunenburg County Will Books, no. 1 (1746–60), pp. 3–162; no. 3 (1778–91), pp. 75–255; no. 7 (1803–16), pp. 52–281.

38. The most useful analyses of slave life in the colonial Chesapeake are Allan Kulikoff's "The Origins of Afro-American Society in Tidewater Maryland and Virginia, 1700 to 1790," *William and Mary Quarterly*, 3d ser., 35 (1978): 226–59; and Russell P. Menard's "The Maryland Slave Population, 1658 to 1730: A Demographic Profile of Blacks in Four Counties," *William and Mary Quarterly*, 3d ser., 32 (1975): 29–54. See also Peter J. Albert, "The Protean Institution: The Geography, Economy, and Ideology of Slavery in Post-revolutionary Virginia" (Ph.D. diss., University of Maryland, 1976).

39. Semple, *History*, pp. 291–92.

40. John Boles, *The Great Revival, 1787–1805* (Lexington, Ky., 1972), pp. 194–95, notes the general unwillingness of Southern evangelicals in this period to see slavery as a moral evil, relying instead on the argument that, though hardly benign, the institution was preferable to the "wage slavery" of the North. As Albert Raboteau, Mechal Sobel, and others have noted, however, this hardening of white religious attitudes toward slavery did not necessarily diminish the slaves' enthusiasm for their own form of Afro-Christianity. Indeed, slave attachment to evangelical religion in the nineteenth century seemed to increase just as the proslavery attitudes of their white co-religionists became more militant.

41. Kulikoff, "Origins of Afro-American Society," esp. pp. 249–56.

42. Free Negroes and Mulattoes, 1814, Lunenburg County, Va., Miscellaneous Manuscripts, Alderman Library, University of Virginia. Luther Porter Jackson, in his study of *Free Negro Labor and Property Holding in Virginia, 1830–1860* (New York, 1942), pp. 247–51, lists all the free blacks in the state who appeared on the tax lists as holding one hundred or more acres of land. No one from Lunenburg appears on Porter's list of 169 property holders.

CHAPTER NINE
The Creation of a Southern Identity

1. Wilbur J. Cash, *The Mind of the South* (New York, 1941), pp. 5, 9, 4.

2. Ibid., pp. 19–20.

3. Bell, *Old Free State*, 1:90–92; Foote, *Sketches of Virginia*, 1st ser., p. 104.

4. Jackson T. Main, "Sections and Politics in Virginia, 1781–1787," *William and Mary Quarterly*, 3d ser., 12 (1955): 96–112. See also Norman Risjord, *Chesapeake Politics, 1781–1800* (New York, 1981).

5. Richard R. Beeman, *The Old Dominion and the New Nation, 1788–1801* (Lexington, Ky., 1972), esp. pp. 221–36.

6. Kathryn Malone, "The Virginia Doctrines, the Commonwealth, and the Republic: The Role of Fundamental Principles in Virginia Politics, 1798–1833" (Ph.D. diss., University of Pennsylvania, 1981), explores the essentially conservative character of Virginia republican ideology.

7. William Brodnax, "Address to the Citizens of Dinwiddie on the Occasion of the Constitutional Convention, 1829," Brodnax Family Papers, Virginia Historical Society.

8. Ibid.

9. Roeber, *Faithful Magistrates*, esp. pp. 203–61, argues that the county courts were being forced to turn over much of their legal power to district courts as a consequence of legal reforms passed by the General Assembly in 1787. The overwhelming body of evidence, however, indicates that the legal and, more important, the social functions of the county courts remained virtually intact right up to the Civil War.

10. Brodnax, "Address."

11. Ibid.

12. Frederika Teute Schmidt and Barbara Ripel Wilhelm, "Early Proslavery Petitions in Virginia," *William and Mary Quarterly*, 3d ser., 30 (1973): 133–46.

13. Ibid., pp. 140–43. The original of this petition is in Petitions to the Legislature, Lunenburg County, November 29, 1785, Virginia State Library, Richmond, Va.

14. Petition to the Legislature, Lunenburg County, November 29, 1785.

15. Ibid. See, e.g., Robert McColley, *Slavery and Jeffersonian Virginia*, 2d ed. (Urbana, Ill., 1974); and Gerald Mullin, *Flight and Rebellion: Slave Resistance in Eighteenth Century Virginia* (New York, 1974), esp. pp. 19–33, 70–72.

16. Schmidt and Wilhelm, "Early Proslavery Petitions," p. 144.

17. Petition to the Legislature, Lunenburg County, November 29, 1785; Real and Personal Property Tax Lists, Lunenburg County, 1782.

18. The best treatment of these growing fears and the consequent retreat from even limited racial egalitarianism is Winthrop Jordan's *White over Black: American Attitudes Toward the Negro, 1550–1812* (Chapel Hill, N.C., 1968), pp. 375–428.

19. The full text of the slavery debates in the General Assembly was printed in the *Richmond Enquirer* from January 19 to March 30, 1832. The debates are also excerpted in Joseph Clarke Robert's *The Road from Monticello: A Study of the Virginia Slavery Debates of 1832* (Durham, N.C., 1941).

20. *Richmond Enquirer*, January 12, 1832.

21. Ibid.

22. Ibid., January 19, 1832.

23. Ibid., February 11, 1832.

24. Ibid., January 21, 1832.
25. Ibid., March 28, 1832.
26. *Richmond Constitutional Whig*, January 28, 1832.

Epilogue

1. Bell, *Old Free State*, 1:575–76.
2. Ibid., pp. 576–77.

Index